ERASMUS AND VOLTAIRE:
WHY THEY STILL MATTER

ERASMUS
AND
VOLTAIRE

Why They Still Matter

RICARDO J. QUINONES

UNIVERSITY OF TORONTO PRESS
Toronto Buffalo London

© University of Toronto Press Incorporated 2010
Toronto Buffalo London
www.utppublishing.com
Printed in Canada

ISBN 978-1-4426-4054-2

Printed on acid-free, 100% post-consumer recycled paper with
vegetable-based inks.

Library and Archives Canada Cataloguing in Publication

Quinones, Ricardo J.
Erasmus and Voltaire : why they still matter / Ricardo J. Quinones.

Includes bibliographical references and index.
ISBN 978-1-4426-4054-2 (bound)

1. Erasmus, Desiderius, d. 1536.   2. Voltaire, 1694–1778.   3.   Erasmus,
Desiderius, d. 1536 – Criticism and interpretation.   4. Voltaire,
1694–1778 – Criticism and interpretation.   I. Title.

B785.E64084 2009   199'.492   C2009-905616-x

This book has been published with a generous subvention from
Pamela Gann, President of Claremont McKenna College.

University of Toronto Press acknowledges the financial assistance to
its publishing program of the Canada Council for the Arts and the
Ontario Arts Council.

Canada Council   Conseil des Arts   ONTARIO ARTS COUNCIL
for the Arts   du Canada   CONSEIL DES ARTS DE L'ONTARIO

University of Toronto Press acknowledges the financial support for its
publishing activities of the Government of Canada through the Book
Publishing Industry Development Program (BPIDP).

Contents

✿

Preface / vii

Abbreviations / xix

Introduction / 3

PART ONE / CAREER EPISODES

1
Names for Bastards / 21

2
England, Always England / 35

PART TWO / WORKS: CHILDREN OF A FORTUNATE HOUR

3
Erasmus's Letter to van Dorp and Voltaire's Letter to
Rousseau / 67

4
Works Finding Their Ways / 81

5
The Survivors: *Praise of Folly* and *Candide* / 123

PART THREE / DUALISMS

6
Never a Peace: 'Thus always Cain or Abel' / 145

Epilogue: Recurrence and Recognition / 177

Notes / 195

Works Cited / 211

Index / 219

Preface

֍

In several ways *Erasmus and Voltaire: Why They Still Matter* is something of a rarity. Quite literally it is the only book that compares Erasmus and Voltaire at length in their various career episodes, their works, and their historic afterlives.[1] The lack of fuller attention is all the more baffling since, as Bruce Mansfield informs us, in the course of the nineteenth century comparisons between Erasmus and Voltaire became commonplace; he largely credits Coleridge for this development.This book might be even more of a rarity in that it keeps a promise. In the course of my previous study, *Dualisms: The Agons of the Modern World* (about which more below), I became convinced that one line of cultural affiliation, at the head of which stood Erasmus and Voltaire, was being reduced in value – hence I promised another volume, something of a companion piece, that would offer some remediation. While referred to only as a 'future study,' the future arrived more quickly than I anticipated, and we have before us a work concerning such preeminent figures whose 'discernible markings, resemblances of thought, style, intellectual positioning, habits of mind and character' (*Dualisms* 200) are portrayed in all their fascinating and surprising deteails.

There is some ingratitude here, particularly as the thesis turns against Coleridge and his final verdict that Erasmus and Voltaire were 'essentially different.' Our first and foremost theorist of dualisms, Coleridge had recognized from the past centuries the two dominant cross-rivalries, those of Erasmus and Luther and Voltaire and Rousseau. He selected them because he saw in them the larger embodiments of profound yet differing cultural principles. Not only that, but he went beyond the crossing pairs to construct lines of affiliation – those linking Erasmus with Voltaire, and Luther with Rousseau. Here he engages in a remarkable comparison between Erasmus and Voltaire, whom he finds alike in their *effects* (which extended throughout Europe), *circumstances* (both lived in ages of hope and promise), and in their *instruments* (those of 'wit and amusive erudition'). But after such analysis he proceeds to his unexpected conclusion (*The Friend* 1:129–30).

But two things should not be forgotten. First, in his choice of historical characters and in their lines of affiliation, Coleridge was laying down a broad runway – a line of continuity – between the Reformation and the Enlightenment (which is even more apparent in his discussion of Luther and Rousseau). Second, and more important, in his critical discussion of the two most important dualisms of the preceding centuries, Coleridge introduces the powerful principle of 'recognition.' This is the hallmark of his method for bringing two historically separated and even diverse authors together. Relying on examples from music he cites recognition's capacity not only to recall the past but also to revive it under different circumstances, making it 'another and yet the same.' As in music so in history: 'The events and characters of one age ... recall those of another, and the variety by which each is individualized, not only gives a charm and poignancy to the resemblance, but likewise renders the whole more intelligible.' The searching out of individual differences can lead to a better understanding of the larger union in which they thrive. He further shows these resemblances to be non-imitative. There are real resemblances that by the exercise of judgment may be distinguished from those of 'intentional imitation,' 'the masquerade figure of cunning and artifice.' Recognition responds to the powers of spontaneous similarities, which, not trying to resemble past models, emerge from within the very disparity of things themselves (*The Friend* 1:129–30). Coleridge's analysis includes individuals as well as epochs: 'I have myself ... derived the deepest interest from the comparison of men, whose characters at the first view appear widely dissimular' (130). Such is the case of the convergences that bring Erasmus and Voltaire together. This method does not discount dissimilarities; rather it relies on them. From out of the midst of such unlikenesses within similar situations (and certainly they are visible in the career episodes and works of Erasmus and Voltaire), we are in a position to detect remarkable convergences of mind and spirit. Going beyond Coleridge's final judgment (and this is certainly the sign of a great theory, that its own boundaries may be transgressed) we can still rely upon his method. This involves no miracle of bread and fishes, but rather the ability to pass beyond first impressions and to make use of a 'transhistorical' imagination. It means a willingness to withstand an easy literalism that stops at the first stage of difference and to penetrate to the core of resemblances. The choices are actually quite simple: do we posit unalterable differences between Erasmus and Voltaire, or, using that proposition only as a starting point rather than as a stone wall, do we proceed to uncover more fully the compared affinities of the two? This is a 'quest' story, one that, going beyond the 'first view' of differences, is in search of the major convergences, some of which have as yet been unacknowledged but when brought together help restore Erasmus and Voltaire to their merited places of intellectual honour. It is thus also a story of recuperation, of recovering areas of their thought in common that makes of them spokespersons for an abiding dimension of Western thought.

Comparative literature, of which this study is an example, thrives upon such recognitions; in fact, there is a methodological merger between the two. We are far from the time when comparative literature needed a defence, particularly of the kind trotted out when I was an eager and dutiful graduate student and tried warhorses would hold forth on such topics as 'Qu'est'ce que c'est la littérature comparée,' or 'Est-ce qu'il y a une littérature comparée?' I left these lectures dissatisfied and convinced a simpler formula would do, such as, comparative literature is best determined by the works that acknowledged comparatists produce. Yet, such pragmatic solutions themselves require clarification. Comparative literature is not given over to randomness; comparisons that are heady and far-flung, and that, while appropriate for undergraduate courses (I remember with bemused attention moving from lectures on Boethius to those on Benjamin Franklin, or from those on Abelard to those on Kafka), hardly fulfil the requirements of a discipline. There must be points of genuine association, historical connection, and spiritual convergences between the figures involved.

Satis est quod sufficit. Enough is as good as a feast. But if enough is only enough, why not try for a feast? Such may be the relation between comparative and single-author studies, or studies limited to a single topic. Too many good things are passed up. Many a splendid essay, or monograph, has been written that quite diligently and even brilliantly follows the course of an individual career. But one can speculate how much more that scrupulous scholarship would have been enhanced, its horizons of judgment and speculation enlarged, by several well-matched comparisons. Here I am not merely referring to simple associations, but to the higher purposes gained when by the very nature of comparisons one arrives at unanticipated questions that yield unexpected responses. From beginning to end, from the shared intellectual commitments prompted by their origins and name changes to the quite similar criticisms Erasmus and Voltaire independently directed against their intellectual rivals, Luther and Rousseau (see chapter 6), the following study has its share of such surprising turns in its argument. In their compared affinities Erasmus and Voltaire provide richer fare than we have ever imagined.

Two essays by Jean-Claude Margolin may serve as trial exhibits: 'Érasme et l'Angleterre' and 'Érasme et la France.' The first, justifiably enough, has little international flavour, and ends with the comprehensive judgment that the spirit and the ideas of Erasmus have never ceased being appreciated in England and in the Anglo-Saxon world (67). But in the other essay, 'Érasme et la France,' Margolin, one of the major European Erasmian scholars, enlarges his perspective, remarking that in the crucial years during and after the Council of Trent, Erasmianism was forced to go underground, even to move into clandestinity (61), and thus was able to survive before resurfacing in the century of the Enlightenment, when it had a 'singular' impact upon the French in general and Voltaire in particular. Margolin then makes the grand comparison, introducing the affinities between these two great letter writers (at last count Erasmus's correspondence totaled some 3100 letters, and Voltaire's in excess of 15,000), such masters of satire and irony, and such rulers of European thought from their seats in Basel and Geneva (63–4). These are just a few tastings of the fruits from their shared garden of surprises. One can go on, and I will go on to discuss their career episodes and their fund of writing, but perhaps their greatest area of association is their psychological matrix: they may be brought together in the complex of psychological characteristics that made of each a reformer rather than a revolutionary.

This book comparing preeminent figures of cultural history has its precedent and prospective programs. It refers back to the debates that constituted the argument of my preceding book, *Dualisms*, and it looks forward to the convergences that join Erasmus and Voltaire. These two aspects may be regarded as facing planes of a cornerstone, with meaningful inscriptions etched on each. They may look in different directions but are joined at the angle and share a common matrix.

For the reader new to the discussion of dualisms it may suffice to rehearse their basic aspects along with a few general principles. By now dualism has earned its alcove in the halls of literary discussion and scholarship: it represents both a mode of inquiry and an area of study. Dualisms exist as major cross-rivalries between two major figures of an age, such as Erasmus and Luther, Voltaire and Rousseau, Turgenev and Dostoevsky, or Sartre and Camus (to which foreshortened list many more could and have been added). In their times and places, other debates and skirmishes simply subside in contrast. As Lewis Spitz wrote, echoing or anticipating other commentators, in the turmoil of the early sixteenth century quarrels were plentiful, 'but the battle of the giants was the great debate between Luther and Erasmus over the freedom of the will' (104). The same might be said of the other cross-rivalries. It is as if at a party two people had their attention directed only to each other, such is the magnetic draw and the constant attentiveness existing between them. Mindful of this special chemistry, awestruck, the others stand aside, absorbed by the momentous clash of such protagonists. The quarrel is in-house, as in a nuclear family, yet fissionable extending to and involving the community at large.

In their origins, class backgrounds, education, aspirations, and temperament, clearly the central figures are different, in fact, antitypes. Thus a formidable collision was practically unavoidable. Yet, oddly enough, it required stages of development, what I call an itinerary of encounter, before any outright intellectual warfare could occur. In all four instances the itinerary was similar. At first they were thought to be comrades-in-arms, leaders in the intellectual vanguard. Both began as reformers. This meant that from the first they spoke a common language, with shared goals, and were united against well-entrenched enemies. But suspicions and misgivings were always lurking, the nagging sense of differences that did not go away. Finally an episode or episodes occur that reveal just how far apart they were in their temperaments and expectations. As a first general principle, we observe that it was not in spite of but because of their early affinities, their very closeness, that the animosity of their debate became so explosive and extensive. Secondly, this was not a quarrel between liberal and conservative but rather between two preeminent figures who had been in the same camp, or so it was thought, and who occupied the height of the times, the best against the best. Finally, they came to represent opposing plans for the future of their own equally divided society. It was this combination of powers that made their clash so definitive, so epochal.

These remarks help clarify the relationship between my previous book and this study of Erasmus and Voltaire. Furthermore, recognition helps resolve a crux. It was thought (somewhat mistakenly, I believe) that *Dualisms* presented a more favourable picture of the writers I called daemonic, the line of Luther, Rousseau, Dostoevsky, and Sartre. Such depiction did not represent to my mind a preference for the one over the other, but rather a matter of historical and psychological fact – what one reviewer has termed a 'brute fact' – as the writers of consciousness, Erasmus, Voltaire, and Turgenev (and even Camus to the Parisians of 1952) seemed subdued by the greater tenacity and conviction of their more dominant, spiritually convinced rivals. Such it may always be. If *Dualisms* did inadvertently convey a preference, here *Erasmus and Voltaire* may constitute a substantial rectification. It shows in dramatic portraiture the strengths and the durability of the lines of thought and thinkers whose leaders will always be Erasmus and Voltaire.

Dualisms depended upon what I termed a lateral poetics, one indeed where intellectual enmity was inveterate and enduring, where in Luther's great formula one was either Cain or Abel – there being no intermediate kingdom, no purgatory in his world where the dominant rhetorical figure is either/or. So, too, William Blake (see McGann) insisted when surveying major divisions among English writers that it would be a grave error to seek to reconcile Byron and Wordsworth or Chaucer and Milton: 'whoever seeks to reconcile them seeks to destroy existence' (20). *Erasmus and Voltaire*, however, employs a vertical poetics. Across the centuries a meeting of the minds occurs, a common front is formed, one that, transcending mere coincidence or even connections, provides a better picture of a type of mentality that is just as enduring as that of the cross-rivals. It is certainly a question, left us yet to prove, whether the 'dynamism' of the one is of greater appeal than the less tumultuous, less challenging demeanour of the other.

Dualisms centred on differences, deep-rooted, contentious, and recurrent, and on enmities that were unending, not even abbreviated by death. This book differs from the first by focusing on similarities, on couplings across the centuries that bring two prominent intellects together in their fates and fashionings. Major elements of their thought, points of contact, that are underrepresented, perhaps even unrecognized when confronted alone, come back with a renewed force when they are considered in tandem.

This is what happens when two figures such as Erasmus and Voltaire are brought together: they experience a change in nature and relationship and become capable of entering into relations with other entities, and thus establishing a line of continuity that overcomes or transcends 'mere' difference. Thus it was with the writers of consciousness extending from Erasmus and Voltaire to Turgenev and Camus. And thus in the epilogue to this book, Erasmus and Voltaire are linked with Cassirer. Brought out of the unitary by comparison, the two are transformed substantially and are ready to enter into other significant relationships.

Such morphological change is meaningful as it sets this methodology apart from that of those great and admirable studies that, with a multitude of expert witnesses, copiously express the defining characteristics of an age. One can think of many such classic studies, but here I bring to mind only two, Ernst Cassirer's *The Philosophy of the Enlightenment* and Jean Ehrard's *L'Idée de nature en France dans la première moitié du XVIIIe siècle*. Each is compendious in its references and rewarding in its thought. The latter in particular shows that the thinkers of the early French Enlightenment were given to compromise along a number of conflicting issues. Nature itself provided its own constraints. On the one hand it was an *idée-force*, while on the other, it was an *idée-frein* (Ehrard 2:786). As an idea of force it served as an argument against superstition, fanaticism, and despotism, but as a braking idea it kept the individual within well-defined boundaries, those of the 'honnête homme,' a devotee of good taste and reason. This may be regarded as a simplified picture of Voltaire. But the problem presents itself in that, while typical of the century of the *lumières*, such a reliance on *idée-force* and *idée-frein* is not new. The same compromising qualities are present in Erasmus as well, and will be explored abundantly through such works as *The Praise of Folly* and others. To be caught on the horns of this dilemma and obliged to accept two such competing ideas and impulses, while characteristic of the period of Ehrard's study, is not unique to it. Thus enters the usefulness and legitimacy of typologies, or transhistorical comparisons, showing that in the cases of Erasmus and Voltaire the ideas of liberating force combined with a salutary restraint are precisely the qualities that bring them together (and in the greater affiliation of *Dualisms*, join them with Turgenev and Camus as well). The hard-headed positivism that sees a thing for what it is and only for what it is (which is realistically impossible) has some things to recommend it. But hard-headedness can soon become wrong-headedness and even imperialistic, denying the imaginative possibilities of transformative changes that comparison brings to entities, where they no longer are things in themselves but things in common relationship with other things. Through time the build-up can comprise a formidable way of presenting and possessing knowledge.

Knowingly or not, even the most individualized of subjects still function within some historical paradigm. In this case, the interpretive syntheses offered by W.K. Ferguson and H. Trevor-Roper provide for fuller comprehension of the presiding conditions that brought Erasmus and Voltaire together and along the way they make possible a response to a lingering question that this study has inherited.

The coincidence of the developing social milieux and intellectual culture is apparent. Where Erasmus and his predecessors and cohorts both participated in and gave expression to the new social conditions that helped bring about a 'decisive break' with the preceding culture of the Middle Ages, these same conditions persisted and even increased in scope and power from the time of Erasmus to that of Voltaire. The prelude to the Renaissance was marked by a break; the postlude by continuity.[2] As Ferguson has argued in a series of sparkling essays that are among the best syntheses of Renaissance culture that we possess, that period (1300–1600) was an age of crisis, an age in transition. At its beginning European culture depended upon a feudal economy with a 'universal' church of large temporal designs. At the end of the period the economy of Europe was increasingly urban, moneyed, with commerce and industry thriving (despite the cyclical economic downturns), with nation states dominant, and with the church compelled to surrender its territorial ambitions and restrict itself to addressing the spiritual needs of its adherents. In more progressive societies it was prevented from establishing a 'fatal union' (Trevor-Roper) with the state, that kind of theocracy that shut down the borders of Italy and Spain and which led to the emigration of some of their better intellects and entrepreneurs. What is important is not the generalized clarity of these observations but rather their easy applicability, what Ferguson calls their 'applicability to historical facts' (*Europe in Transition* 9). And, we can add, their applicability to particular faces, to the men in the trenches and their individual needs and pursuits.The changes are enormous in their repercussions – from a feudal landed economy, with aspirations of a universal church and all its permeating institutions and orders, to a moneyed economy, with an emerging more powerful laity and centralized national state. As we survey that change we can see that the world in which Erasmus was an early participant, an aid and abetter, Voltaire represented something of the fulfilment (as Margolin has suggested, see above). Rather than a break, or differences of degree leading to differences of kind, or quantitative leading to qualitative change, we can follow a developmental continuity. To be sure, the Christian humanists of the sixteenth century had to undergo startling changes in their original thought and belief before finding accommodations with the more secular humanists of the eighteenth century, but this occurs within a gradient of development provided by the larger social changes.

Where Ferguson describes the controlling forces of social milieux, Trevor-Roper in a celebrated essay, 'Religion, the Reformation and Social Change,' calls the conduit connecting the Renaissance (or Reformation) and the Enlightenment, 'Erasmianism.' By this he does not mean Erasmus or his doctrines, but rather the ambient social attitudes that would only grow in time. This entails the rejection of 'a great deal of the external apparatus of official Catholicism': the defence of the life of the laity from marriage to the dignity of many 'callings,' and in general a kinder, gentler less theologically restrictive attitude of tolerance (33). This, as it turns out, is a crucial distinction, for many a journey that Erasmus could not make, Erasmianism did.

This brings us to the question that has been frequently asked: why should discussion be limited to Erasmus and Voltaire and not include Turgenev and Camus? One could dodge the question and assert that by discussing the two one is also discussing the others. And that would be in part true. But there is a better reason: Erasmus and Voltaire stand in the same line of historical continuity. There are direct and indirect connections as well as convergences, even situations in common and enemies to boot. Put more succinctly, the Christian humanists of the sixteenth century who represented moderation and peace, but who were constrained by the 'confessionalists' (see Rummel, *The Confessionalization of Humanism in Reformation Germany*), may have found a well-qualified modicum of vindication, as certainly an altered Erasmus may have, mutatis mutandis, in the formidable more secularized humanism of the Enlightenment. We have no way of knowing. But what we do know is that rather than being rejected, a newly reborn Erasmus, via Erasmianism, was clearly appropriated by the thinkers of the Enlightenment.

Advisements. Throughout this study I have resorted to the French *Voltairien* and *voltairienisme* rather than 'voltairian' because in their original denotations they indicate the more embattled reputation of Voltaire throughout the nineteenth and into the twentieth centuries. Also I refer to radical protestantism with a lower case 'p' when it involves attitudes but to an upper case Protestantism when it is a matter of creed. This volume is primarily a study of those 'moments' when the lives and intellectual interests, the character and the thought of Erasmus and Voltaire intersect. This means that some works of great value are omitted; it also means that some issues, far-fetched for the text, can still find comfortable berthing in the notes. For instance, 'Erasmian' and '*Voltairien*' in their separate historical developments do not have any special roles in the text, but the diverse paths they travelled and disputes they engendered are necessarily followed in notes 4 and 5 of the introduction. With the addition of works cited, notes have expanded their purpose beyond that of simple citation and now may be used for amplification and clarification. Thus there are notes that give fuller treatment of Voltaire's disastrous – even dangerous – experience at the court of Frederick II. This tells us much about Voltaire but very little about Erasmus's relationship with Charles V. Hence a perfect occasion for a note. Similar opportunities arrive in the epilogue where the separate routings of Cassirer and Heidegger are elaborated.

As for textual sources I simply refer the reader to the Works Cited section and where the series of quotations from a main source is uninterrupted by other allusions I simply use page numbers without further reference.

Acknowledgments. Three friends, Jay Martin, Nancy van Deusen, and David Michael Hertz, have in particular made significant contributions to this study; they offered keen insights on both style and structure. My personal assistant Anthony B. De Soto, who was most helpful particularly in the final stages of the manuscript, deserves much praise. Everybody knows that no book arrives at its destination without the directing force of a strong editor, and so many thanks to Ron Schoeffel. The last two books of my life would not have been possible without the loving encouragement of Roberta L. Johnson.

Abbreviations

※

Allen Allen, P.S. *Opus epistolarum Des. Erasmi Roterodami.* Oxford: Clarendon, 1906–58.

AS Erasmus, Desiderius. *Encomium Moriae Erasmus von Rotterdam.* Ausgewählte Schriften. Darmstadt: Wissenschaftliche Buchgesellschaft, 1976.

ASD Erasmus, Desiderius. *Opera omnia Desiderii Erasmi Roterodami.* Amsterdam: North Holland, 1969–.

CEBR Bietenholz, Peter G., and Thomas B. Deutscher. *Contemporaries of Erasmus: A Biographical Register.* Toronto: University of Toronto Press, 1985–7.

CWE Erasmus, Desiderius. Collected Works of Erasmus. Toronto: University of Toronto Press, 1974–.

LE Rupp, E. Gordon, and Philip S. Watson. *Luther and Erasmus: Free Will and Salvation.* Library of Christian Classics 17. London: SCM, 1969.

OC Voltaire. *Oeuvres Complètes.* Paris: Garnier, 1877–85.

RC Voltaire. *Romans et Contes.* Paris: Gallimard, 1979.

ERASMUS AND VOLTAIRE:
WHY THEY STILL MATTER

Introduction

🜎

Why Erasmus and Voltaire, and why now? To ask these questions is not for the purpose of eliciting as from a prompt sheet a calculated and dutiful response. Rather it is to open up the larger vistas that their presences evoke. From the enormous changes the crisis of the Renaissance provoked down to the hazardous implications of twentieth-century philosophy in Germany and throughout Europe they provide patterns of response. To see them as figures of critical change in the first period extending from the Renaissance to the Enlightenment and as bulwarks of common reason in the second is to express the complex natures of their characters and appeal. They still possess a permanent hold on our interests by virtue of the notable roles each played at decisive turning points in the development of Western culture; and the living reality of their contributions is still with us, especially enhanced when joined together. They are representative figures and leaders in a mode of thought that continues to possess a great validity and that resurfaces whenever a true dualism occurs. These considerations should be sufficient to argue that the time is ripe to open a new front, to establish another balance sheet in estimating the values and appeal of Erasmus and Voltaire. The call is clear to universalize and to intensify the languages of each that once held such celebrated sway.

The coincidences in the lives of Erasmus and Voltaire are striking and remarkable. They may come under the heading of 'career episodes,' including such matters as their changes of name, the stigma of bastardy, or their formative experiences in England. But coincidences as material circumstances may be like footprints in the snow; however arresting, unless they lead somewhere they rank among the accidental, the ephemera. Rather than a story told, they may represent only a story half-told. The foot trail must lead somewhere, and indeed in both of the instances explained in chapters 1 and 2, their coincidences are generative, what James Joyce called 'portals of discovery.' In each case their name changes were products of a sense of genuine aspiration, of their need to become the persons of accomplishment that they had promised themselves to be. While inspiration or cause may have differed, their aspirations and goals were remarkably similar. In each case their 'accidents' of birth led to a lack of attachment, even a grant of freedom, or rather a reattachment to a greater family, a brotherhood, a common cause of kindred spirits, whether London-Oxford reformers, or the programs of the *philosophes*. The very circumstances of their birthing and change of name led them to become what they truly desired, and that was to be free-standing public intellectuals. They were cosmopolitan by choice: Erasmus found a home wherever there was a library and an active printing press; Voltaire finally situated on the border between France and Switzerland and found his own perch, one of complete financial and intellectual independence. While causes differed, results were remarkably similar. Each attained the freedom that was his life's design. Coincidences, even the larger ones described in chapters 4 and 6, are not incidental, perhaps not even accidental, but fundamental drives of a personality seeking expression, here the unexpressed intimations of a greater need for citizenship in the republic of letters. What is not accidental is that each of these earlier coincidences opens the way to what I referred to above as a 'thicker' reading of the conjoined careers of Erasmus and Voltaire.

Coincidences may be bubbles in the air; historical connections follow subterranean routes. Such were the underground streams that brought Erasmianism to the surface once again in the late seventeenth and early eighteenth centuries. In their attachments to the independent achievements of free-standing intellects, the revered *res publica litteraria*, Erasmus and Voltaire may be spiritually joined through the centuries; but as F. Schalk (see below, page 00) has abundantly shown this was no accidental association across time, but rather a series of ideals bequeathed from intellectual to intellectual, prominently joining Erasmus at the headwaters with Voltaire at the river's mouth. The pedigree is not conjectural but historically specific.

Another connection is more conjectural but also intriguing because it involves the illusory goal of ascertaining a 'first' from all
the antecedent 'firsts.' Voltaire was certainly not the first to realign
the map of Europe along a north/south axis, but he was among
the fullest in his commitment to such a redrafting. The argument
of this study suggests that before Voltaire it was the leaders of the
early Reform who first proclaimed the spiritual superiority of the
North, thus preparing the way for all the political and civil benefits that emerged in the wake of a nascent protestant mentality.
An entire schema of historical and geographical assumptions – of
history entering geography – were being forwarded. If Voltaire
was the recipient of this new historical landshift, one of the initia-
tors was certainly Erasmus, particularly in his *Julius Exclusus* (see
page 205, note 7).

This is not a book about people who lived with a wild and passionate abandon, who responded to events from the nerve ends of
their instinctual life; nor is it one about figures of such stature that
they changed the course of history. Erasmus and Voltaire founded no churches, nor any sects or schools.[1] Yet, as religious intellectual, the one, and rational philosopher, the other, or simply
the most notable writers of their times, they held their allure for
rulers of church or state, who persistently tried to entice them to
their court or camp. In the midst of his increasing hostilities with
Luther, Erasmus repeatedly declined a compromising invitation
to Rome, with a forthcoming high office (bishopric or cardinal's
hat) implied. And Voltaire entered into one of the most fascinating relationships of philosopher-with-king when he accepted the
invitation of the remarkably talented Frederick II of Prussia (who
referred to him not without irony as 'le roi Voltaire'). The disaster produced by this visit only promoted their bountiful correspondence, a necessary recourse since they found that they could
not live with one another or without one another.[2] To be sure,
Erasmus and Voltaire continued to find their singular admirers
throughout history (perhaps among those 'ironic points of light'
that, in Auden's poem, 'Flash out wherever the Just / Exchange
their messages').[3] They rank among those who are undeceived
even by their own self-deceptions. Yet, they came to represent
much more; they were the literary giants of their age; witness
that their names became standards and they the epitomes of their
times. 'Erasmian' and 'Erasmianism' became catch-words by

which to identify his beliefs and those of his followers,[4] just as in the nineteenth century *'Voltairiens'* and *'voltairienisme'* served to identify with favour or with hostility – but always with ardour – a set of beliefs in the radically polarized intellectual and political life of nineteenth-century France,[5] which extended down through the Dreyfus affair and even up to the contentiously rival camps of the 1930s. Adding a third name, that of Petrarch, nineteenth-century progressive historians were able to conclude 'that only three times did a single name so dominate European intellectual life: the times of Petrarch, Erasmus, and Voltaire.'[6]

Of course each is subject to special claims on the part of advocates, but such claims frequently serve only to enforce similarities. A major scholar of the Reformation was able to conclude his brief biography of Erasmus with these words: 'Never again would anyone be able to combine such learning with such unceasing devotion to the issues of the day.'[7] Already, however, Theodore Besterman, one of the most knowledgeable *Voltairiens* of the twentieth century and who certainly did the most to advance studies in Voltaire, had made the same claim of uniqueness for his star: 'Voltaire was in fact the first great man of letters who used his fame and literary skill in the active promotion of his social convictions.'[8] Jean-Paul Sartre justifies both declarations, joining their subjects in their respective dual functions, when he writes of the *philosophes*: 'Pour la première fois depuis la Réforme les intellectuels interviennent dans la vie publique.'[9] They were each public intellectuals whose words were anticipated and controverted, studied, admired, and condemned. Whatever they said carried with it considerable public weight. They were teachers in fact, if not in name, and their classroom was the commonwealth of letters.

This is a book of many such convergences. The first – the starting point of this study – is one where they are probably unique and that is the remarkably similar fates they experienced in their historical afterlives. Rarely in modern cultural history have such dramatic displacements occurred as those that have attended the reputations of Erasmus and Voltaire.[10] Each underwent similar degradations. Each was deprived of his commitments to the preferred and prestigious 'grands genres' of his time. Theirs is not a story of dislodgement but rather of a radical change of perspective as they became known for works and qualities to the near-total exclusion of those for which they were famous among their contemporaries. Seldom if ever have such preeminent figures been so totally transformed. In being altered they were also diminished, reduced in the number of works that attract attention and reduced to the single status of great satirist (thus even misreading the two works that have survived). Erasmus and Voltaire had their works splintered and they were given new personalities. Summarizing the emergence of a single work to the subtraction of all the others, it has been asked: with the exception of *Candide* does anyone still read Voltaire? (Groos 1:v). Such reduction can also lead to irrelevancy. Voltaire had dropped off the desks of active intellectuals acquiring at best only a historical importance. The same might be said of Erasmus and *The Praise of Folly*.[11] Not only might it be said, but it *was* said by no less a creative imagination than that of Stefan Zweig, who entered so intimately into the character of his 'revered master,' Erasmus. In his *Triumph und Tragik des Erasmus von Rotterdam* (I quote from the translation with the less telling title, *Erasmus of Rotterdam*), Zweig laments that while Erasmus's numerous works sleep quietly on library shelves, 'hardly a single one of them, though they enjoyed in their day worldwide fame, has any message to our epoch' (3). But in the pages that follow Zweig does everything to bolster the double understanding his original title portends, and that is the relevancy of Erasmus for the clouds gathering over Europe in the 1930s.

Yet, eluding and defying the generalized neglect, *The Praise of Folly* and *Candide* continue to live. In fact, having grown still grander in their historic afterlives, they have subsumed, if not consumed, other works for which Erasmus and Voltaire were even more highly regarded. Erasmus was the prince of Latin letters and the most important biblical humanist of his time; his earliest works bespeak an ardent Christianity, one to which he remained constant throughout his life. Voltaire's first play, *Oedipe*, had a longer consecutive running than any play of the century and immediately brought its young author into comparison with Corneille and Racine. And when he wrote his at times brilliant epic poem *La Henriade* in praise of Henri IV at the siege of Paris, his work instantly invited comparison with that of Virgil. His *Siécle de Louis XIV* is a masterpiece of historiography. Yet these works have been pushed to the sidelines of disregard, and it is by virtue of their surviving masterpieces that Erasmus and Voltaire now enjoy whatever acclaim, or even limited attention, they receive.

How this all happened is a complicated story of canon formation (or deformation) because the roads they travelled were substantially different, and yet the outcome and the patterns were
remarkably similar. What is anomalous in this historical refrac-
tion is that leading Erasmian and *Voltairien* scholars, far from
lamenting this process of deformation, actually declare the judgments of history to be correct, and they do so for the same reasons
and, I might add, for the right reasons. As early as 1924, with the
publication of his biography of Erasmus, Huizinga argues for the
distinctiveness of the *Praise of Folly*, claiming that of all the publications of Erasmus, 'in ten folios' 'only [it] has remained a truly
popular book' (77). He does not treat this as mistaken but rather
credits the justice of historical record. If the *Praise of Folly* (he includes the *Colloquies*, which I would not) has remained alive, 'that
choice of history was right.' It is not because that work is light
in contrast to being ponderous, but rather because it is his best
work, charming the world by its sparkling wit (155). Marcel Bataillon, summing up a three-week-long centenary conference at
Tours, was able to congratulate his audience of scholars for not
'underestimating' *The Praise of Folly*; in fact, it occupies 'le sommet lumineux de son [Erasmus's] oeuvre' ('Actualité' 2:886). At
such a luminous height it does not cease to be republished and
read. And like Huizinga, Bataillon provides some of the reasons
for its continuing success. It is an instrument of self-comprehen-
sion (quoting Robert Klein) and an ironic critique of the humanist
himself (quoting Margolin 2:888). As for Voltaire, André Billaz,
writing under the entry *Zadig* in the authoritative *Voltaire Dictionnaire*, can claim that 'for us' the poems and plays are 'unreadable'
(a somewhat harsh judgment), but that 'le conte est le sommet
privilégié de l'improvisation liberé et heureuse, ou l'on peut
écrire selon son fantaisie' (the *conte* is the privileged summit of
a free and happy improvisation, where one can write according
to one's own fancy). It fell to the genial insight of Zweig to bring
the two together in their isolated grandeur: among the numerous volumes of Voltaire's works, 'Candide ... is the only one to
survive hardily and remain of vital interest. So also, among the
innumerable folios written by Erasmus's ready pen, [the] brilliant
and spirited [*Praise of Folly*], the child of a fortunate hour, is the
one which continues to amuse and edify us' (Zweig 79). The reasons for this ascendancy of these two works will be discussed in
chapter 5, but obviously they could not have jumped so far ahead

of the pack unless they contained some elements normally absent in their authors' other works, unless they contained elements of self-exploration and self-contestation where Erasmus and Voltaire pitted their best hopes against their worst fears. Rhetorically, intellectually, and personally these works have earned their positions of preeminence.

But this is not the only convergence. Clearly it is time for a restoration of Erasmus and Voltaire not only in the singular achievement of these two classics but also in the deeper recesses and the larger vistas of their works, the far-reaching import of their thought. This book aspires to take its place in that league of renewal. On the larger screen there are three areas where their vital cotenancy comes into view. The first is their rhetoric, which in the works of each is established according to a scale of proportionate value. For Erasmus, works and ceremonials are not to be rejected provided one keeps the main spiritual values in view. For Voltaire, his culture of mundanity, an ingrained part of his character, occupies a defensible position, but only a subaltern one in comparison with the discoveries of Newton, or the sheer triumph that was *Tartuffe*. This hierarchical rhetoric is the basis of much misunderstanding. Voltaire was accused of playing a double game. But like Erasmus he should not be blamed for this two-handed habit. Rather than a balancing act, it is for each the expression of a larger virtue, and that is their adherence to this scale of proportionate values. The quip that Voltaire used against Frederick II may be used against him. Frederick invoked another rising star (Baculard d'Arnaud) to replace the setting sun of Voltaire. To this challenge Voltaire replied that Frederick scratches with one hand ('égratigner') while he protects with the other. Not only *could* this quip be turned against Voltaire, it was. Later Roland Barthes would repeat this royal insult, declaring that Voltaire would rather *bâtonner*, to beat, and *esquiver*, to dodge, or to duck, at the same time (*Essais critiques* 100). He bobs and weaves. Naves employs the same trope: Voltaire 'encourage d'une main et freine de l'autre ...' (Naves 15). But it was this latter capacity – shared with Edward Gibbon – that accounted for their warm receptivity to Erasmus, discussed below. Each, Erasmus and Voltaire, was credited with knowing where to draw the line that prevented excess.

Their rhetorical code of incorporation, of subordinated inclusions, naturally enough can cause confusion. And both Erasmus and Voltaire became objects of aphoristic witticisms, oxymoronic insult: Voltaire being credited with possessing the 'genius of mediocrity,' while presenting a 'chaos of clear ideas' (Trousson, *Visages* 440), and Erasmus with the 'perfection of unclearness.'[12] If this study has one purpose – as the preceding arguments indicate – it is to expose the inadequacy of such expenditures of wit in the presence of the extent and seriousness of their presumed victims' thought and achievements. Such restoration of Erasmus and Voltaire requires understanding them by other means than simply their historical importance, by entering the deeper recesses of their procedures, the eventful changes in their lives and thought, and the far-reaching import of their thinking.

Here we come to what even for this author was a major discovery and the source of a new engagement with the thought of Erasmus and Voltaire. However different the spiritual and practical dimensions of their epochs, however divergent their versions of humanism, however at variance their visions of the past, Erasmus and Voltaire shared a fundamental philosophical propensity and need. The philosophy of each was to be suspicious of philosophy and the need of each was to establish direct contact with what they valued. Unheralded and untold is the fact that what shines most clearly is their mutual need to go beyond the obfuscations of metaphysical and theological speculation and to establish direct contact with the living sources of their thought. Of course these waters of life differ in their origins and their natures: Erasmus and the Christian humanists of his day were obliged to brush aside the accretions of theological dogmatics in order to drink from the pristine waters of an early Christianity, found in the simplicity of the Gospels, in the words and acts of the apostles and in the works of the church fathers. In their view, these pure streams had been muddied and clogged, and every effort on Erasmus's part was devoted to clearing away the underbrush that thwarts direct contact. For Voltaire the broader reaches of philosophical thought and the great systematizations have similarly prevented vivid reaction, not to the teachings of Christ, which he had despoiled, but to the realities of existence, to the genuineness of original human response. It was perhaps their much-noted absence of self-absorption that directed their sights outwards onto clear and direct evidence, onto real objects that absorbing the self's attention helped maintain in each the notable quality of balance.

It is at the juncture of these dual enterprises that Erasmus and Voltaire are united historically in their efforts and goals. As in the construction of a transcontinental railroad, they had to meet half-way. The golden spike of their meeting was the notion of a 'second Reformation.' One of the many virtues of Mansfield's second of his three volumes, *Man on His Own*, is the leitmotif he strings through of 'two Reformations.' How to formulate and bring together the several contributions of Luther and Erasmus to modern culture was the problem. Some saw Erasmus as a defector, others saw Luther (and Calvin) as perverting into another kind of absolutism their very rebellion against absolutism. Others preferred to see a joint effort; the vehemence of Luther was required to fight the obstinacy of the Roman curia but after time, the moderating virtues of an Erasmus were required to initiate a 'second Reformation.' Edward Gibbon in chapter 54 of *The Decline and Fall of the Roman Empire* writes that 'since the days of Luther and Calvin a secret reformation has been silently working in the bosom of the reformed churches; many weeds of prejudice were eradicated, and the disciples of Erasmus diffused a spirit of freedom and moderation' (2:892). He cites the liberty of conscience and the practice of toleration that had spread to Holland and England. But another reason for Erasmus's appeal was to be found in Gibbon's fear of 'the boundless impulse of inquiry and skepticism,' particularly from among those 'who indulge the licence without the temper of philosophy' (2:893). Erasmus's reputation thus underwent a renewed afterlife among the liberal theologians following the Enlightenment. One such was Charles Beard (1827–88), who also tried to reconcile the separate roles of Luther and Erasmus, concluding that events justified each. 'The Reformation that has been,' is Luther's monument; perhaps the Reformation that is to be, will trace itself back to Erasmus,' to which Mansfield adds: 'This is probably the most famous formulation of the doctrine of the two Reformations, first stated by Gibbon and generally accepted by nineteenth-century liberals' (*Man on His Own* 173). Under the entry 'Reformation' in the index to Mansfield's second volume one can retrieve more names of the eminent theologians who found a way out in the notion of two Reformations.

While Erasmus had to be stripped of his *philosophia Christi* and his allegorical means of interpretation, Voltaire coming from the opposite direction needed to add some baggage, and this was his defence of and belief in a Supreme Intelligence, a 'Dieu unique' who was God of all the peoples and not subject to appropriation by any one of them, thus avoiding the contentious lines of separation necessary to form a cult, a sect, or a religion. Erasmus, by sub-terranean streams and indirect means, and Voltaire, by his active presence, thus are brought together in that much vaunted and historically valuable 'second Reformation.' If God did not exist, it would be necessary to invent 'him.' But for Voltaire God does exist in the immediate sensory apprehension of the unity and radiant power of the universe. This remarkable presence serves two func-tions; he is the policeman of the world, the cop walking the beat, who thus restrains while not fully checking the criminal impulse. But it is for the second reason that God would require invention: his divine presence is the guarantor of intellectual justice, the con-necting medium between humankind's mind and the world, the charter of the reality of things, and thus a guard against nihilism (see below, page 115).Voltaire's greatest and most implacable foe is this acquiescent submission to the ultimate disposability of all things. The destruction of the great systems of thought produces its own nemesis, the blight of an atheistic materialism and ulti-mately nihilism, a hollowness at the core of existence. Without a belief in God, humankind would thus fall victim to nothingness, and forfeit its primary resource, the legitimacy of the individual voice and the validity of genuine human response. Voltaire's God is the warrant of the proportionality between words and things, the adequacy of relationship between our minds and the world. Thus Voltaire adamantly insists that our minds treat 'objects,' and that 'moeurs' and 'esprit' are themselves constitutive of reality. But more than that, his God stands for the validation of human emotions and humane outcry. Whether in protest or in prayer, in outrage or in pacification, this validation would be lost without the sense of the divine presence. Voltaire's finest moments occur when he rises up in vocal protest against the human evils that compound the indignities of man's fate. His sense of a supreme being saves even this voice.

These three areas – their rhetoric of proportionate value, their need for a direct contact, and their coming together in the eigh-teenth-century hope for a 'second Reformation' – are like atmo-spheric elements that cover and are present in all phases of the thought of Erasmus and Voltaire. They colour and envelop the separate chapters that are built around more specific career epi-sodes, their works, and their crucial dualistic involvements. But one of the more surprising convergences occurs in another dis-covery. Almost inadvertently and certainly reluctantly Erasmus and Voltaire, each in his early fifties, underwent something like a 'mini' aesthetic conversion. Each had shifted gears and under some external persuasion and inducement took readily to a genre that they had formerly practically discounted, Erasmus to his colloquies and Voltaire to his *contes*. This change was nothing short of remarkable and a stunning anticipation on their parts of the preferences that posterity would show not for their works of high seriousness but for those that came easily to their pens. In fact, so easily did they come that both Erasmus and Voltaire may have overproduced. These issues will be aired in chapter 4, but one thing is clear: both the colloquies and the *contes* became virtual storehouses of their authors' best thoughts and reflections.

The largest and most critical convergence, one that stands out in the intellectual biography of each, representing the major engagement of their lives, is their participation in a dualism, Erasmus with Luther, and Voltaire (whether he wanted to or not, whether he acknowledged it or not) with Rousseau. In these defining debates of their ages, the two poles of the Western psyche exert their magnetic draw one on the other. They are set on a collision course. This study in canon formation naturally enough involves biography, but biography raised to the level of basic typologies. Because I neglected Zweig's work in my prior book on *Dualisms*, where I fully discussed the theory and practice of dualistic encounters, I may properly turn to him to suggest their presence and their impact. 'Seldom does destiny provide such fundamentally contrasted men as Erasmus and Luther, differing completely both as to character and as to physique ... Even when two such antagonistic temperaments work toward the same goal, they are bound to clash ... The conflict thus arising was inescapable and proved to be of worldwide significance' (Zweig 132, 136, 139). Not *even* when, but *especially* when they also have shared affinities, they are bound to clash. Such temperamental differences but linked in a common cause made conflict inevitable.

Their great differences and confrontations will be the subject of the last chapter, but there I introduce new materials, not discussed in *Dualisms*; for instance, I discuss their different 'temporalities' – not their conventional descriptions of Time as a concept but the way their experience of time enters into their blood and becomes part of their metabolism of life, and thus differs profoundly from the 'temporalities' of Luther and Rousseau. Next, where reductive pathologists passing as literary critics are normally concerned with 'le cas' of Rousseau, his troubled spirit, even his persecution complex, I explore the equally volatile and troubling 'case' of Voltaire, who strangely, inexplicably insisted on hounding the unsuspecting and helpless Rousseau. I suggest that Voltaire's own motivations may be explained by the demands of his participation in a dualistic encounter. Lastly I extract the quite similar deficiencies Erasmus and Voltaire found in their opponents, and the transformations this involvement brought to the lives and spirits of both of them. In thus faulting their opponents they also defined themselves.

The faded appeal of Erasmus and Voltaire derived in part from the personal and dynamic contrasts with their cross-rivals. Undoubtedly both suffered some diminishment in their controversies. Dualisms are stories of impact and transformation, of struggle and supersession. More than any other this engagement revealed their beings, elicited by a constant shadow companion, who alternatively thwarted, challenged, but in large measure defined them. Not effecting a total transformation, this opposition brought out qualities, made character traits that were always there more evident and more pronounced. Carducci's historical paradigm is accurate. Petrarch, Erasmus, and Voltaire at the acmes of their acclaim were the prime representatives of the progressive 'civiltà europea' but when confronted with Dante, Luther, and Rousseau, for whatever cause (fear, egotism, some internal resistance, or simply better thinking), they became more 'conservatori' (*Dualisms* 203). In the characters of Erasmus and Voltaire, despite their earlier heydays, it is obvious that, judging by their rhetoric, their methods, their positions taken, these qualities were resident but latent, needing only to be struck to be revealed.

But it is also clear that involvement in this dualism helps to sustain their continuing *actualité* and appeal. It has been argued that if we possessed only his *De servo arbitrio* (*On the Bondage of the Will*) we would be getting the 'full scope' of Luther's thought, but that would be because we would also be hearing Erasmus as well (Oberman 212). Conversely, Bataillon has argued that the significance of Erasmus's *De libero arbitrio* (*On the Freedom of the Will*) would have been slight but for the fact that it provoked Luther's formidable response (161). Like Voltaire and Rousseau, whose deaths were separated only by weeks in 1778, inevitably they are joined together in remembrance as they were in life. The linkage is indissoluble. And Zweig, with another remarkable insight, knows the dispute to be unending. Near the end of Erasmus's life, he tells us, Luther made something of a peace gesture, but Erasmus, personally wounded and blaming Luther for the 'tumult' that engulfed his century, turned it down (219). Similarly, when Rousseau offered to contribute to a subscription drive for the purpose of erecting a statue in Voltaire's honour, Voltaire declined to accept any subvention from that source. Indissoluble and unending, it is thus a mistake, I believe, to untwin the twain, to sever the symbiotic relationship that did so much to reveal and define the character and characteristics of each of the antagonists, and of their times as well.[13] Clearly, one additional reason among several is that participation in a dualism turns out to be a survival mechanism, where one's identity is preserved by its contrast with that of a natural opponent, one so different in character and purpose, one so unlike, that together they constitute in their grand opposition two dominant and competing types. Paradoxically, although diminished by it, this very liaison, this agon of debate, has contributed to the continuing presences of Erasmus and Voltaire.

Discussion of their historical fates seems to hover and linger over any discussion of Erasmus and Voltaire, mainly because it involves so much of their character and works. These are the two sources of both their attraction and their faded appeal, the simple directness of their works and the complexities and ambivalences of their characters. In each there seems to be required a double column of enormous credit and notable deficit.

In *Zadig*, amounting to a second preface as well as a defence of his work, Voltaire counters the kind of criticism which he must have heard in his time and which would continue to be heard prominently from the French Romantics. An envious courtier and his wife find fault with the justly acclaimed practical wisdom of Zadig; he doesn't make the mountains and the hills dance, the sea does not open up: 'il n'a pas le bon style oriental'; 'Il est sec et sans genie' *(Romans et contes* 73). But Voltaire responds by asserting that Zadig 'se contentait d'avoir le style de la raison.' Huizinga writes similarly of Erasmus, who is eternally *à propos*: 'What he writes is never vague, never dark – it is always plausible' (113). This is a major defence, but it also means that if there is a clear stability in their styles (not altogether true), there is a great lack: their works are never multilayered, are not open to what William James has called 'the deeper parts of our mental structures' (quoted in *Dualisms* 3). They are easily encompassed, never exceeding the level of their intent. Not only was each committed to direct contact with objects and events, but each also wrote in a style that was 'portable,' conveying easily absorbed material truths that the reader could carry with him or her. Thus they wrote to and for the lessons of the day. And this very topicality may have undone them. Victimized by their own success, their thoughts had become commonplace in the history they helped to forge.[14] But genius should have no need to go abegging. Their own works pointed the ways to higher aspirations. Both in their efforts to remodel the culture of their times showed their appreciation of the higher attainments of art and learning.

Their complex personalities both benefited from and were hampered by ambivalences. Acutely aware of the contradictions and contrasts in existence, they never sought unity of being, to be at one, but rather lived in response to the many pleats and bends of experience. Cautious, sceptical optimists, they were reconciled to the slow changes of time, and knowing observers they were aware of the complexities and contradictions of history. In other words, they acquired a wisdom that was more than practical, that contained its appropriate dosage of scepticism, rationalism, and reasonableness, with no tendency toward or appreciation of transcendence.[15] Reformers they always were, but they become more moderate in their aims and purposes.

Their diminished appeal has much to do with other less admirable traits of character. Erasmus was guarded, circumspect, and in most cases he shied away from direct combat. He himself owned up to a satiric style that wished to strike but not to draw blood. What attracted the fiercest criticism was not his mind but his character. From the earliest days, Ulrich von Hutten, a once devoted follower, learning of his intent to attack Luther, denounced Erasmus's abdication, his imputed traits of cowardice and fear, fear of giving offence (see Klawiter 45). Divided, wishing to have it both ways, Erasmus was, as Augustijn concludes, more content to be a spectator than a participant, a mediator, a spirit above the dust, never an antagonist. But this not unexpected defection took place after he had already established himself – well before Luther – as a leader in reform. Huizinga famously remarked that there was no Tarsus in Erasmus's life (33) and Erasmus himself on more than one occasion expressed doubts about his readiness for the full exercise of the Christian spirit, finding himself more than likely to follow the safer road. (CWE 8:259, quoted in Augustijn,

Erasmus 125). He feared that he would repeat Peter's denial.[16] Despite his many exhortations to follow in the footsteps of Christ, despite his spiritualized interpretations of biblical passages, Erasmus felt acutely his unwillingness to sacrifice all and to live by the commands of the spirit. This was more than an unwillingness to be a martyr for Luther's cause; rather it was more of an inbred hesitancy, a caution that responded to both sides of an argument, a practically minded attention to the ills of the world, and an ethical concern with simple steps of correction. It was in contest with Luther that he found himself to be wanting. He could not relieve himself of that critical habit of mind that tied him to the needs and purposes of the world. This was his dilemma, and one he suffered through with anguish.

But neither did Voltaire have any taste for martyrdom. Yet obviously, unlike Erasmus, he did not experience any anguish because of this lack. Erasmus could not bring himself to live the life of the spirit, but he also acknowledged this fact, and in so doing may have possessed more than his self-detraction allows for. And Voltaire, by the very means of his 'gamesomeness' and duplicities, never kept quiet, never accepted the safeguard of silence. In essence each was a lowlander rather than a mountaineer (Augustijn, *Erasmus* 200, repeating Huizinga 164, but deriving ultimately from Erasmus, 'Auris Batava' [The Dutch Ear], Phillips 211), but in the forthrightness of their responses they each revealed uncommon and redeeming virtues.

History hovers but it also beckons; it waylays and it uncovers far-flung affinities and attachments. Perhaps the real source of this present book on Erasmus and Voltaire is a personal one, involving the encounter of a member of the generation of the 1950s with the crushing debates and demands of the 1960s, and not only the antiwar, civil rights, and wholesale educational reform movements, but practically all aspects of social and intellectual life. Here the personal and the historical merge and a psychohistory intrudes. The generation of the 1950s, liberal and tolerant, product of the optimism created by victory in the Second World War, yet still descended from the lowered expectations of the formative Depression years of the 1930s, was similarly distracted by ambivalence. Here William Strauss and Neil Howe's *Generations* (1991), in its thematic of collective generational differences presenting another pillar of knowledge, is of immense usefulness. Members of this generation, they declare, 'respond ambivalently to anything they confront' and competing theories 'yield a consensus or "compromise" solution' (10). Trusting in a predictable order in future events, they were unexpectedly passed on the outside by a horse they had not anticipated or foreseen. Caught unawares, superseded by history itself, despite their own willingness to seek out reform, they were mired in foot-dragging, holding back and hesitant in the face of a younger generation's more radical sentiments. They could not stay their ground because it was shifting under their feet. According to Strauss and Howe, they 'reflect a lack of surefootedness' but they also had 'a keen sense of how and why humans fall short of grand civic plans or ideal moral standards' (282) and here the contemporary sociologists might just as well be describing Erasmus and Voltaire (as arguments below will indicate). Members of the 1950s generation were caught in the middle, betwixt and between. In the middle of their ways they came across a historical onslaught that they could neither quite join nor ignore. From their own dilemma they were in a position to understand the ambiguous roles that history imposed upon Erasmus and Voltaire, with one hand enlisting their forward movement but with the other tearing out their hearts. Given a world view of such 'enormous complexity' this generation suffered 'a wounded collective ego,' and it is not surprising that as they got older they also found refuge in 'resignation' (292). This hardly enviable perspective does, however, draw one closer to the predicaments and problems faced by Erasmus and Voltaire, and if it does not constitute a complete restoration of their reputations, it can at the very least make of their lives and works a true cornucopia for current literary discussion, a bridge uniting opposite shores where those coming and going can convene. From this new vantage point, the revitalized forms of Erasmus and Voltaire make an especially compelling call on our attention.

PART ONE

CAREER EPISODES

ONE

Names for Bastards

꿏

Names! What's in a name?
James Joyce, *Ulysses*

In his brilliant discussion of dualisms, his attempt to get at the 'radical' nature of dissimilar personalities, Coleridge dismisses 'similarity of events and outward actions' as not being indicative of real resemblance (*The Friend* 1:130). Yet, career episodes can be essentially revealing, particularly when they carry with them deeper motivations and emotional consequences. It is typical of the natures of Erasmus and Voltaire that small, unobtrusive beginnings have their ways of opening out onto larger endings.

An early 'outward fact' that establishes the first affinity between Erasmus and Voltaire is that each changed or altered his name. By itself this might mean little. But sometimes a name is more than a name; names can imply things, particularly when they are chosen, as if one were rebaptized, self-determind, and free to become the person one wanted to be, and thereby choosing one's own affinities. A change of name is often the outward sign of a new beginning, of a new freedom, a freedom to follow one's aspirations. But the open road is not a road leading anywhere. There are powerful obstacles as well as false routings. Standing in the way of each of these men is the father figure, whether by his absence or his presence, but whose name in the process is being undone. Jacques Chomarat, for instance, attributes Erasmus's unwillingness to accept a leadership role in the reform movement of which he was the nominal leader to his failure to 'interiorize' the father (2:1165–6). Where Erasmus tried to live down the fact that he was by birth a bastard child, Voltaire chose to spread the rumour that he was born from his mother's love liaison. He fought all his young life with the presence of his father, who was a highly placed state bureaucrat. But this rebellion had its consequences as well; his cutting up, his acting-out in behaviour that could be considered a little more than strange, exacted a price that later would have to be paid. In all of this mix of different and yet similar starting points and character traits, one thing stands clear: each managed to find his own way to his genius.

The names chosen by each as well as the reasons for the new elaborations were resoundingly different. Why Erasmus may not have been totally satisfied with his given name might appear to be only a minor quibble. He would have preferred the name Erasmius (closer to the Greek original 'erasmios,' in its adjectival form meaning 'amiable' or beloved, rather than the noun form indicating simply 'Love'). Erasmus thus implied beloved of God (O'Rourke Boyle 12). However, memorials to St Erasmus, martyred under Diocletian, were not uncommon – 'he enjoyed a lively cult in the fifteenth century' (O'Rourke Boyle 12). Erasmus could have seen his memorials in a chapel in Westminster Abbey and at the Church of St Peter in Louvain. But as Marjorie O'Rourke Boyle reminds us, 'Erasmus of Rotterdam was not inclined to indulge in hagiography' (13), particularly of a saint whom one beseeched for material wealth and riches, or for relief from ailments of the bowels. Quite simply, she concludes,'there is no biographical evidence that Erasmus's patron saint influenced his spiritual aspirations' (14).

But the matter changes completely when it involves his choice of a new name. Better than he knew, there was a strong correspondence between Desiderius, indicating a 'longing for,' and Erasmus's own personality There is also some coincidence between the historical figure of Desiderius and Erasmus's own dawning spiritual vocation. He first used the name in a letter to his former patron Hendrik van Bergen in 1496 and again in a letter to John Colet in 1499. The full form Desiderius Erasmus Roterodamus first occurs in the preface to the first edition of the *Adagia collectanea* of 1500 (O'Rourke Boyle 16). While both O'Rourke Boyle and Schoeck remark upon the conventionality of such name changes within classicizing humanistic circles (it is even satirized in *The Praise of Folly*), with Erasmus the name addition was more than a nod toward convention. It represented several spiritual awakenings, first as a humanist devoted to belles-lettres and then subsuming this as a scholar devoted to sacred literature.

The new name is a figure in self-fashioning. In a letter to a former pupil Erasmus describes his boredom in attending a scholastic lecture in Paris. At the time he was residing at the Collége de Montaigu. He playfully asks his correspondent to imagine him, Erasmus, a man committed to letters, forced to endure and trying to absorb a dense lecture: 'If only you could see your Erasmus sitting agape among those glorified Scotists, while "Gryllard" lectures from a lofty throne. If you could but observe his furrowed brow, his uncomprehending look and worried expression, you would say it was another man' (CWE 1:136–8). This important excerpt suggests a beginning phase of Erasmus's self-fashioning. Already Erasmus was framing a self-image, that of a humanist (with some ambitions as a poet), one which he exploits to show the humorous discrepancy of Erasmus residing among the scholastics.

But there is more to the name-addition than this. If at the earliest dating of his own self- naming he could not be counted among the new theologians, by which enterprise he would make his later fame, still it showed the future directions of his thought. It constituted a 'presentiment' of his greater vocation. 'It coincides suggestively with his growing theological vocation' (O'Rourke Boyle 20). Desiderius was a correspondent of Jerome, Erasmus's favourite among the church fathers. Huizinga with his intuitive insight suggests this as the reason for the name adoption (6), abundantly supported by Professor Boyle's more detailed gem of scholarly investigation. The addition of Desiderius brings together his genuine aspirations of combining virtue with eloquence and his future devotion to biblical studies as well as his numerous editions of the early church fathers, aided by his long immersion in classical authors. As he looks backwards from a letter of 1501 (which later became the opening and closing paragraphs of the *Enchiridion* (1503), his first major statement of theological import), this is the ulterior purpose he sees as being behind all his earlier literary efforts. The letter finally provides Erasmus's own understanding and clarification of his genuine motives throughout this trying period, starting with his departure from the monastery at Steyn (never to return), to his three-year stay at the court of the bishop of Cambrai, to his ill-advised studies in Paris, to his period of self-discovery and self-confirmation amid the English humanists. Finally he makes a clear record and defence of the purposes that were driving him. He had always felt the need to justify himself against his critics at Steyn; now he feels he can do so fully and faithfully. When in his youth he embraced the finer literature of the ancients – 'not without much midnight labour'– this was not out of a desire for fame or selfgratification, but rather according to a 'long ago determined' program to use these classical ornaments to adorn the Lord's temple that had been desecrated by 'ignorance and barbarism.' He then goes on to employ a phrase that captures our attention. Such treasures 'can inspire even men of superior intellect' (et generosa ingenia) to love the scriptures (CWE 66:127; Allen 1:374–5). There is that in the essence of Christianity which can appeal to the intelligences (called 'noble' or 'lofty') of worldly successful men – not simpletons, not children. The language is astonishing: it is men of superior intellect, and presumably of worldly accomplishment, who have been alienated and are now in need of persuasion. These adults active in the world were to become Erasmus's intended audience throughout his life. As a Christian intellectual, Erasmus will always reach out to such people, eminent lay people who may have been put off by the apparent childishness of common religious practices and thought.

François-Marie Arouet also changed his name but the nature of the name, the reasons for the change, the occasions from which it emerged, and the effectual consequences in his thought and work differed enormously from those of Erasmus. Having been twice exiled and once committed to the Bastille (for some particularly suggestive and pungent verses concerning the sexcapades of the Regent, Philippe, duc d'Orleans, which lines Voltaire denied writing), Voltaire resolved to turn over a new leaf. The young man who had a bon mot for every occasion and a reception in every sheltering chateau avowed a change of life, a new dedication. For a few years he had been engrossed in writing his first play, *Oedipe*, the production of which had been delayed by his internment, as well as by disagreements with the actors, who had a controlling voice. While in prison he also composed hundreds of lines of his future epic, *La Henriade* (earlier known by the more opprobrious title, *La Ligue*). These works would bring a blaze of fame not to Arouet, but rather to the newly adopted identity of Voltaire. It is in a letter to the earl of Ashburnum that we first find the valedictory signature, Arouet de Voltaire, and on the title page of the first edition of *Oedipe* (1719), we find 'par Monsieur de Voltaire' (Besterman, *Voltaire* 76; Pomeau, *D'Arouet à Voltaire* 115–18).

Not only does the change of name mark a new beginning, it carries with it many of Voltaire's characteristics. To change from

Arouet was not a hard choice. As Casanova remarked, 'Voltaire would not have become immortal under the name of Arouet. He would have felt himself degraded by hearing himself always named 'à rouer' ('to be beaten,' Besterman, *Voltaire* 76). But the new name itself exerted a positive attraction. While Erasmus's changed name would indicate a smiling benevolence, a religious piety, as one 'beloved' of God, 'Voltaire' indicates a sprightliness, a verve, a vivacity of spirit, a leap in the air, the bubbly effervescence of champagne, as memorialized in his poem, *Le Mondain*. Indeed he redeemed his early tutelage under the wits and wags, the so-called *libertins*, relics from the court of Louis XIV, by his remarkable wit, which had become an integral part of his manners as well as his mores. One overcomes the awkwardness of any situation by a well-timed and well-turned remark. And so Voltaire paid a courtesy visit to the Regent, the man who had imprisoned him, soliciting his continued interest in his board ('nourriture'), but begging him not to bother further about his bed ('logement'); in short, patronage is preferable to imprisonment (Pomeau, *D'Arouet à Voltaire* 115). Such are the winning effects of the bold effrontery of wit.

There are other more contentious contrasts that emerge from the change of name. The first has to do with bastardy. Again the different reactions are notable. While Erasmus struggled to live down and even erase the taints and handicaps of being born of an illicit union, it was Voltaire himself who was behind the story that he was not the son of an irascible highly placed tax accountant, but was in fact the offspring of an affair between his mother and the duc de Rochebrune, a minor librettist and a nobleman to boot. Voltaire, with his flair for liveliness awash with scandal, revelled in the very situation that understandably constrained Erasmus.

In construing Erasmus's birth and early years, modern commentators are not so much beset by a dearth of information as by its one-sidedness. In 1524 Erasmus dispatched a *compendium vitae* to one Conradus Goclenius, the designated keeper of the flame (CWE 10:230–8). The document, while valuable, is still one of artful self-fashioning (whenever was a cv unflattering, or devoid of self-enhancements?). As to his birth, the story he tells – here the over-utilized modern term 'narrative' is appropriate – is that his father, Gerardus, was being steered toward the priesthood by a large family not interested in a further division of the patrimony. While in Italy Gerardus was deceitfully informed that his beloved Margareta, then pregnant with Erasmus, had died. Distraught, Gerardus then entered the priesthood, thus curtailing any possibility of marrying Margareta and bestowing legitimacy upon Erasmus. This taint hampered Erasmus throughout his life, particularly since bastardy disqualified one from obtaining a university degree, ecclesiastical benefice, or even from writing a will (Rummel, *Erasmus* 3). Born out of wedlock and beset with penury (both of his parents died when Erasmus was between thirteen and sixteen), Erasmus was induced by his guardians to enter the monastery at Steyn. Both of these impediments, that of being born out of wedlock and entering the monastic life for which he had no true calling, Erasmus worked to remove by dispensations. In 1506 Julius II granted Erasmus 'because of his merits' the right to receive ecclesiastical benefits despite his being the offspring 'of an unmarried father and widow' (Schoeck 1:28). A later dispensation, granted by Leo X in 1516, is however more severe in its language, claiming Erasmus, as he himself fears, to be the offspring of 'an incestuous and condemned union' (Schoeck 1:30, 39n20). From personal experience, I know that church documents can be terribly revealing, as my own father's baptismal certificate indicated that his mother's long-gone husband could not have been his father. Moreover, there are some indications that Gerardus may already have been a priest at the time of the liaison, and the fact that Erasmus had a brother older by three years possibly indicates that the relationship may have been one of longer-standing.

Brothers are not for the sons of history, or for heroes. While Huizinga records that the relationship between Erasmus and his brother Pieter was cordial in their earlier years (8), later Erasmus turned with unusual venom against his brother, who 'had an eye toward the main chance, was not above stealing money, a sturdy drinker and a wencher far from idle, in short so unlike his younger brother that you might think he was a changeling' (Rummel, *Erasmus* 3). Voltaire harboured great hostility toward his (by ten years) elder brother Armand. Their differences apparently came early on. Armand attended Saint-Magloire from which he emerged an ardent Jansenist; Voltaire attended Louis-le-Grand, where Jesuits encouraged his genius for letters. The father despaired of each, claiming them both to be crazies, one with devotion and the other with impiety. But it is no secret that Armand was regarded as the more reliable son. When the senior Arouet died in 1722 he left Voltaire a substantial inheritance, but only to be meted out annually by an executor. The father was well acquainted with his son's prodigality. Evidently the father himself underwent a change of heart and attempted by means of a codicil to his will to restore young Arouet to his full inheritance, but he died before he could sign the amendment.

Given his background, his uprooting, and his strivings, Erasmus's nature was of a mixture of critical intelligence and deeper needs. His historically critical mind served to disallow many a legendary saint, just as his abhorrence of a materialized religion demoted the popular veneration of quite dubious holy relics. At the same time he was reluctant to exclude them totally. His rhetoric, based upon the hierarchical scale of proportionate values, is filled with 'take back' clauses, where practices that had been formerly rejected are brought back when given their proper spiritual or allegorical understanding. On a larger plane, this rhetorical tendency toward reconsideration shows itself in his reluctance to break with the mother church, with his 'matrix' view of time and history, and with his search for consensus. It anticipates and makes less surprising his later reversals. Despite his sharply critical mind Erasmus is filled with longing, thus providing an insightful psychological basis for his added name.

One exemplary instance occurs in 'A Pilgrimage for Religion's Sake' ('Peregrinatio religionis ergo,' 1526), where visits to the shrines of Our Lady of Walsingham and St Thomas at Canterbury are recounted. Unlike Dante, unlike Chaucer, who regarded pilgrimage as the true spiritual metaphor for *homo viator*,[1] but very much like Luther, Erasmus frequently argues against pilgrimage per se, reminding his readers that it is much better to remain at home and discharge one's responsibilities to family and neighbours than to waste one's resources visiting other lands. On this issue there is no equivocation, but when it comes to 'ceremonials' or to the veneration of saints and the adoration of relics, Erasmus can be of two minds. The most notable example might be the so-called letter from Mary, which Erasmus inserted to express his own ambivalences. The first part of the letter abhors the misdirected use of prayer as extortion, whereby petitioners turn to the Virgin for all manner of worldly gain and assistance. As in another colloquy, 'The Shipwreck' ('Naufragium, ' 1523), Erasmus deplores such error not only for its obvious recourse to bargaining, but mainly for the deflection it represents from a primary reliance on Christ. But in the latter part of the letter Erasmus stoutly defends the place of Mary in serious Christian belief. He deplores the neglect, abandonment, and desecration of her places of worship by some zealots of reform. Despite Erasmus's disclaimer that it was intended as a satire of Zwingliite iconoclasm, the letter came under attack from the University of Paris. In his argument Erasmus yields to elegant sentiment, even in the manner of George Santayana, to a kind of aesthetic appreciation. She, the Virgin Mother, cannot be ejected 'unless at the same time you eject my son whom I hold in my arms. From him I will not be parted. Either you expel him along with me, or you leave us both here, unless you prefer to have a church without Christ' (CWE 40:628). The argument, Erasmian in its effect and frequency, is twofold: it is wrong to turn to Mary in lieu of turning to God or to Christ, but it is equally wrong to remove her from the hospices of Christian belief. This would be tantamount to truncating the Christian family. Do we hear in this plea the voice of the orphaned Erasmus, who requires a matrix view of human history and experience, and who has endured separation himself and thus does not wish it in the Holy Family? Recall Kierkegaard's comment that Luther devised a religion for the adult male!

Chomarat, in his brilliant study of Erasmus's rhetoric, remarks on Erasmus's role as a satirist to 'steal himself away,' to remove himself (2:1165). Furthermore, in Erasmus values are hierarchical; thus they may be subordinated but not totally rejected. Once primary values are assured, lesser values, compromised in themselves, such as ceremonials, fasting, aural confessions, and other human ordinances, may be reintroduced. This is also part of Erasmus's 'relativism' and the Pauline doctrine of expediency. In 'The Whole Duty of Youth' (Confabulatio pia, 1522) one of the characters lauds the proverb, 'Not everything, not everywhere, nor to everybody' (CWE 39:97), which later receives its confirmation heard throughout Erasmus's works: 'If something commonly accepted by Christians is not clearly at variance with Sacred Scripture, I observe it to the extent of not offending anyone' (99); or more notoriously, 'The truth does not always have to be told, and it matters greatly how it is told' (Rummel, *Erasmus* 12). Thus, Ogygius, the simple-minded visitor to the shrines mentioned above, is naive in his acceptance of the more shadowy objects of spiritual show. He does accept as authentic the pseudoletter from Mary, but also asks for some accounting of the milk that Mary allegedly spurted onto a rock. He also provides a more acceptable interpretation of how the milk should be understood and venerated in prayer: the human soul, cleansed by the blood of Christ, 'longs without ceasing for the milk of gospel doctrine, until it attains to the perfect man, to the measure of the fullness of Christ' (CWE 40:633), and (on the next page) it is by emulation of Mary that people are made ready to receive Christ.

Erasmus's mode is concessionary, at first indicating abuses but then taking pains under proper circumstances to reinstate. Not willing to exclude them totally, he is in need of a saving remnant. Personally he is content to be a spectator, a commentator and not an arbitrator. One of Luther's constant complaints is that in his satiric mode Erasmus fails to advance an argument for effectual practice. To enter Erasmus's works is like riding a carousel, where many points are touched but a handhold is much more elusive. He is like Proteus, hard to pin down, and slippery as an eel.

This line of thought that we have been following, the orphaned boy, the poor scholarship student with a need to please, the elusive satirist, the failure to interiorize the father (and a far more serious wanting, the failure to interiorize the love of a mature person), sets him off in many ways from Voltaire, who had an imperturbable sense of belonging, who managed by wit to overcome social unpleasantness and more. Rather than a matrix view of nature, society, and history, one that looked for and required consensus, Voltaire was consumed by a need to break with the past. He felt no need to interiorize his father but rather he killed him off.

The theme of parricide is present in Voltaire's drama, but is not as rampant as is thought. *Brutus* culminates in filiocide, and *La Mort de César* does end in parricide, but relies upon the mythical belief that Brutus was actually the son of Caeser.[2] Even in *Oedipe*, the play that has attracted unsurprisingly most of the psychological examination, the major and revealing themes do not involve parricide at all. To be sure, there is a personal urgency in *Oedipe* not present in other Voltaire works; it shows the years of attentive labour, when he as a young man was undergoing his most strenuous trials with his own father and learning to hate his brother's religious devotion to Jansenism. In this play, Pomeau reports, Voltaire was carried away by his subject (*D'Arouet à Voltaire* 126). So, it is practically inescapable that such familial tensions should penetrate this first work. They are present but overcome and that is the play's real meaning.

The play naturally carries with it interpretations of parricide and of *frères ennemis*. Voltaire rightly criticized the play as not being one but two plays (OC, IA, 365–6). With the introduction of the heroic wandering Philoctète, who had once loved and still loves Jocaste, he complicates the plot centred on the original nuclear family. But where a drama critic senses an anomaly, a reader given to *psycholecture* senses an opening. Whence comes this untoward intervention? What are the psychic pressures at the root of the dislocation? For J.-M. Moureaux, who provides an admirable example of such *psycholecture*, Philoctète is the character in whom Voltaire has 'probably' put most of himself (55). Against the malicious charges made against him, Voltaire is upholding his personal honour (see *Première lettre*, OC, IA, 325–31) just as Philoctète is emerging from the horrendous triangle by a sense of a higher calling, with a better model to support him and lead him on. Philoctète returns to Thebes, only to find Jocaste married to Oedipe, who had once represented a 'menace' toward her previous husband Laius. Not only is there some spirit of rivalry now with Oedipe but their relationship is exacerbated when Oedipe accuses Philoctète of having killed Laius (based on their previous history) and thus being the one responsible for the plague afflicting Thebes. Philoctète's wounded sense of honour prevents him from even responding to such an accusation. The two anomalous strands thus find their unity in the different fates of the two 'brothers.' Philoctète manages to rescue himself from this psychic disorder, from the infernal triangle, by bringing to mind his higher calling. He was the warrior-companion of the incomparable Hercules, who destroyed the many monsters of the land. Hercules now stands as his model in recuperation, the model to emulate. This renewed calling rescues him from any imagined or imputed parricide. He has better things to do than to participate in any sibling rivalry for the affections of the mother. The other brother, Oedipe, is however caught up in the entanglement and does not achieve his independence, but rather a self-inflicted blinding and exile. The preferred son suffers his own fate.

Such a reading is highly suggestive and up to a certain point legitimate. These deeper tensions help account for the play's tremendous success and are the result and reward of Voltaire's long preoccupation with it (in contrast to other works that he dashed off in a matter of weeks). But we must remember that Philoctète and Oedipe are not brothers, although they are rivals, in a fashion, for Jocaste's love. Above all, the characters in the play act with a rectitude, self-denying on the parts of Jocaste and Philoctète, and kingly on the part of Oedipe, who behaves with a stern righteousness in his pursuit of the culprit. While their fates are horrendous their characters are all good, even noble. Perhaps Pomeau is right in seeing the play as being anti-Jansenist, and that Voltaire in the warfare between the two factions is siding with his early teachers, the Jesuits (128). But there can be no question of the association of Philoctète and Voltaire, as a kind of self-portrait of choice and aspiration. Philoctète chose the path of honour and glory by following his recovered model, the heroic Hercules. Voltaire in the midst of writing *Oedipe* was already on the way to discovering his own model, the great Henri IV. The poet had found his prince, 'le poète, son chevalier,' and the acknowledged heir of Corneille and Racine was soon to become the French Virgil.

Whether right in claiming the true theme of the play to be *amitié*, Pomeau is certainly correct in placing friendship on one of the highest rungs in Voltaire's scale of values (129). But there is more to it than this. Friendship is part of a broader aggregation of virtues, those that go into the making of a *republique littéraire*, the free association of like-minded individuals who together or apart are independently advancing the cause of freedom, reason, and knowledge. It is this association that elevates Voltaire above the accommodating culture of mundanity, and represents his true ideals and aspirations. Membership in this select grouping is his goal. In his schedule of the highest honours, culture and politics come together, as occurred, he tells us, in *Le siécle de Louis XIV*, in Periclean Athens, in Augustan Rome, in Florence under the Medicis, and most recently in the century of the great Louis XIV. In fact it could be said that, rather than the dead Laius, the real presiding genius of his *Oedipe* is the recently departed monarch. In his wake and in diminished circumstances the children must carry on, defining themselves in the aftermath of the grandeur of the preceding century. For his part, Erasmus may briefly entertain an ideal where politics, culture, and primarily peace converge (see page 92 below, and where Erasmus's letters are aglow with the promise offered by the accession to power of Henry VIII, Leo X, Charles V, and François I), but his ideal kingdom is that of Christ, which may have found its worthy human representation in the original spiritual inspiration at the time of the apostles – 'the primitive church with its strict commandments' (Augustijn, *Erasmus* 85) –

even extended forward to the great age of the church fathers. But degeneration attends all human matters. And it is to restore the purity of the earlier communities, to clear away the accretions that have blocked the paths to a true Christian faith, whether by the decadent and disputatious scholastics or the rivalries within the various monastic orders, that Erasmus seeks out a community of scholars, laymen as well as ecclesiastics, who adhere to the spiritual principles of Christianity.

It is by these qualities, with all their differences, that finally, under the aegis of a more comprehensive truth, Voltaire and Erasmus enjoy their more affective affinities. No longer representative men, but rather as individuals, they share several spiritual principles, first, a devoted attachment to friendship and then the larger interest in cultivating, protecting, and advancing the republic of letters. The insightful and eminently readable Huizinga quotes from an early letter of Erasmus: 'My mind is such that nothing can rank higher in this life than friendship' (12). And throughout his life Erasmus sought with some success to engage himself in discourse with a circle of like-minded friends who willingly brought together piety and learning (104). In fact, his greatest colloquy, 'The Religious Feast' (Convivium religiosum, 1522), describes such a gathering in practice. From different sources he did arrive at the same embrace of the 'res publica literaria' (Rummel, *Erasmus* 41). But, more than a community of interests, there is a direct filiation between the two men, as F. Schalk has shown in a thorough piece of historical scholarship, 'Erasmus und die *Res Publica Literaria*,'[3] which traces the spread of Erasmus's ideal through the various Academies, to Leibniz and ultimately to Voltaire. In Voltaire's argument what is most important is not the organization of effort (that does come later – he was after all an academician), but the fact that the common arguments of scientists and philosophers were arrived at '*insensiblement*,' or independently, thus forming what could be called a movement. Thus the shared interests of Erasmus and Voltaire emerge and then merge together as one of the large sustaining poles of Western thought and culture.

Such intellectual cosmopolitanism came with some cost as well as reward. Their jointly held allegiances to *res publica literaria* and the broad culture of enlightenment involved both Erasmus and Voltaire in conflict with their rivals in the famous dualisms. And at the same time, their wide-ranging cosmopolitanism required an intellectual vagabondage. Erasmus was a roaming scholar feeling at home wherever there was a library and an active printing press. He spent many years in England, moving to Louvain in 1517. When things in Louvain among his Catholic critics began to heat up, Erasmus felt obliged to move to Basel. When the Protestant faction there assumed controlling power, he moved to Freiburg im Breisgau in 1529. His own ability to move about and to set up shop in different areas was obviously abetted by the scholarly prevalence of spoken Latin. For his part, Voltaire, according to Besterman, spent 'half his life' in England, in the Netherlands, in Prussia and other parts of Germany, and in what is now Switzerland. He was able to carry on effective correspondence in English, Italian, German, Spanish, and Latin. The last twenty-eight years of his life were spent far from the Paris of his great triumphs. The republic of letters was the necessary recompense and refuge for a scattered life, shared by each.

What is most indicative of the characters of Erasmus and Voltaire is that instruments of potential bondage became episodes of self-transformation. Their name changes and bastardies were of a piece. What these accidents and actions purveyed above all was the freedom to choose, to be what one most earnestly and tenaciously decided to be. Thus their very lack of attachment, their capacity to move on, brought with them the sense of a higher calling. Far from impediments – although in Erasmus's case these were cause for worry – they provided both the incentive and the opportunity to pursue their own goals. Even their much utilized scale of proportionate value afforded them the shifting possibilities of choice. By virtue of their enormous gifts and personal determination both found in this freedom the power to surmount obstacles, to pursue earnestly their callings and to emerge as freestanding men of letters and defenders of culture and civilization. In this, their first convergence, we can detect the scaffolding for their respective later achievements.

TWO

England, Always England

Another major affinity between the two is that protracted stays in England marked genuine turning points and milestones in each of their careers. It was in England during his first visit in 1499 that Erasmus found the recognition he had so earnestly sought; in England Erasmus was 'discovered' (Augustijn, *Erasmus* 32). But there is more: in England Erasmus found a circle of highly placed Christian intellectuals who combined learning with piety. He came upon his heart's desire, that is, a group of enlightened, pious, and learned friends, and in their confluence of interests he gave as much as he received. Yet, in altogether six visits to England (not including the brief excursion of 1517 to receive the papal dispensation), the astonishing fact is that despite such extended exposure Erasmus never acquired any fluency in English (although it is hard to imagine him not acquiring some smattering of conversational English). Such was the extent of the Latinate culture of his time that this did not hold him back nor impede the vigorous exchanges among his newly found friends and allies.

Erasmus came to England at the invitation of his tutorial student, Lord Mountjoy, and with some reputation as a promising humanist (Seebohm 16; Huizinga 27).[1] Voltaire visited England as part of a plea bargain which cut short his second stay in the Bastille. This was 1726; he did not leave England until 1728. He was greeted and entertained as France's most illustrious writer, but at the time left little imprint on the culture of England. England in the two centuries since Erasmus had changed considerably. Erasmus met a brilliant but limited circle of striving Christian humanists and an England that was just beginning to venture out onto the seas.[2] Voltaire encountered an England that had flourished in literature, philosophy, and science, with Shakespeare and Milton, with Bacon, Locke, and Newton. So, Voltaire brought back to France more than he left in England. He altered the nature of French drama, was the first to translate a Shakespearean play (the first three acts of *Julius Caesar*) into French, appropriated Locke, and popularized Newton. The astonishing fact is that prior to his two-year visit, Voltaire had never heard of Shakespeare and yet he was responsible for converting France from rampant Anglophobia into something approaching Anglomania. He did this in part because of his extraordinary gift in acquiring foreign languages, by assiduous study, by constant conversation, and by being a devoted playgoer. Within a short period of time Voltaire became so proficient in speaking and writing English that the first version of *Lettres philosophiques* was written in English as *Letters concerning the English Nation* and he also wrote his major essay on epic poetry in English as well. By changing himself Voltaire changed the tastes and interests of his people. His first dramas upon his return were *Brutus* and *La Mort de César*, both plays showing the influence of Shakespeare both in subject and effects. But Voltaire also came back with a greater interest in being a philosopher, one that was armed and ready for combat, noticeable in the additions to the *Letters concerning the English Nation* to be found in *Lettres philosophiques* (essays on Bacon, Locke, and Newton, and, beyond all, a lengthy addition disputing Pascal).

While hardly fledglings (each was in his early thirties) both Erasmus and Voltaire found their new wings for flight in England. Erasmus's first visit was in 1499, the next in 1505–6. The third more extensive visit went from August 1509 to August 1514, prompted by the death of Henry VII, the accession of Henry VIII, the return to power of his friends, including Thomas More, and the great hopes for literary patronage, for the sake of which he cut short his long-awaited but disappointing trip to Italy. There were two additional visits in May of 1515 and in the summer of 1516, but it was the first three that brought Erasmus together with John Colet (1467–1519), John Fisher (1469–1535), William Grocyn (?–1519), William Latimer (c1460–1545), Thomas Linacre (1460–1524), Thomas More (1477/8–1535), and William Warham (c1456–1532).[3] These were men of scholarly note or highly placed in government, the university, or the church. They were attached to the new learning and in particular the acquisition of Greek (with some stabs at Hebrew). In their various fashions they could be called the Oxford-London reformers. Erasmus was himself one of the centres of their circling attention, as again in various degrees they collaborated with him, sponsored him, or otherwise provided him with benefices, emoluments, or pensions. It should be remembered that these financial rewards did not go toward a high style of living; rather they provided him with the means to purchase books and to pursue the study of Greek, which led to the scholarly work and publications to which he was so fully committed. And their support was well repaid. Craig R. Thompson in his classic essay, 'Erasmus and Tudor England,' attributes *The Praise of Folly* (*Moriae encomium*), Erasmus's work on new editions of the *Adagia*, and the supreme accomplishments of Jerome's letters and the Greek New Testament to the third lengthier stay (31–2).[4] This listing does not include the earlier *Enchiridion*, for which Seebohm makes special claims, nor the first collection of the *Adages*.

Every one of his newly won circle of friends had benefited from visits to Italy. In fact, H.R.Trevor-Roper refers to the movement as being Florentine-Oxford. Most of them brought back a knowledge of Greek (Grocyn, Latimer, Linacre). Grocyn had begun his study of Greek at Oxford before leaving for Italy and upon his return introduced a course in Greek ('the first to be offered at the university' CEBR 136). Seebohm notes that Grocyn had 'for some time been publicly teaching Greek at Oxford' to which statement he adds, 'not altogether to the satisfaction of the old divines' (8). Colet never learned that language to his regret, as he wrote in a later letter to Erasmus, but nevertheless encouraged fully the 'new learning.' These young Englishmen encountered not the pagan Italy of disrepute, but an Italy (particularly in Florence, and in other parts as well, such as Padua and Ferrara) that was undergoing its own spiritual revolution. One source of this spiritual awakening was the Neoplatonic academy of Marsilio Ficino, where the Aristotelianism of the scholastics was abandoned, replaced by an attractive alliance formed between Platonic eloquence and Christian doctrine and influenced by the dominating calls to a Christian piety and ecclesiastical purity on the part of Savonarola (who unfortunately met the fate of the 'unarmed prophet' for which he stands as Machiavelli's exemplar). While the general reader might be surprised by the introduction of the name of Savonarola here, there is no question but that translations of his sermons and commentaries on the Psalms were another source of the later Erasmian reforms of Tudor England (McConica, *English Humanists* 195).

The greatest Italian poet of the age, Angelo Poliziano, was also a scholar of merit and so recognized by the English. This was not the lax Rome of Luther's Italian experience, but rather a Florence of ideal religious aspiration that left its own imprint on the young English scholars who sought in common a new learning based upon new sources and linguistic capabilities.

From his first arrival in 1499 to his departure in 1506 after his second visit, Erasmus leaves us abundant evidence of how the England of the Oxford-London reformers fulfilled his dearly held dream of a scholarly community of like-minded men. Writing to John Colet from Oxford in October 1499, he does not hold back: 'Now, one of the many reasons why I find your England most agreeable is this in particular, that it is well supplied with that without which life is disagreeable to me, I mean men who are well-versed in good literature ...' (quod iis rebus abundant, praeter quas nihil mihi solet esse iucundum, hominibus bonarum literarum scientisssimis... CWE 1:201; Allen 1:245). Leaving London after his second visit of 1506, Erasmus writes similarly 'that there is no land on earth in which he has found such groupings of men, so sincere, so learned, so dutiful ... so imbued with every virtue as he has found in the single city of London' (CWE 2:119; Allen 1:428; also quoted in Seebohm 114).

While others joined forces, thus creating if not a movement, at least an intellectual 'circle' of impressive credentials, it was John Colet and Thomas More who entered into the closest working relationship with Erasmus. Colet, in particular, had a profound impact on Erasmus's Christian belief and practice. Having returned from Italy Colet began giving very popular lectures on Paul's Epistles. These lectures were unusual not only in subject matter but in method. Colet confronted Paul's Epistles in their totality, deriving meaning from the literal story as it was told as well as from the historical context. As a means of elucidation, he also introduced comparisons with other works of the gospels, the Epistle of John, for example. He did not adopt the method of the current scholastics, who would choose an isolated text and then tease many sorts of meanings from that passage, some quite abstruse or far-fetched. These were frequently virtuoso performances in distancing ramifications. Colet was different and what endeared him to More as well as to Erasmus was their interest in effectual Christian practice, in those qualities that appealed to men of the world. Colet's lectures drew attention because of the personal

incursions he made into the meaning of the apostolic letters. He
spoke directly and freely, not as a doctor of philosophy but as
a man speaking to men. He said what he meant and he meant
what he said (Seebohm 19). When after 1503 he became Dean of
St Paul's, his sermons continued to be well attended; among his
auditors, Erasmus tells us, were 'most of the leading men in his
native city and in the king's court' (CWE 8:235).

In October of 1499 Erasmus and Colet exchanged a series of
letters over a disagreement concerning Christ's words in the garden of Gethsemane, 'Let this cup pass from me.' The dispute is
not incidental as it reveals an abiding aspect of Erasmus's own
Christology, its concern with the very human nature of Christ that
expresses itself in a natural aversion to the agony awaiting him
(CWE 1:208). However serious and revealing the disagreement,
it is overshadowed by the preceding letter (#108) because in it
Erasmus fully expresses his comprehension of the revolutionary
nature of Colet's lectures on Paul, the great following they elicited, and the opposition they provoked. He indicates that together
they share a mutual hostility to the methods of the current crop of
theologians, representatives of the so-called new theology. These
qualities and their enemies in common were in part responsible
for bringing Colet and Erasmus together. Erasmus puts it clearly,
'When you tell me that you dislike the modern class of theologians,
who spend their time in hair-splitting and sophistical quibbling,
you have my emphatic agreement...' Thus they engender a taste
for arguing but do not instil wisdom. Lacking eloquence, which
is to be garnered from a familiarity or seasoning with the older
classics, they render theology, which ought to be the queen of all
the sciences, unattractive. An intellectual hubris drives them to
settle all questions, one outdoing the other until they are reduced
to trying to get wool from a goat, or blood from a rock. Thus they
debate such questions as whether God could have taken the form
of the devil or an ass (CWE 1:203). The consequence of this is what
always happens when a discipline falls into decadence: the best
and the brightest turn to other endeavours while it attracts those
of 'sluggish or disordered wits,' who are 'scarcely fit for letters at
all.' A tell-tale sign of such decadence is that there is greater intelligence and scope of ideas outside the university than within it.

The letter is important in another way: it shows Erasmus at
a crossroads. Colet had evidently invited Erasmus to lecture at
Oxford on Moses and that 'eloquent stylist' Isaiah, by the latter

appealing to Erasmus's reputation as a rhetorician, a *litterateur*. But this role as a literary critic concerned with style Erasmus now rejects as being beneath him, while lecturing on the full meaning of sacred scripture is above him. 'Hoc recuso quia minus est instituto meo, illus quia maius viribus' (CWE 1:205; Allen 1:248). Simultaneously the letter discards Erasmus's acquired reputation and announces a new departure: his as yet undeclared determination to acquire Greek. In a letter of 1501 to Antoon van Bergen (CWE 2:25) he acknowledges that no knowledge of scriptures can be complete without the knowledge of Greek (and proceeds to give some pointed examples from the Psalms as proof). 'It was, perhaps, amongst the more important results of his first visit to England that Erasmus returned to Paris with the single determination to read the Greek authors at first hand' (Woodward 135). If this determination as far as we know was unexpressed in England, however implied, there is every indication of his commitment to acquiring Greek in his letters to Jacob Batt and others (see Epistles 123, 124). But there is more: the attainment of proficiency in Greek would aid him in his corrected edition of Jerome's letters, leading from there to his true avocation: sacred letters. Arriving as a man of letters, Erasmus left England zealous to acquire the tools of a true theologian. That is, both Erasmus and Voltaire returned from England with their goals in sight, Erasmus as a theologian and Voltaire as a wide-ranging philosopher.

Rather than seminar think-tank cerebrations (which have their justifications) Erasmus and Colet sought a method and a means of reaching out to a general public, educated and accomplished, but which were being neglected. One can understand why Seebohm sees some influence and inspiration of Colet's methods and goals in the composition of Erasmus's *Enchiridion* (1503): 'The *Enchiridion* was, in truth, a very re-echo of the key-note of Colet's faith' (106). 'The decisive turn in his life and studies was associated with John Colet ... and it hinged on a conviction that Colet had found the method for restoring true "theology"' (McConica, *English Humanists* 24). Preferring a confluence of interests, an 'association,' rather than a unidirectional influence, one can also say that the experience with Colet gave Erasmus a push in the direction he was already intent on taking.

But this congruence does not exhaust the ongoing relationship between Colet and Erasmus, and more especially Erasmus's importance for England. Erasmus has given us an early biographical outline of Colet's life (in a letter to Jodocus Jonas (1521), CWE 8:232–43); it is combined with that of Jean Vitrier, forming 'parallel lives' of two men, quite similar in their impact on Erasmus and on those who knew them. In their modest ways of dealing with others, they represented combined models of life and learning intended to serve as counter-myths to the more aggressive ways of Luther. As was Erasmus, Colet was attacked for so-called heretical notions; he managed to emerge from these charges untarnished and even with his standing enhanced. We can only read with awe and some appreciation of the powerful appeal of Colet's sermons, as well as his extraordinary courage, when, for instance, we learn that at the Convocation for the Extirpation of Heresy, he chastises the assembled bishops for their negligence in regard to the spirit of Christ. There are two sorts of heresies, he tells them, that of doctrine and that of misleading worldliness on the part of the clergy. (Seebohm provides an admirable abridgement 138–53.) On one particular occasion, after he had spoken against the notion of a 'just war,' his enemies thought that Colet would receive a well-deserved dressing-down from Henry VIII, who was saber-rattling an invasion of France. After a private meeting lasting more than an hour and a half, during which he was extremely impressed by Colet's mind and demeanour, the king emerged with Colet saying, to the disappointment of the eagerly expectant throng of courtiers, that they might favour whatever teacher they liked, but 'this is the teacher for me' (Hic est doctor meus; Seebohm 165; Allen 4:526). Needless to say, while offering Colet his protection, Henry did proceed to launch several invasions of France, the first ending disastrously and the second only managing to hold on to some unimportant French towns. Colet's great strengths and appeal lay in his sermons, where his personal convictions were in view, and not in his writings. Erasmus attributes the fact that Colet wrote but little to a certain uneasiness about his command of Latin grammar, but also adds that he spoke powerfully and this from a familiarity with the English poets (could he have avoided Chaucer?).

Colet figures prominently in Erasmus's *Colloquies*, chief among them being 'The Whole Duty of Youth,' 'A Pilgrimage for Religion's Sake,' and 'A Religious Feast.' The last is the fullest and best of Erasmus's colloquies, showing his ideal of a gathering of laymen given to serious discussion concerning Christian doctrine and polity. These might well be pages taken from Plato's *Sympo-*

sium, a classical *convivium* reborn. What ought to have been the issues of the cathedral have been taken over by the villa. While it is fruitless and pointless to attempt to identify the historical source of the villa, there is no problem in identifying the source of the practice. Erasmus describes it himself in his brief sketch of Colet's life, where Colet's custom of combining religious discourse with frugal dining is memorialized. While the time spent at table was short, 'the conversation was such that would suit only educated and serious people.' A boy would read from Paul's Epistles or from Solomon's Proverbs, from which Colet himself would chose a passage and make it a topic of conversation. Though religious and serious, the discussion was never tedious or pretentious. His guests were 'so refreshed in mind and body that they went away better men than they came.' (CWE 8:235; Allen 4:516).

Through all of their other qualities, Colet and Erasmus emerge prominently as educators. Upon the death of his wealthy father, Colet used the abundant inheritance to 'refound' St Paul's School (part of the old choirboys' school was still standing). In fact so generous was his benefaction that in his last years he became somewhat hard-up. Erasmus summarizes both of their concerns when he writes: 'Being a far-sighted man, he saw that the greatest hope for a commonwealth lies in the education of its young' (in hoc esse praecipuam reipublicae spem, si prima aetas bonis rationibus institueretur; CWE 8:236; Allen 4:518). The good of the *res publica* depends upon education from an early age based upon good principles (or methods). In 'The Whole Duty of Youth,' demonstrating these principles at work, Erasmus depicts the idealized product of such a school as St Paul's. Of all the colloquies from the 1522 edition, this, according to Craig Thompson, was the 'most widely quoted and imitated' (CWE 39:90). A grammar school boy, Gaspar, discourses with another young man, Erasmus (emended from the previously named Erasmius). Describing his well-organized day from morning to night, Gaspar presents qualified reformist positions on such matters as auricular confession, sermons, fasting, mass, monastic vows, and theologians. 'Erasmus' asks where he acquired such wisdom. Gaspar answers that he had served in the household of John Colet. 'It was he who steeped my childhood in lessons of this kind' (CWE 39:99). Thompson expands on the many pedagogical ways, by means of Christian doctrine, Latin style, and instructional method that Erasmus helped guide the early educational program of St Paul's

(CWE 39:89). Most prominently, however, over the master's chair was a picture of Christ with the inscription, *Audite ipsum,* 'Hear ye Him,' provided by Erasmus, and confirming the centrality of Christ in the educational program of the school (see CWE 39:92, 100n15; Allen 4:352–3; CWE 8:383–5).

Even in the twentieth century accolades continued to accumulate regarding Erasmus's role as an educator (although he developed a distaste for actual teaching). According to W.H. Woodward, 'it may be reasonably maintained that of all of his activities none was more congenial to him, none more characteristic, none of more influence in his own age and subsequently, than that which was concerned with Education' (xxvii). And another expert student of the subject, R.R. Bolgar, was able to assert 'Erasmus is the greatest man we come across in the history of education' (xiv). He was certainly one of the founding fathers of the *studia humanitatis,* the humanities, which, based upon the knowledge of Greek and Latin and the elevated cultures they conveyed and devoted to the imitation of great models, managed to produce for more than three and a half centuries notable writers and statesmen. It eventually ran out of steam and became a slow-moving, if not staid, vehicle, having lost the sparkle of discovery which Rabelais, Erasmus's foremost French disciple, required, that is, a concern with practical cases concerning humanity's state ('quelque cas practicques et concernens l'estat humain'; *Gargantua* XXIII). It involved a strict harnessing of energies, so that not one minute of the day was lost ('qu'il ne perdoit heure quelconques du jour,' ibid). Humanism represented a new dynamic, one that controlled by strict schedules was part of the larger Renaissance need to respond aggressively to Time. It triumphed in its origins because it showed more energetic intelligence and contemporary effectiveness than did the existing methods and products of the schools, and it declined when it too became too limited in subject matter, with new information and focus coming forth from outside its walls (Thompson, Foreward xv). Nor was it uncontested, as we see when Rousseau's *Émile* appeared as a revolutionary tract that directly challenged the philosophical wisdom, educative procedure, and subject matter of the schoolroom regimen that Erasmus had helped install. Even Rousseau's rival figure, Voltaire, showed his own critical independence when, unabashedly modern, he refused to bow before the idols of their past, subjecting such classics as Homer and Virgil to Pococurante's languid cynicism but sharp critical judgment, and maintaining there was more to be learned in a few pages of Locke than in all of Plato. It should be recalled, however, that Voltaire, under the accommodating tutelage of the Jesuits, received the kind of education that Erasmus had fostered.

But all is not as secure as the sheltered halls of academe might promise. The third colloquy, in which Colet figures, became the matter for the stern-willed iconoclastic reforms that Henry VIII introduced into England after the Act of Supremacy. It is tragically more than ironic that the Act of Supremacy, which cost the recusant Thomas More and John Fisher their lives, thus bringing to a temporary end the hopes and promise of the Oxford-London reformers, also brought with it the attendant translations into English of many of Erasmus's tracts, including 'A Pilgrimage for Religion's Sake' (McConica, *English Humanists* 189–90). In the second half of this colloquy, describing a visit to the shrine of Thomas in Canterbury, Ogygius is accompanied by one Gratian Pullus (the cognomen meaning 'colt' for Colet; see Seebohm 179n1), who shows a rational contempt for the worship of relics, and being a fastidious man, as Colet was known to be, he shrinks from the kissing or even touching of the dirty garments deemed to be relics. Immediately he is thought to be a Wycliffite, which Erasmus dismisses (allowing however that he may have read Wycliffe). But the major thrust occurs when Pullus questions the need for such excessive wealth at shrines of worship. Would not the purposes of the sainted martyr and those of the Christian church be better served if some of that wealth were distributed among the poor? Ogygius, the ever-present voice of moderation in Erasmus's mental make-up, tries to soften the blow by showing his preference for splendid churches over dirty and neglected ones.

Erasmus, in the colloquies (rarely are they true dialogues), manages to eat his cake and have it too; he makes his reformist points but also introduces some qualifying palliatives of virtuous moderation. The reforms of Henry VIII were not so moderate: he razed the shrine of Thomas, forbade pilgrimages, suppressed the monasteries, and declared the martyred Thomas a traitor to his king, Henry II. (In his striking descriptions of the changes brought to both pilgrimage sites, Seebohm is effective, 182.) The 'Pilgrimage for Religion's Sake' thus led a particularly active political life. 'No more suitable product of Erasmus's pen could be found for Cromwell's purposes' (McConica, *English Humanists* 189–90). The injunctions of 1536 and 1538, in addition to the Acts of Suppression, also confiscated the monastic wealth. The injunctions further forbade the clergy from making use of images or relics to lure the people into making contributions and pilgrimages to saintly shrines were banned (McConica, ibid. 189; Thompson, 'Erasmus and Tudor England' 48).

The work of Erasmus, particularly the presence of that work in England, did not end with his death, nor did it end with the advent of Luther and the subsequent disillusionment that tempered Erasmus's once buoyant optimism and his ideas of reform. This runs counter to Seebohm's argument, which ends his still-classic study with the death of Colet in 1519. From his vantage point, he looks back with plaintive regret to the ensuing centuries of revolution that, as far as he was concerned, put a stop to the germinating ideas of the Oxford reformers (319). But the Erasmian influence did not end suddenly, not with the even more drastic termination of the lives of More and Fisher, nor even in the longer run that Seebohm envisaged. In fact Erasmus enjoyed a remarkably productive afterlife in Tudor England. He became, in McConica's attractive phrase, 'a prophet with a following' (*English Humanists* 34). While strangely allowing that Erasmus might not have been the most creative of this group of reformers, McConica still maintains that 'he was preeminently the movement's propagandist, by far its most prolific proponent. It is for this reason that his name is chosen to describe the common cause in which they were engaged.' While it is always hazardous to link so widespread a movement to the name of a single person, or to place that person at the vortex of ideas, still, broadly understood as representing a larger phalanx of allies and ideas, the phrase has its simple efficiency. Thus, 'Erasmian' came to represent the combined interests in 'evangelism, laicism and humanism' (23). And it was under all three flags that the Erasmian influence proceeded through sixteenth-century Tudor England. There was enough variety in his works–outspokenness combined with modulation, possibilities for reductions if not elimination of certain ordinances and practices of the Roman church, along with opposition to Luther–with the result that he could find a multliformed appeal to the various 'settlements' of the century, thereby providing the continuing bases for a *via media*. His works thus underwent a flurry of translations, chosen according to how they fit into a particular political or religious need and ethical program. Erasmus's works thus became a part of Tudor reforms. As E.J. Devereux writes in his *Renaissance*

English Translations of Erasmus: 'In 1532 there began what can only be described as a *campaign* of publication and translation, much of it of Erasmus, aimed at achieving a combined religious and political reformation in England by persuading readers to support religious change, the Royal Supremacy, and the break with the Papacy' (xviii). Thus, over a wide range of subjects Erasmus, after his death, continued to enter into the intellectual and social life of the English. McConica traces the subtle and shifting party allegiances of the time and how Erasmus's works fit into the varied reformist agendas. This meant of course an Erasmus who had to be transformed, as all such adaptations require, an Erasmus devoid of his opposition to the Supremacy Act and the break with Rome, bitter over the execution of his friends and allies, and opposed to the total suppression of the monasteries. These aspects of his thought put aside, there was a ready spiritual and practical reception for many of the ideas that first attracted and brought together the Oxford-London reformers, and of which Erasmus became the nominal head.

In these great and yet continuous changes two figures from among many stand out, Thomas Cromwell and Catherine Parr, Henry's 'last queen.' The ideals of the Oxford-London reformers were recovered and redeemed by the strong political programs of the former and by the more professional and scholarly enterprises of the latter. During Cromwell's tenure as Henry VIII's 'principal secretary,' and 'the indispensable manager of all the King's business' (Spitz 237), the *Enchiridion* became a crucial book for its propagation of a simple Christian piety, the Bible through various hands was translated into the vernacular (about which Henry was of two minds), and such colloquies as 'A Pilgrimage for Religion's Sake' were major justifications of reform and change.

The *Enchiridion* should be accompanied by a letter of 1518 that Erasmus wrote to the venerable abbot Volz and which became the justifiable preface to the new edition brought out by Froben. The letter both defines and defends Erasmus's purposes in writing the *Enchiridion*. It is a work of clarification and self-affirmation. Understandably enough the work had little effect on its intended beneficiary, one John Popperuytter, who as an arms provisioner naturally remained in the environs of the court. But Erasmus's purpose certainly went beyond that unregenerate individual. He strongly felt that the Christian doctrine, due to obscurities and difficulties in the biblical text, required a concise and clear digest, a handbook for easy and clear comprehension, thus an *enchiridion*, or small dagger to fend off the evils of the world. In the letter he particularly identifies the current Pharisees as dumping dirt in the pure wells of Christian doctrine. Through their human ordinances, such as indulgences, papal dispensations, and reliance on 'ceremonials,' they clog the genuine springs of Christian belief (CWE 66:12–13). Prior to the 1518 edition the *Enchiridion* was relatively successful and gratifying to Erasmus, undergoing some nine editions. But after 1518 it became enormously popular, obviously benefiting from the raging storm provoked by Luther in 1517. The above allusions to indulgences and the like are Erasmus's indications that he knew and approved of Luther's work, prompting a deferential letter of recognition and mutual support from the German monk in March 1519. A friend to each, Wolfgang Faber Capito, in a letter of 1519, urges Erasmus to join forces with Luther, arguing that this 'will encourage the younger generation to risk something in the cause of liberty in Christ' (CWE 6:294). Unfortunately the pending break between Luther and Erasmus would, within a few years, polarize the people Capito thought to bring together.

The *Enchiridion* would be translated into the vernacular in practically every country in Europe (see McConica, *English Humanists* 16n2). But in England it enjoyed a special favour, particularly with its demotion of monasticism and with its relegation of the monastic vocation to being simply one way of Christian life among others. McConica amply describes the contents of the *Enchiridion* (17–26) but more important he describes the new uses to which it was put by Cromwell. First appearing in 1533 (the translation was thought to be the work of the remarkable but proscribed William Tyndale), 'it far surpassed in popularity, measured by editions, all other works of Erasmus' (145). Thompson credits its appeal to 'its summons to spirituality, its downgrading of externals such as pilgrimages, vocal prayers, images and monasticism; its eloquent silence on clerical authority and hierarchy; its insistence on the importance of one's internal life and on the imitation of Christ' ('Erasmus and Tudor England' 43). Among these persistent ideas, Christ obviously occupied the central position in all aspects of worship. This called for a renewed pietism, but such as was allied with learning, particularly with the acquisition of the classical languages. The subtleties of the theologians were to be avoided. The rage for definition could not accord with Erasmus's deep-seated scepticism over such setting of rules. Human nature is so different, situations vary, there is such obscurity in the sources of conduct that it is impossible to lay down a rule that covers all situations. Here emerges what Erika Rummel has called Erasmus's 'Christian scepticism.' The lines of human conduct are so crooked that no rule can suffice; the only rule that runs straight is that of Christian charity, acquired by a direct, simple and faithful reading of the gospels. Emphasis was thus to be placed on reform of ecclesiastical practices that had no warrant in scriptures. At the same time, Erasmus advocated a return to the learned spirituality of the early church fathers. Thus appeal was made to eloquence and education, where students were taught Christian doctrine and classical languages.

Erasmus's influence further extended into the vernacular translation of the Bible itself. According to Jean Hadot, despite all the criticisms directed against Erasmus's edition of the New Testament, some of it quite justified, it remained the received text into the nineteenth century. Even by way of the various publishing channels and the accretions brought about by Erasmus himself (and others), Erasmus's 1516 edition formed the basis of that jewel of national prose, the 1611 English Bible. This view is reinforced if one acknowledges the presence of William Tyndale's prose in the later crowning achievement, because Tyndale, as has been recently shown by David Daniell, depended heavily upon Erasmus in this and many other matters as well (*Tyndale's New Testament* xvii, xx). Yet, in the machinations of the times, his hand was hidden and various other versions, still in part based upon Tyndale's, were put forward, before the acceptance of the 'Great Bible' of 1539. In fact, because of the king's opposition it was not until 1535 that publication of a translation was permitted, and this only after Henry's open break with the papacy (Thompson, 'Erasmus and Tudor England' 41; McConica, *English Humanists* 162–6). Thus the routing to the Authorized Version of 1611 was circuitous and difficult, as even here it was recognized that a full and more accurate translation of the Old and New Testaments would require the services of many expert scholars.

It is an easy step from the *Enchiridion* and other works sponsored by Cromwell to Erasmus's Paraphrases of the New Testament endorsed by Catherine Parr. This was the particular project of her learned circle, thus providing a link of continuity between the reigns of Henry VIII and Edward VI (see McConica, *English*

Humanists 11, 12, and passim). Begun as early as 1545, the translations of the Paraphrases by various hands were published in two
volumes in 1548 and 1549. They were intended for the use of laity
and clergy alike. They were to be made accessible in some place
where parishioners would most 'commodiously resort.' While
parishioners were encouraged to read, young clergy were examined. They were obliged to own not only the New Testament in
Latin and in English but also Erasmus's Paraphrases as well, and
would be tested by superiors on how diligently they studied the
three. It was intended as a clear digest, in simple terms, of the New
Testament, intended for the laity and even for the clergy with no
degree in divinity. Sentences that might appear dark are made
'open, clear plain and familiar.' Thanks are given for the mercy of
God who through such scholars as Erasmus has opened 'the way
to the pure and perfect knowledge of God's word' (Thompson,
'Erasmus and Tudor England' 52; McConica, *English Humanists*
240–2). Unlike what might have been his reaction to the suppression of the monasteries, this translation and the availability of the
Paraphrases fit perfectly into Erasmus's own goals and ideals.

But obviously, given the changes his own thought underwent
and even the qualifications expressed within his works, there
were many versions of Erasmus available for consumption by
various creeds. Anglicans of a Protestant bent could call upon the
Erasmus of the period prior to 1517. Moderate Catholics could
claim as their own the later Erasmus, who regretted his earlier au-
dacities and recanted. The wide extent of possible interpretations
qualified him better than More to be called a man for all seasons.
Finally there were the outright conservatives who saw in Erasmus the progenitor of Luther, and who repeated the once common saying, 'aut Erasmus Lutherizat, aut Lutherus Erasmizat.'
Even the Paraphrases were utilized to attack Erasmus for being
one with the evangelicals, thus bearing responsibility not only for
Luther and the Lutherans but even for the Arians of their day
(Thompson, 'Erasmus and Tudor England' 62–3).

But Erasmus's detractors also recognized him as being a most
learned man; consequently there is one part of Erasmus's contribution that was used by all parties, and this was his work as a
philologist. Though Erasmus was at first denounced(the Greek
language bordered on the heretical in the Latin church) and then
attacked (see below for Erasmus's dispute with Dorp), eventually
all controversialists, across the very wide spectrum, learned that

a knowledge of these foreign languages helped toward an exact knowledge of biblical texts and of patristics. Debate centred upon the meanings and implications of words; thus Erasmus's greatest and most enduring triumph may have been as a philologist (Thompson, 'Erasmus and Tudor England' 67).

But why was this so? We must recall that in the sixteenth century we are dealing with a God-hungry people; not only mentally but viscerally they had a felt need and hunger for God. At the same time they had a deep-seated and pervasive fear of hell. The correct reading of a text may set one on the right road from sin to salvation. To come across the phrase that justifies one, that gives solace and confirmation, means one has not only found the honey but the honeycomb. This is barely comprehensible in our time when even among theologians the notion of God has lost all sensory apprehension and is paper-thin. But the notion of hell persisted, even past the age when it was supposed to have declined. Rousseau records how Mme de Warens with her benign view of Christianity would alleviate his fear of eternal damnation, and Voltaire wrote his *Épitre à Uranie* to assuage the guilty apprehensions of Mme Rumplemonde, whose fearful attacks frequently followed her quite active sexual life.

But Erasmus's hold on the English mind entered by way of other areas than that of ecclesiastical reform. Its grasp was permanent on the greatest literary imaginations, on Spenser's intent in the *Faerie Queene* to fashion the perfect English gentleman, in the recessive mode of Milton's unheralded masterpiece, *Paradise Regained*, and above all in Shakespeare's comedies and tragedies. While Bruce Mansfield can effectively graph the lines of Erasmus's reputation, his rise, his fall, and then his rise again at the end of the seventeenth century to provide in his new guise as a rational philosopher the starting points and early intellectual affinities for both Voltaire and Rousseau, his taste for folly continues to resonate permanently in such literary masterpieces as *As You Like It, Twelfth Night, Hamlet,* and *King Lear* (Thompson, 'Erasmus and Tudor England' 33; and Welsford, chapter 5 below).

Yet, despite these many reincarnations the handiwork of Erasmus became less and less in evidence. First, he encountered the same fate as would Voltaire. He was lost by the very means of his success. These authors form classic examples of losing by winning. That is, so successful had their recommendations been that they became commonplaces and thus subject to being shrugged off. Accounting for the fallen-off publication records of Erasmus under Elizabeth, Thompson notes that, in addition to the vogue of foreign editions, Erasmus's doctrines had become standards: 'In religion certain battles had been won, monks and monasteries had disappeared, the vernacular Bible was easily available and fairly cheap, a vernacular *Book of Common Prayer* was in use, and relics and suchlike things were forgotten' (Thompson, 'Erasmus and the Tudors' 57). But this does not fully explain why Erasmus himself should have been neglected. For a fuller explanation we should turn to Mme de Stael's lessons for Voltaire (see page 201, note 14 below): he who commits himself to the topicalities of history will be devoured by history. In the flow of generations one wave will override the preceding. It takes exceptional talent and interests beyond those currently pressing to escape the ravenous maw of historical change.

The circumstances that brought Erasmus and Voltaire to England were quite different; what each received and offered by his visit also differed, and yet the consequences were the same: each became a confirmed Anglophile, though for different reasons, superficial or profound. This was in part due to the changes that England itself underwent in the intervening two centuries. Erasmus, though still a minor figure, was well received by the restricted circle of English religious humanists. In England Erasmus attained the recognition he desired; he was 'discovered' and some of his best surviving works, *The Enchiridion*, *The Praise of Folly*, and the 1516 edition of the Greek New Testament, were written, sponsored, or encouraged in England. Erasmus in England gave as much as he got. The circumstances of Voltaire's departure for England were quite different. He had engaged the duc de Rohan in a lively disagreement over lineage; soon thereafter, when Voltaire was dining with the duc de Sully, Rohan called him out, whereupon some of his toughs administered a thrashing to Voltaire. The victim rushed back into the room where he was dining, only to have his dinner companion refuse to take the side of a bourgeois against a member of the nobility. When Voltaire challenged Rohan to a duel, it was Voltaire who was imprisoned in the Bastille. Hence his departure for England was a plea bargain. But despite the cloud over his coming, Voltaire, enjoying the constant support of the recently restored duke of Buckingham, was well received and in the highest circles. The England that he encountered was considerably different from that of Erasmus's time. Literature, the arts, philosophy, and science had flourished (the great *floraison* of literature due, as Thompson has stoutly maintained, to the earlier but continuous influence of the Oxford-London reformers). And politically the first of the Indemnity Acts was passed, a step on the way to granting full rights of subjects to those who did not belong to the established church. The differences with France were, under the circumstances, all too striking – the revocation of the Edict of Nantes (1685) was merely the culmination of a long series of hardships imposed upon the Huguenots. Understandably, in Voltaire's enthusiastic reaction – which was to undergo some qualification – England became the land of hoped-for liberties. The various 'settlements' of the sixteenth century, while temporarily effective, apparently·'settled' nothing and it was primarily war-weariness by the late seventeenth century that served to make England a beacon of liberty and a recognized centre of modernizing thought. Voltaire left only a minimal imprint on the England of his day, but what he took away in his sense of literature and philosophy was enormous. 'Si l'Angleterrs n'a pas été marqué très visiblemente de l'empreinte personelle de Voltaire, cette nation ... l'a influencé de manière profonde et durable' (Besterman, *Studies* 145:9). While Erasmus was discovered in England, Voltaire by discovering England discovered a larger part of himself. Of course, at the age of thirty-two (a striking coincidence, as Erasmus was also in his early thirties when he first visited England), having reaped the successes of *Oedipe* and of the *Henriade*, Voltaire was far from intellectually unformed; in fact, he had already experienced something of a religious coming of age. During a stay in Holland, he was astonished by the religious tolerance in evidence at The Hague (Pomeau, *La religion* 156), where many religious sects lived together in peace. But several years later what England brought to his religious base of tolerance was a deepening interest in politics and philosophy, which would stay with him all his remaining life (Besterman, *Studies* 145:10–11). He became the future multitalented writer of *Le siécle de Louis XIV*, with wide-ranging and knowledgeable interests in politics, economics, and philosophy (an imprint left most clearly in the *conte*, *Micromégas*). Most important, these interests all came together to forge his attachment to an international republic of letters.[5]

Obviously Shakespeare beckons, with whom Voltaire's notable and long-standing encounter reveals both the credits and liabilities of his complex character. The relationship to Shakespeare also signals a genuine clash of cultures, even a kind of *translatio* or epoch-making changing of the guard in matters of dramatic taste and sensibility, and finally an even more profound convergence with Erasmus. This is an argument requiring some extension. Shakespeare, who was emerging as not only England's but modern Europe's greatest dramatist (his subsequent reputation would exceed even those boundaries), presented a vivid challenge to Voltaire not only in matters of taste and dramatic values but also in the larger issues of national pride and accomplishment. This became political warfare carried on in the galleries of culture.

Voltaire lived in the afterglow of the great age of French theatre, and he was the designated heir of Corneille and Racine. The experience of the live theatre of Shakespeare in London was nothing less than a shock to his system. What is surprising is not the later hostile remarks that remain in the memory because they are so fulsome but his earlier willingness to incorporate elements taken from Shakespeare that he found wanting in the French theatre. Moreover, these criticisms were not ad-libbed but expressed an integral part of Voltaire's personality and indeed of his aesthetic ideal. The Shakespeare that Voltaire found early he continued, despite the controversy, to regard late with almost unchanged language. A diamond in the rough, a natural genius who was barbarous in many ways, a monstrous beauty – are only some of the epithets that are piled upon Shakespeare from first through last, with only changes of emphasis and some alterations growing out of a national defensiveness born from polemics. Both Besterman and André Michel Rousseau make it known that these were far from Voltaire's judgments alone, but in fact were the shared opinions of many English critics of the time, upon whom Voltaire may have depended. John Dennis, Nicholas Rowe, Rymer, and Pope (even down to the much later Lord Byron) all measured Shakespeare's natural beauties, the products of genius, against imputed barbarities of style and action. (Besterman, *Voltaire* 143–4; Rousseau, 146:449–50 , which is to say that much of the reigning English criticism had been influenced by the tenets and triumphs of French classicism of the seventeenth century. Faguet has remarked that Aristotle was the first French dramatic critic (Jusserand 65); Boileau, with his emphasis on 'unity, clearness, regularity, selection, logic … qualities rare and noble' (ibid. 104) was the exponent, and Racine, Corneille and Moliere the embodiments and models. By such standards of taste, there was no easy fit for Shakespeare; in fact, it was considered normal to cut Shakespeare's plays: 'On abrège tous les jours Shakespeare.' The actor David Garrick removed the grave-digger's scene from *Hamlet*, and cut almost the entire fifth act. Nor should we forget that the *King Lear* that English audiences saw from 1681 to 1834 was that of Nahum Tate, who sought with some mercifulness to avoid the true terror of Shakespeare's ending by concluding it more happily with Edgar marrying the surviving Cordelia. If this is what happened to Shakespeare at home, one can well imagine the constraints abroad.

There are many twists and turns in Voltaire's engagements with Shakespeare. The first and most obvious one was that Voltaire on more than one occasion takes credit for having been the first to introduce Shakespeare to his French audience. This claim runs into the problems of historical antecedence, the fact that in the long drawn-out string and continuum of historical diachronics, there are always firsts before the first (see below, page 121). Besterman summarizes the issues as well as anyone.[6] He quotes from Voltaire's later address to the Académie Française, where the now aged and venerated man of letters informs his auditors (the address was actually delivered for him by d'Alembert) that he was the first Frenchman to learn English, the first to introduce Shakespeare to the continent and to translate him, the first to make known Pope, Dryden, and Milton, even the first who had dared to explain the great Newton, and do justice to the profound wisdom of Locke (*Lettre de M. de Voltaire à l'Académie française*, 351). André Michel Rousseau, in his splendid three-volume study, *Angleterre et Voltaire* (which Besterman sponsored), as does David Williams, shows that these claims are not quite the whole truth; still, as Besterman maintains, they are 'justified,' or in the main true. There were 'mentions' of Shakespeare prior to Voltaire, even some brief literary comparisons, but with Voltaire Shakespeare entered into the working program of an active dramatist. Voltaire may not have been the 'firstest' to refer to Shakespeare but his involvement and exposition was the 'mostest,' that is, the fullest and most consequential use of Shakespeare, who became for him an object of constant if shifting attention. Thus we may distinguish between 'false firsts' and those that bore consequences.[7] Voltaire's importation of Shakespeare had enormous and long-range consequences for the French theatre, and by this attraction Voltaire helped transform French literary tastes from Anglophobia to something like Anglomania, or from one distasteful excess to another. Of course in this process Voltaire's own attitudes underwent some revision. If the contrasting terms of his attitude remained constant, the emphases shifted drastically. There may not have been a volte-face, but there were certainly some sharp alterations of judgment. In his own defence Voltaire will constantly remind his readers of his own priority in the French Shakespearian transaction.

Three moments distinguish Voltaire's varying attitudes toward Shakespeare. In his *Lettres philosophiques* of 1734, Shakespeare is judged from within an English context. Native speakers are able to respond to Shakespeare's beauties so well that they are willing to forgive his barbarities. Later imitators bungled so badly in imitating Shakespeare that by a kind of reverse English he shone in comparison. This explains Shakespeare's divine status among the English, despite his failures in plot, language, and morale, about which Voltaire remains vehement and unrelenting. Thus the English tragedies are better remembered by detached sections (Voltaire offers a translation of Hamlet's 'To be or not to be' soliloquy as an example.) But in most things that matter – *bienséance*, order, *vraisemblance* – the plays are barbarous. Voltaire will thus delight in exposing by plot summaries (always very superficial and frequently erroneous) the strangely alluring tumult of the English tragic stage (*Mélanges* 81–4).

A certain politeness or restraint toward his host country characterizes the expositions in the *Lettres philosophiques*. Thereafter polemics will rule and a literary war inserts itself between the English theatre (Shakespeare) and the French theatre (Corneille, Racine, and Molière). The second phase derives from the *Appel à toutes les nations de l'Europe* of 1761. Because national tastes are self-favouring and beyond dispute, Voltaire makes an 'appeal' or a 'call' to international judgment (192–3). It is one of Voltaire's axioms that any national literature may be truly considered great only when it triumphs beyond its country's borders, and thus establishes an international order of excellence. This is what happened to Corneille and Racine in tragedy and to Molière in comedy: they reached beyond the frontiers of France and set the standards of dramatic taste for most of Europe. As of Voltaire's time this was not true of Shakespeare, whose genius and appeal remained local, that is, it could not escape from being tainted by the uncultivated taste of its time (*Appel* 192–3, *Lettres* 367).

Voltaire then proceeds to two tests. First he gives an elaborate plot summary of *Hamlet* (as he will do on more than one occasion), a summary which in the very telling sensationalizes the piece and shows its manifold complications. Voltaire is thus able to conclude scornfully: 'This is the sort of play that they prefer to [Corneille's] *Cinna*' (200). A strange beauty in certain speeches, which the English learned by heart, has contributed to the success of the play, thereby obscuring its obvious deficiencies of plot. Yet the beauties do persist, which beauties, Voltaire (writing anonymously, and thus able to refer to himself in the third person) claims to be the first to have made Shakespeare known in France. 'M. de Voltaire est le premier qui les ait fait connaitre en France...' (201). He then juxtaposes his earlier 'imitation' of Hamlet's monologue with a more literal one, in order to expose the faults of Shakespeare's language. He does this while pretending to praise its qualities, its 'naturel,' which has no fear of the basest of ideas, its energy, which others might regard as effrontery, and its daring qualities which some *esprits* not quite accustomed to such unusual excesses might simply take to be gibberish. Nevertheless, underneath these covers there is some power that carries one beyond the need for mere elegance. Shakespeare is a diamond in the rough; if one seeks to smooth out the irregularities one risks losing some of the weight (203).

The next paragraph proceeds to provide Voltaire's own dramaturgical ideals – observance of the unities, of decorum, of regularities of speech and action – all quite simply and eloquently expressed. He again concludes ironically: 'Il est clair qu'on peut enchanter toute une nation sans se donner tant de peines' (Clearly, one can enchant an entire nation without taking very great pains). Voltaire insisted on playing tennis with a very high net and within narrow lines. The *Appel* offers some reasons for Voltaire's great respect for the strenuous discipline of the stage. In a section that has been disparaged ('Des divers changements arrivés à l'art tragique') Voltaire conducts a quite stunning and knowledgeable historical survey of tragedy, starting with its origins in the sacred mysteries through its many fluctuations and abuses until it reaches Corneille's *Le Cid*, 'la première pièce qui franchit les bornes de la France' (the first play to pass beyond the borders of France; 217). This section, which reveals Voltaire to be a true historian, shows why owing to its earliest origins he holds dramatic art in such revered estimation; it remains a com-

munal experience, a binding together that displays the highest
values of a people. Consequently there must be a sharp spiritual
divide between what passes on the street and what is permissible
in the confines of the theatre. Theatrical acceptance bestows the
sanction of social permissibility. Such a license must not be degraded. Thus he deplores the language of Iago (208–9) when that
astute criminal psychologist describes in the most graphic terms
to the desperate imagination of Brabantio (as he will to Othello)
the sexual coupling of his daughter, Desdemona. Where earlier
Voltaire had insisted on translation as the art of imitation – carrying over from one language what was suitable to the spirit of
another language – here he insists on literal word-for-word trans-
literation in order to disclose the desecration, and for him it is
just that, when decorous language is abandoned. The historical
origins of drama, the inviolable dimensions of the stage, are up-
permost in Voltaire's attitudes toward the abuses represented by
Shakespearean drama.

Of course he misses much. Iago's lurid imagery is a tool of his
scheming by which he manipulates and inflames the fearful sexual imaginations of his victims. So, too, in his succinct abstracts
of the plots of Shakespeare's plays, Voltaire neglects the 'design,'
the architectonics, the reciprocal developments of speech, character, and the unfolding action. When he renders Hamlet's speech
into *Voltairien* language and sentiment, he has made it spiritually
his own. This 'method' removes the mainspring of the originality
and singularity of Shakespeare's language, which is expressive of
character in a developing dramatic situation. The speech reaches
great heights because it indicates the turmoil and indecisiveness
of Hamlet's agitated and searching mind. Not only the language
but the thoughts figure into the unfolding dramatic action, the
internal order of Shakespeare's play. The 'undiscovered country'
certainly anticipates Hamlet's invidious comparison of himself
with Fortinbras, who defies (or, more graphically, 'makes mouths
at') the uncertainties of the 'invisible event.' Every step along the
way – the emerging internal order of the play – emphasizes the
thoughtful Hamlet's march toward and willingness to enter into
the unknown, to attain the 'purification of [his] motive' and to acquire the simple faith of letting be. Voltaire's translation removes
this quality of self-inspection, self-reference, and self-incrimina-
tion, the way the soliloquy discloses the nature of Hamlet's mind
and thought and the essential progression of the dramatic action

of the play. Voltaire's version might be termed a philosophical abstract of the situation in which Hamlet finds himself.

Eva Jacobs, in an insightful essay, 'Tragedy and Didacticism: The Case of Voltaire,' readily accepts that for the modern reader 'Voltairian tragedy is a corpse beyond resuscitation' (51). Despite attempts at historical understanding, 'no amount of such effort will alter the public's perception that Voltaire failed as a tragedian' (55). But the reason for the failure in the judgment of modern taste is not in the so-called didacticism or even the gap between tragedy's 'irreparability' and the optimism of the Enlightenment, but rather 'the shift in the main focus from the portrayals of individuals to general propositions about mankind' (58); 'the characters and what happens to them, fade into insignificance when compared to the weight of ideas' (60). The tendency of Voltaire's plays, and here it is in accord with the taste of the times, is to extract moral generalizations. And this returns us to the issue of diction. Shakespearian diction particularizes and personalizes: it reveals the dimensions of individual characters, whether the searching qualities of Hamlet's mind or the scabrous ingenuity of Iago. Diction identifies. 'Why, man, they did make love to this employment. They are not near my conscience' (V.ii.58–9). To Horatio's indulgent regret at the deaths of Rosencrantz and Guildenstern, Hamlet responds with great strength of personal conviction, all the more powerful because of the colloquial nature of his language. He is responding ardently, instinctively. This is not a moment for moral abstractions (although thoughtful defences do follow) but for the revelation of character in situation. The multivalent language of Shakespeare's plays draws us into the quests and natures of his characters; the noble language of Voltaire draws the attention away from 'individual destiny' and toward 'general ideas' (Jacobs 65).

Lastly, the *Voltairien* critique that is most remembered is the letter of response addressed to the Académie Française when Pierre Le Tourneur's translations began to appear in 1776. In his *Preface* Le Tourneur neglects even to mention Corneille and Racine (and Voltaire as well). Voltaire's blood boils, he writes, when he thinks of this faker, who dares to disparage his great national patrimony to the advantage of a semi-barbaric upstart (Voltaire, *Correspondence* 45:231). Le Tourneur's point in his *Preface* is a very simple but offensive one. Shakespeare was fortunate in that he

wrote his tragedies before rules were codified, before criticism
began to dictate to creativity. He was free to roam wherever his
dramatic tastes and talents brought him. But of course the rules,
according to Voltaire, were those that had developed through a
long historical process before reaching their perfection in the art
of Corneille and Racine. Furthermore, Le Tourneur weaves into
his defence of Shakespeare the arguments of critics who rightly
claim that if one can imagine a scene as taking place in Egypt
or Rome one can equally well imagine some fourteen or sixteen
years passing. Voltaire's fault lies not in his defence of the three
unities but rather in his converting them into universal principles.
Obviously there are impressive works from stage or screen (*The
Tempest, High Noon*) where the unities are well observed, just as
there are others of even higher distinction where they are not. But
Voltaire could not let go. It has been said that with Voltaire one
epoch ended and with Le Tourneur another began. But this is to
treat them as two ships passing in the night, headed for different
destinations, when in fact there was a dramatic clash. The changing of the guard brought about a new change of order. A curtain
has fallen. Le Tourneur won by silence, by simply ignoring the
three dramatists, and Voltaire lost by defending the standards of
a lifetime.

Yet one could expect better from Voltaire. One is tempted to
surmise that it is Voltaire's own taste for anomaly, for contrast
and contradiction, and for paradox that drives him. After all, in
the short essay on Chancellor Bacon, he reminds the reader that
'the compass, printing, engraving, oil-painting, mirrors ... eye
glasses, gunpowder' were all discovered prior to the time of experimental science. Yet, it would be natural to suppose that these
sublime discoveries were made by greatest scientists in times
more enlightened than his own. 'Not so,' he exclaims, 'it was in
the age of the most mindless barbarism that these great changes
were made on the earth' (*Mélanges* 59). He finds the same contradiction in Homer and Shakespeare, who are brought together
in the French version of his essay on epic poetry (but not present in the English original). The example of Shakespeare confirms
the paradox that he uncovers in Homer: that the same author can
rise so high and fall so low. Shakespeare's inclusion in tragedy
of drunkards, clowns, and singing gravediggers – such mixtures
of personages and style – is most abhorrent to Voltaire's insis-

tence on a constant nobility in speech, actions, and morality in true tragedy. Here Shakespeare falls short of the *Voltairien* ideal: whatever one can imagine of the 'most monstrous or absurd' can be found in Shakespeare. Yet the insights and dramatic effects can be dazzling, like 'des éclairs qui ont brillé dans la nuit la plus profonde' – an obvious borrowing from *A Midsummer Night's Dream*, where the conventionality of 'profound night' measures poorly in linguistic power against Shakespeare's 'collied night'). Later imitation only served to augment Shakespeare's reputation. He had the original genius that 'without guide, art or rule' may go astray himself from time to time, 'but he leaves far behind him those who rely only on reason and exactitude' (OC 3B 418–19). In these remarkable pages – the thoughts are repeated in his inaugural address upon his reception into the Académie Française and in a letter to Cardinal Quirini – Voltaire comes very close to Le Tourneur's arguments and to those of Giambattista Vico who credits the natural brilliance and artfulness of Homer and Dante simply because they wrote before the right way became critically codified.

But Voltaire could not go all the way with Vico, even if he had known of his work, and the nature of Le Tourneur's *Preface* was too challenging to ignore. While the above citations indicate that it would not have taken much to tip Voltaire into a broader and freer interpretation, still, through some national pride and personal defensiveness, Voltaire continued to require the values of French drama that insisted on retention of *vers rimés*, a full accord with the unities, particularly that of time; he abhorred the mixture of kings and clowns and the debasement of language and sentiment below the noble. His introductory essay to the publication of *Brutus* (OC 5) and the discussion of Shakespeare in his *Lettres philosophiques* provide reasoned arguments for all of these points. They also reveal the defects of his arguments.

The great tragedian for Voltaire is above all a great poet. *Vers rimés* by compounding the difficulty accentuates the achievement. Blank verse seems nothing other than prose made verse by typographical concession. Rhymed verse also enhances moral instruction by its greater memorability. But is memorable language, that which is retained and carried with one, only expressed in rhyme? Certainly rhyme cinches the point to be made. But is there not memorability in such lines as 'Reason not the need,' 'Unaccommodated man,' 'How all occasions do inform against me' 'What's

Hecuba to him or he to Hecuba?' – to mention only a few of the hundreds that comprise the Shakespeare quotation book? These are not commonplaces but discoveries made by the unfolding dramatic context and expressed in an uncommon or unpredictable mixture of diction. The dramatic context elevates the language, and extends it beyond what was commonly thought into new revelations. This is because Shakespeare was extremely attentive to the internal order of development of his tragedies and their characters, which in turn carry him beyond what he may have at first envisioned.

What hampered Voltaire's insight? As we try to 'pluck out the heart of [his] mystery,' we turn to his last statement, that which d'Alembert read to the Académie Française in 1776. Clearly a kind of patriotic zeal informs Voltaire's outrage and Le Tourneur comes off as a turncoat. Voltaire can well understand, without condoning, Shakespeare's divine reputation among the English, but for a Frenchman to place Shakespeare ahead of Corneille and Racine – without even naming them – is treasonous. At this time, in the early stages of the American Revolutionary war, which the colonials seemed to be losing, anti-British sentiment ran very high in France. Still, it is unseemly for Voltaire to confound the aesthetic issue with political betrayal. Thus, suiting up for one last battle, the aged general calls all his sad captains – d'Argental, de la Harpe, d'Alembert – and they respond to the rallying cry. But one senses that this is a rear-guard action rather than an advancing front. The battle has already been lost. Voltaire is witness to the end of an era. 'J'ai vu finir le règne de la raison et du goüt. Je vais mourir en laissant la France barbare...' (*Correspondence*, 43:241). And what galls is that he is being beaten with his own stick (239). The height of calamity and horror is that he was the first 'autrefois' to speak of Shakespeare, the first to extract for the French the diamonds that were buried in the dung-heap (231–2).

What incites Voltaire's anger is the suggestion that the genius of Shakespeare had eclipsed the greatness of Corneille and Racine – a nativism to be sure, and essentially an aesthetic one, the one on which Voltaire was nurtured and to which he remained faithful. We return to the formative place of the *Siècle de Louis XIV* not only as a work of history but as the cultural centre in Voltaire's life. It was then that under Richelieu Corneille was formed, and under the king himself that Racine was honoured (*Lettre* 365, 'Lettre a l'Académie Francaise'). Voltaire concludes his *Lettre* by asking his auditors, the distinguished gentlemen academicians, to imagine how Shakespeare's *Troilus and Cressida*, with the loutish Thersites, would have played before the court at Versailles. France has passed from one extreme to another. Voltaire complains that it is now enduring a large- scale cultural invasion (involving the import of foreign solecisms, where his countrymen now ask for '*roast-beef* de mouton'), and French sensibilities habitually do not take well to such invasions, particularly when represented by vulgarizations to the exclusion of good taste.

Was it only an adherence to a reigning aesthetic ideal? Besterman makes much of the aesthetic and political differences, quoting Voltaire to the effect that the English writers, given the greater climate of liberty, write what they can, but the French are constrained to write what they may (*Studies* 1:156). While such discriminations are more than adequate they are not fully satisfying. Other matters intrude. We can refer to temperament and ask whether there was some internal reserve and restraint on Voltaire's part that kept him from any revolutionary break-through and made him seek out balance. Why could he not move with the Shakespearean genius and follow more wholeheartedly what he truly admired? Here we come to a better comparison, a more comprehensive truth, one that unites him with Erasmus. Like Erasmus, the familial younger brother, he has been brought up to fulfil the role of the older brother, that is, to become the defender of the values of a culture, who sees himself and his values as being threatened and replaced by a new wave of interests, a new generation with different thoughts and feeling.[8] The rebel founder, the initiator, even the newly 'first-born' now finds himself bypassed, supplanted. Furthermore, in their character types, Erasmus and Voltaire labour under the special sign of reformers who recant. Like Erasmus he came to regret the 'excesses' of a movement that he helped initiate. In his attempts to rejuvenate French drama by importing English action and spectacle he only asked for a little rain not a tempest (Williams, *Studies* 340). The regrets of recantation are now his refrain. Unfortunately, he would later lament, he was the first to make English poetry known in France.

When France moved its fixations from Anglophobia to Anglomania, he resorted to balance. In this as in other matters, he was a reformer not a revolutionary. Just as Erasmus could not break with mother church, or the consensus of the ages, so Voltaire was held back, hobbled by his notable restraint, his unwillingness to be more than an ameliorist, an accommodator. Certainly, in his surprising sixties, he was able to give expression to outrage, but this was over palpable miscarriages of justice, the harmful reactionary policies that posed a threat to the great enterprise of the *philosophes*. Voltaire remained a man of his time, as did Erasmus, because of some inner 'occult' emotional hindrance. Here they are at their most fascinating psychologically. Perhaps it is egotism, a defensive refusal to accept the challenge of the new, an unwillingness to follow the voice of the spirit and instead to fall back on an inherent reserve. But this is as far as analysis can burrow before hitting something irreducible in character that prevents the individual from going all the way he may in fact have wanted to go. All reportage, all data, all facts shrink in importance before this bewildering aspect of human character. There is some tragedy here as talented people, great figures who initiated change, and thus having enjoyed a once appealing ascendancy, unexpectedly find themselves ejected by the changes of history's larger sweep and are forced to confront the limitations of their own persons and purposes. Voltaire remained a man of balanced judgment, which is in itself laudable, but which also prevented him from giving full expression of his ideals, from revealing with firmer resolve the qualities that he genuinely stored and retained. How sad it is to see a man of Voltaire's stature and abilities backtrack, engage in a war in which he ties his own hands, and utter pronouncements which he only half believes, and denounce that which he would truly embrace! A sense of limits remains a limitation. To hold to the commonplace is still conventional. To quote Naves again, 'Il ne se laisse aller.' Such self-restriction would come to an end with Romanticism (in Le Tourneur we can detect the emerging lines of the pre-Romantic). Romanticism, in contrast with Voltaire, has one distinguishing quality (beyond all the other more recently discussed ideological or mythic or ironic qualities), and that is a true consultation with one's own emotions, a movement beyond public consent to the freedom of personal preference and expression.[9]

PART TWO

WORKS: CHILDREN OF A FORTUNATE HOUR

Erasmus's Letter to van Dorp and Voltaire's Letter to Rousseau

In his thin-skinned response to criticism, Erasmus was far from saintly; in fact, as a controversialist he was very imperfect. Of course no one escaped fault-free and unscathed from the bitter controversies of the times, such were the animosities, the personal rivalries, the jealous guarding of status and position, the genuine generational conflicts between innovation and tradition, as well as some just and fearful concerns about the hazards of future change.

Pitch defiles, and so does controversy. And Erasmus, despite his many winning and edifying arguments, was not always at his best as a controversialist. Three traits emerged as particularly bothersome to modern observers: he was disingenuous, he seemed to suffer from acute amnesia, and he was moved by a spirit of denial. Tiresome in its disingenuousness is his insistence that because he names no names in his satirical works he brings no injury to the professions as a whole. It was only wishful thinking on his part to believe that he could strike and not draw blood or inflict harm (except on those with already guilty consciences), or that humour and satire were games, not to be taken seriously, or that he was merely raising questions rather than making pronouncements – forgetting that a question is still a remark.[1] His forgetfulness went to the extreme when he declares in later periods of revocation that he may have somewhere perhaps spoken ill of monks and theologians, or when he avows that he has only dipped into Luther, reading him by bits and snatches, as if he did not devote total attentiveness to everything coming out of Wittenberg; there is hardly a letter after 1519 that does not contain some references to Luther or his cohorts. It is with a similar tic of defensive self-protection that he dismisses many of his works as tossed off in haste because of other more pressing duties. Perhaps the spirit of denial is his most serious default and brings us close to some persistent traits of Erasmus's personality. He declined to take a leadership role in the movement of which, at least in its earlier days, he was the nominal leader, much to the pointed disgust of von Hutten and others, who resented the abdication of their acknowledged *chef d'école*.[2] He abhorred being singled out, as if this were to turn him into a target.

The accent of bleating is most audible in his *Hyperaspistes*, when he complains that Luther, under attack in Germany, in England, and in other countries, and by some parties even within his own camp, should choose to direct his vehemence against him (CWE 76:98). Resorting, as was his wont, to the precedent of the ancients, he wonders why his views that are found in Origen and Jerome, when directed against Luther, should be called Erasmian (CWE 9:398–9). Hence his distaste for this designation as a distilled system of belief. In the dispute with Jacques Masson (Latomus) he refuses to acknowledge that he is the real target of attack (yet Erika Rummel in her meticulous investigations shows that phrase after phrase in Masson's arguments can be traced back directly to Erasmus's writings).[3] Erasmus preferred to be a discreet, self-marginalized counsellor, one who exerted influence at a polite distance. As Augustijn remarks, he absents himself from the contest. In fact, his earliest words in *On the Freedom of the Will* express his distaste for hand-to-hand combat: 'And so I have always preferred sporting in the spacious plains of the Muses to engaging in sword-play at close quarters' (LE 7). Yet these very aspects of his personality are those that plunge him into depths of self-analysis and self-reproach, particularly when he is obliged to enter into contest with Luther, and all occasions seem to inform against him. He fears that he will make the *gran rifiuto* and mimic the real denial of Peter. But as Augustijn points out such self-reproach is the product of intensely honest introspection (an even greater example will be the letter to Marcus Laurinus of February 1523).[4] The Holy Spirit, the lack of which caused him anxious moments, takes many forms and may have been with him when he knew it not.

All of these weaknesses are real in the character of Erasmus, and have remained as subjects of scholarly scrutiny from his time to ours; from von Hutten to Huizinga, his character was disparaged while his learned mind was admired. His faults thus are out-standing until we begin to examine the tactics, the arguments, and the goals of his opponents. To have made servile mouthpieces of their junior dependent colleagues is truly deplorable – a tactic that enabled them to retain a veneer of amiability. It is even harder to credit their arguments as they were marked by nit-picking, by absence of any true wit or intellectual liveliness, and mainly by the presence of self-concern. Their obvious motivations were self-preservation and territorial control, and they were wary of any incursions into their academic prerogatives. If we put aside such all-too-human motivations, we may find it hard today to believe that much of the acrimonious debate was over the introduction of classical foreign languages, notably Greek, Hebrew, and of course Latin, into the collegiate curriculum, the three forming the bases of the new *Collegium Trilingue*, whose growth at Louvain Erasmus was most instrumental in fostering. That it and similarly formed institutions have by now endured for nearly 500 years, that instruction in foreign languages (even the use of the term is demeaning and primitive-sounding) has become a required part of learning at all levels and is of particular service to national poli-cies, should not make us forget the role which the issue played in the heated controversies of the past. When fear in all its forms is in the driver's seat, people can be spooked at every turn, and at times quite needlessly.

These are the attributes that Erasmus scorns and against which he inveighs, and the contrast prompted the emergence of the Erasmus whom his contemporaries chose to admire and history to honour, the Erasmus who is a staunch defender of Christian lib-erty, providing support for the adult Christian conscience against the ordinances and reliance on 'works' promoted by the church. This same Erasmus, having become an advocate and defender of genuine learning, was in the forefront of the battle of The Book. He understood that many of the attacks against Luther were in re-ality directed against the new learning that he advanced. Erasmus was the leading 'biblical humanist' of his day, dedicated to using his erudition and his skills as a *literatus* to embellish the temple of the Lord. He stood for human liberty, for freedom of inquiry, for a faith in the testimony of one's senses, and for the proofs offered by the critical intelligence. Moreover, like his great contempo-rary, Thomas More, he had a confident faith, one that did not fear gradual change, particularly when it was supported by genuine learning, good information, and sound doctrine. Coleridge will attribute Erasmus's conspicuous intellectual role to his being the beneficiary 'of the first vernal influence of real knowledge' (*The Friend* 1:132). Erasmus expresses bewilderment that prominent theologians should think the sky is falling, and are 'terrified, as though it were something perilous and pestilential' that anyone should attempt to acquire Greek. Finally, he makes the simple assertion, 'I see nothing here that much affects the genuineness of our Christian faith' (CWE 3:136).

This is the Erasmus that shines through, particularly in the earlier controversies with Dorp, Masson (Latomus), and Lee, and with each debate the shadow of suspicion increases, brought about by the spread of Luther's doctrines. The dispute with Dorp, which this section emphasizes, was largely concerned with matters of philology, but gave way to graver matters of theology and biblical interpretation. The exchange of letters with Dorp occurred before the fateful years 1519–20, that is, before the renewed outbreak of hostilities over the formation of the *Collegium Trilingue* and most crucially before the advent of Luther's more polemical writing, with whose ideas Erasmus could then be associated. Nevertheless, despite the later softening, if not revocation, of his positions, perhaps even because of them, Erasmus's letter of defence may be rightly allied with Voltaire's famous letter of 1755 to Rousseau, where Voltaire takes to task the latter's 'defence of ignorance.'

In the days of his great success, travelling back to England after a triumphal journey up the Rhine to Basel in 1514 where he was crowned with such epithets as the German Socrates, the Star of the North, famous for his *Praise of Folly*, and his yet unpublished editions of Jerome and the New Testament, he was met by a copy of the letter Maarten van Dorp had written to him from Louvain. Erasmus's response was not made until his next return from England in May 1515. It was thus from a position of well-earned ascendancy that he was able to respond to Dorp with magnificent eloquence, with a driving force of conviction that makes of this letter one of the sterling defences of human knowledge, of a commitment to genuine learning, Ostensibly written by a friend issuing a timely warning, Dorp's letter, showing the tactics of the conservative theologians of Louvain, was actually a 'put up' job, criticizing Erasmus for the satire of *The Praise of Folly* and raising alarms about the pending edition of the New Testament. Such was Erasmus's stature at the time that even future projects were anticipated and thus subject to warnings. Erasmus's tone is more forgiving because he realizes that his one-time protégé, now a doctoral candidate in theology at Louvain, was under the thumbs of his lead professors, and was being used as a 'stalking horse.' He was thus willing to make allowances and, indeed, such largesse was vindicated when Dorp later became a stout defender of the trilingual lectureships in Latin, Greek, and Hebrew that Erasmus had worked to introduce into the collegiate curriculum at Louvain (CWE 71:xvii–xix).

If we conflate both of Dorp's letters, that of September 1514 and the second in response to Erasmus from August 1515, it is possible in summary fashion to reduce Dorp's arguments to four, two of which will come back with a terrible vengeance to haunt Erasmus in his quarrels with Luther. Dorp's letter first takes aim at *The Praise of Folly*, arguing that Erasmus's satire will in the mind of the lay person constitute a slur against all theologians. In responding to this Erasmus is not his own best advocate, as he is responding to Dorp's fears with his own brand of defensiveness. Dorp's somewhat tepid argument means that one cannot criticize offensive behaviour of some, even many, of a group for fear of tainting the entire group. It is as if people were devoid of powers of discrimination. Erasmus argues that the just will be amused and know themselves not to be inculpated, while the tainted will accuse themselves by their protests (CWE 3:119). He further argues that his style is so accommodating, so qualified, so given over to humour that little offence can be taken (125). Erasmus does not understand the impact of his own words. Wit and humour do not insulate the topic but have powers of seductive appeal. The fact that he names no names can set people off on a guessing game, trying to figure out who is intended and they can, when clues are sufficient, have the pleasure of identifying the culprit. And his argument that by naming no names he harms no one was cleverly met by the counterstatement that it is precisely because he names no names that he damages the profession as a whole. Against Dorp's charges that he implicates Christ, Paul, and the apostles in madness Erasmus is far more effective. He explains that by this lunacy he means a kind of ecstasy, where one is taken out of oneself (125–6). That this may be construed as ordinary madness exists only in the minds of the worldly wise who cannot comprehend such selfless devotion to Christian ideals. Let us be fools for Christ's sake (see below, chapter 5).

It is when Erasmus turns to invective and when the power of his denunciation strikes fire that he shows the true fervour of his commitment and his apologia attains its just status. He denounces those so consumed in the battle of words that 'they have no time to read what was written by the evangelists, the prophets, and apostles' (124). Pronouncements of theologians and bishops lead to further more intricate pronouncements so that 'there is no hope of recalling the world to the old true Christianity' (125). His detractors, those who have led Dorp astray, have closed themselves in their own authority, and invoke the fear of popular disbelief merely to conceal their own ignorance. They are not concerned with the people at all but solely driven by the need to protect their academic turf. 'Bonas litteras metuunt et suae timent tyrannidi' (They are afraid of the [humanities] and fear for their own dictatorships; Allen 2:108; CWE 3:132). It is for this reason that they raise the threat of popular uproar and disturbance. 'They fear that if there is a renaissance of the humanities, and if the world sees the errors of its ways, it may become clear that they know nothing.'[5] How much better would it be to avoid nit-picking over errors that are minute or corrigible and participate in a collaborative effort of common cause (122).

There are more serious charges and complaints as well as some valid defences in Dorp's letters. This is made clear in his second letter where he develops a strict dichotomy between the roles of the grammarians and the theologians (CWE 3:165). The theologians in their original drive and purpose felt called to answer very practical and current questions that were left unresolved or untouched in holy scriptures. These are serious problems that cannot be solved by the grammarians' memorizing the Bible letter by letter, or by allegorical interpretations. These are questions concerned with the sacraments, 'how the sacraments ought to be administered, what their proper forms are, when absolution should be given to a sinner, when he should be rejected, what according to the commandment ought to be given back, and what retained, and countless points of this kind' (165). While hardly productive or the result of a profound philosophy, it is in this sense of an evolving Christianity that the theologians considered themselves 'modern' and Erasmus and his followers to be mere antiquarian *litterateurs*. But neither Erasmus nor More (more forcefully) was persuaded, answering that in their time the arguments of dialectic produced no plentiful harvest, but rather legalistic discriminations that only lead to further subtle distinctions and pave the way of sophistry (Erasmus's favourite term for his opponents was 'sophists'). We can recall von Hutten's judgment that but for their involvement with Erasmus these celebrated divines would be unknown in Germany.

Even granting some legitimacy to his claims of a higher purpose, Dorp obviously errs in two ways. First he makes a straw figure of the grammarian, restricting that role to correcting accent marks, or poring for hours over four words. But for Erasmus knowledge of grammar is justified in its application to the establishment and proper understanding of texts. Like the knowledge of languages it is a tool in their elucidation and never an end in itself. Furthermore when Dorp scorns the grammarians' futile pursuit of insignificant matters he shows himself to have been a poor reader of *The Praise of Folly*. Far more poignantly and with painful understanding Erasmus himself laments the waste of a lifetime in what the wiser world considers petty knowledge. But as Betty Radice, the editor of *Praise of Folly* in the *Collected Works*, indicates in her introduction, some of the descriptions of the grammarian's sorrowful lot were added in 1516 *after* Dorp's letter – but the materials surrounding it abundantly make the same point.

Two further issues loom large both at the times of these exchanges and even later in the course of Erasmus's dispute with Luther. Dorp fears that Erasmus's faulting the Vulgate for the errors of scribes and copyists will have a nefarious effect on 'the purity of the faith' (CWE 3:161). Rather it must be shown, 'so that the faithful do not waver,' that other texts were rejected and the Vulgate alone, as corrected by Jerome, was the one accepted by the church in the interests of uniformity (162). But this perceived threat to the faith of the people is allied with and based upon Dorp's more fundamental argument, one that will be heard again and again: 'For it is not reasonable that the whole church, which has always used this edition and still both approves and uses it, should for all these centuries have been wrong' (CWE 3:21). The continuity of culture, the weight of custom, and the authority of the church and its learned doctors all combine to form the emotional basis of opposition to change. Oddly enough, tragically enough, it will be these very arguments – fear of tumult among the masses and discredited divergence from the customs of the ages – that Erasmus will redeploy in his debate with Luther. Representing the profound changes that he underwent in the 1520s, and the transformations of his thought brought about by his contest with Luther, Erasmus makes use of the arguments that he had successfully rebutted against Dorp. This changed reaction has been well remarked by both contemporary and modern followers of Erasmus's development. Even the very sympathetic Augustijn regrets the changes brought about by the contest with Luther. This is the 'tragische Moment,' he writes, the huge 'Veränderung' and even a 'Verschiebung' (the tragic moment that brought about the 'change' and 'slippage'; Erasmus: *Der Humanist* 275–6) and about which in his time von Hutten laments. Hutten's fallen leader will have the sad task of comparing his former contributions with the arguments he has currently adopted in his opposition to Luther. It is in his own mind that Erasmus will suffer most and in this judgment von Hutten was partially right.

But at the moment of his debate with Dorp in 1515 Erasmus was the obvious victor. To Dorp's charges Erasmus replies that the Vulgate was not exclusively the work of Jerome (CWE 3:135); moreover, the argument accrediting the customs of the ages means compounding the errors of negligent scribes and copyists. The errors in transcription are too obvious to be ignored. Hence the versions used by Jerome, Ambrose, and Augustine all differ (133–4).And as for popular belief, Erasmus 'sees nothing here that much affects the genuineness of our Christian faith' (136).

Erasmus's arguments go even farther and deeper. He obviously argues for the acquisition of the three essential languages and urges the study of pagan authors so as to sharpen one's sense of grammar and syntax. Moreover, he boldly incorporates the wisdom and aspirations of the classical world into the framework of Christian belief. Against the theologians' complaints that this represents a turn to pagan authors, he answers, How can you deny the acquisition of learning from classical letters when you depend so much upon Aristotle (CWE 3:124)?

What attracts our attention is not so much the arguments – although they are effective – but rather the buoyant tone. The responses are obviously those of a man confident in his purpose, one who has discovered his life's work. His declared intention from the *Enchiridion* onwards was to bring people into a more direct contact with the spirit of the gospels and the understanding of the early church fathers. By reaching back he was reaching out to the laypersons of his day and reaching forward to a better grounding and understanding of biblical texts. Instead the theologians were clogging these fresh springs with the debris of their proliferating '*Questiones*.' Erasmus's true purpose, his genuine contribution and originality was, as Augustijn quite rightly maintains, the renewal of theology. This was the meaning of Erasmus's efforts, the unifying feature throughout his mature career, to bring to piety the added adornments of good letters, and here is where, in his view, the modern theologians fail. Good letters depend upon sound learning, and this in turn requires accurate understanding in the languages of the text. Erasmus is convinced that the general decline in learning in his time is attributable to the neglect of instruction in Greek and Hebrew, as well as Latin (CWE 71:66, ¶67). But there is a graver accusation: Erasmus attributes the widening divisions within the church to the decline in learning. The responsible parties are those who refuse the guidance of available knowledge 'and not ... those who are striving to use languages to help the development of sound learning' (66, ¶64).

Such a challenge to the existing practice of theologians requires an even greater strength – there is a philosophical charge behind the arguments of philology – and that is the argument of freedom that both Erasmus and More at this phase of their careers put forward (however much they were later to change). In his *Apology against Latomus* of March 1519 Erasmus puts in question form the urge toward freedom that is the real force and justification of his efforts: 'But why should writers of the present age be denied a right that the saintly Aquinas demands for himself ... Why, when we review opinions should we be denied the freedom of commenting upon them? Not only Jerome claims this freedom, but every more modern writer takes advantage of it' (CWE 71:82 ¶118). Again and again similar expressions of this need for intellectual freedom will unite More, Erasmus, and their colleagues and represent their defence and justification. Moreover, they were not afraid of changes that were supported by solid evidence and genuine piety, changes that could only contribute to the renewal of faith that the increasingly secularized and alienated society sorely needed. In regard to biblical studies it is clear that Erasmus's attempts (but certainly not his alone) to reformulate the study and establishment of texts on a sound linguistic and philological basis succeeded remarkably. This may have been his finest triumph. But in the extension to society as a whole, as later years and experience dictated, theirs was a reformation that did not totally succeed, and breaks occurred even from within. More became a zealous foe of heresy, unlike Erasmus, who was never quite as willing to brandish that threatening bolt but who underwent his own retrenchments nevertheless.

Voltaire himself was quite instrumental in the rehabilitation of Erasmus's reputation and the extension of his influence. In his *Essai sur les moeurs*, in the trialogue between Erasmus, Lucian, and Rabelais (later joined by the much admired Jonathan Swift), and in the *Anecdote sur Belizaire* (all duly noted by Mansfield (*Man on His Own* 2.18–25), Voltaire praised Erasmus the satirist, one who worked to disestablish the practices of the Roman church and spread tolerance all under Voltaire's 'God unique,' who includes in his fold even the virtuous pagans, as is most memorably expressed by the phrase, 'Saint Socrates pray for us.' So plentiful are the allusions and connections that one wonders why there has been such a paucity of specific studies bringing them together in more detailed analysis.[6] For Carducci as for Conrad Busken Huet (1826–86) they are aligned with Petrarch as eponymously representing their times. One does not need to rely on such hero-fetishism to establish the extraordinary correspondences that exist between Voltaire and Erasmus. Beyond the plentiful references to Erasmus in Voltaire's work, Voltaire was if not the first at least preeminent in promoting the notion of another Reformation (see above, page 11), and thereby helping to secure the return of Erasmus. In the inflammatory *Sermon des cinquante* Voltaire abhorred the personalities of Luther and Calvin (who had 'une âme atroce'); nevertheless he credits 'nos pères' for having given the tree of Christian practice and belief a good shaking and effecting some major reforms (*Melanges* 269). But despite the removal of such doctrines and practices and beliefs as transubstantiation, the adoration of saints and the bones of the dead, aural confessions, indulgences, exorcism, false miracles, and ridiculous images and relics, they still left the work 'imparfait.' There are large movements underway, such as Socinianism, all working to finish, to 'achever' the work that was left incomplete. They are all ready to adore a single God. Voltaire clearly is advancing the notion of a second reformation, but one without Christ. This sanitized reformation becomes necessary for another reason. And here Erasmus's moderating scepticism, much appreciated by Gibbon, enters the argument. Some weak spirits, in the unthinking and unquestioned simplicity of their fervent belief, are staggered and even undone by the arguments that pretend to demolish official Christianity. Thus they abandon ship entirely and leap just as fitfully into no religion. In Gibbon's phrase, 'They want licence without the temper of philosophy' (893). And to be just Voltaire's reformation is a religion for philosophers – perhaps even Masons, or the contemporaneous Phi Beta Kappa, whose anagram, revealing its origins in the Enlightenment, means 'Philosophy as the Helmsman of Life.' The moderating virtue of Voltaire (somewhat belated after his blistering attacks against all facets of the Old and New Testaments) calls for a willingness to apply the brake, and not to go too far in the opposite direction. This same principle both Gibbon and Voltaire found available in the more conservative tendencies of Erasmus's thought.

Behind such defences of religion lay a strong commitment on the parts of Erasmus and Voltaire to the values of civilization, to letters, and to learning, thus forming a link between Erasmus's letter to Dorp and Voltaire's famous witty and admonitory letter to Rousseau. This letter is much briefer – barely two pages – and not complicated by the abstruse points of textual and interpretive matters that were so crucial to the Erasmus-Dorp exchanges. By indirect means Voltaire had received a copy of Rousseau's second *Discours* (*Discours sur l'origine et les fondements de l'inégalité parmi les hommes*). But as Besterman correctly states, 'It will be noticed that much of Voltaire's letter is relevant to the *Discours* of 1750 rather than to that of 1755' (Voltaire to J.-J. Rousseau, OC 16:262n1). Voltaire's letter is a model of how to respond to radical discourse. Operating on three levels, it combines down-to-earth humour, with the yes/but provisions, and a simple but ardent defence of the necessary and ample benefits derived from learning.

While Erasmus was a brilliant satirist the strange paradox remains that he never seemed to master the art of humour in his apologetics. It was as if under attack he became a different person, utterly abandoned by any sense of firm confidence and riddled by defensiveness. With Voltaire, however, the presence of wit, the legacy of his tutelage under the waggish *libertins* of his earlier years, never abandoned him – particularly when it came to polemics. Thus his very first sentence brings Rousseau's theory out of the clouds down to everyday existence: 'I have just received your new book directed against the human species' (J'ai recu, Monsieur, vôtre nouveau livre contre le genre humaine,'

259–60). While complimenting Rousseau on painting in their true colours the horrors of society (which, however, allow us so many sweet things of life), he doubts whether such complaints will ever correct human vices. He finishes the paragraph with a classical summary of the paradox involved in an intellectual's detraction of learning: never was such intelligence ('l'esprit') employed to make us stupid ('nous rendre bêtes'). In fact, so effective, he continues, is the argument, that it makes Voltaire want to crawl on all fours. But having lost the habit some sixty years ago, he will leave that 'démarche' to those more worthy than either of them. This is Voltaire at his comic best, taking an intellectual argument and reducing it to its everyday inconsequence. The balloon of theory is pricked by humorous inversion.

The next and largest part of the letter is in the concessionary yes/but mode. By personal experience he knows the shameful tactics of the brigands of literature, of the pirates who have stolen his works, manhandled them, and sold them for profit. These are people who would have been better off being lackeys, or performing some other useful function. But are these not the thorns that accompany any flowering and thus must not be kicked against? The 'but' argument is the most telling because here he argues against the loose causality that still hampers discussions of literature and politics. How often have we heard it wondered how, as if asking a question but instead making a statement, the country of Bach and Beethoven could have produced the Holocaust, or how one can go directly from Luther to the same grim events, or how the Enlightenment could have produced Hitler. Next, Hannah Arendt was known to quip, they'll be reaching back to Adam and Eve. Only the grossest leaps of the historical imagination, compounded by causal negligence and obfuscation, the classical confusions of *post* and *propter*, could manage such contaminations between the creative artistic genius and the distorted mentalities of thugs and criminals who shed the blood of innocent fellow citizens on so massive a scale. Thus Voltaire is able to remind Rousseau that Marot was not responsible for the St Bartholomew Day massacre, and Corneille contributed nothing to the wars of the Fronde (the civil strife that tore France apart from 1648 to 1653). In an excised passage he points out that Petrarch and Boccaccio were not responsible for Italy's troubles. Great crimes were only perpetrated by gigantic ignoramuses, whose crimes speaking for themselves, whatever animal cunning they may have possessed, indicate enormous mental shortages.

Far from being incentives to murder and mayhem, letters, or literature 'nourissent,' 'rectifient,' and 'consolent.' Such justifications while not grandiloquent are even more prepossessing by their very simplicity. Such literature that Voltaire defends brings sustenance, moral adjudication, and solace. And how can that be wrong? These two letters, certainly not inconspicuous in their times, will continue to be cherished for their defences of learning and humane letters.

FOUR

Works Finding Their Ways

🦂

The fascination of what's difficult
Has dried the sap out of my veins, and rent
Spontaneous joy and natural content
Out of my heart.

W.B. Yeats

The comparative method adopted by this study receives its fullest justification in the discussion of Erasmus's *Colloquies* and Voltaire's *contes philosophiques*. The similarities existing between these genres in the course of their authors' careers are nothing short of remarkable, and these include how they came, when they came, and what they represented. Reluctantly, if not inadvertently and by accident, Erasmus and Voltaire turned in their later years to styles and genres that would go far in accounting for their acclaim. They thus accomplished individually and apart one of the miracles of literary biography – that which occurs when a noted writer pivots and brings into being a style of writing which his own ingrained tastes and training had only belittled. Eventually, they each found their newly adopted genre a great source book and repository for contemporary events, for individual incidents, for skewering opponents, but more importantly for gathering up the accumulated thoughts that made them public intellectuals of such wide interest. So fully did they commit themselves to these new styles that the colloquies and the *contes* may be regarded as roadmaps of their intellectual developments. In some ways changed estimations on the parts of the authors themselves anticipated the changed perspectives of posterity. Each of the genres looms extensively in their authors' oeuvre; in fact, in their originality they have become identified with their authors' names. Although there were numerous *dialoghi* during the Renaissance, colloquies, as such, now belong almost exclusively to Erasmus, while *contes*, or the *roman philosophique*, was virtually 'inaugurated' by Voltaire (Naves 82). Lastly, each encounters the same critical problem, and that is one of superabundance. So readily did they take to their new-found genres that they overproduced; the supply exceeds the demand and hence is in need of critical selectivity.

Each author entered into his new venture by external persuasion; in both cases, they needed to be pushed. Each then underwent and benefited from what could be called a miniconversion. Such miniconversions should be differentiated from the major religious conversions whose beginnings, middle, and ends William James has described so fully in his profound meditations on American life in *The Varieties of Religious Experience*.[1] James's detailed discussion of the aspects of conversion provides a useful template for uncovering the nature of the miniconversions; it shows profound difference as well as compliance. While undergoing change, both Erasmus and Voltaire adhered to their essential natures and in the beginning, middle, and end of the conversion process continued to show their great differences from Luther, in the one case, and Rousseau, in the other. Their changes derived from no melancholia, no egregious discontent; nor did they require self-submission, or self-effacement. Nor were their revelations bolts out of the blue, or blinding light; there was no burning bush, or other life-altering experience (among the many aspects of James's discussion of the conversion experience). In fact, their changes represented something of a *revirement*, a return to a part of their natures that had been suborned in their quest of more 'serious' works. The change complied with their more conscious intentions and not with response to some ulterior purpose. Representing no drastic overhaul of their lives (they still continued to write works of great significance), their 'conversions' showed a new conscious consistency. The 'fascination of what was difficult,' or the labour involved in rising to 'high seriousness,' also gave way to ease, as it did for Erasmus in the composition of *The Praise of Folly* (despite its many later revisions and the fact that it led to no serious replication). Ease is a cause of wonder. But it was more than mere facility that took hold of their efforts; rather, it was the accumulated experiences of a lifetime, their reflections on the world they had witnessed, and more important, their own involvements that now came pressing to the front. As with more fundamental conversions this rediscovery of their more natural bent opened the ways to a fresh out-pouring, to a major expansion of their thoughts. What matters is not how these breakthroughs were attained – inadvertence has its own varied means – but what was attained. These two formerly deprecated genres became havens for the developing and mature thoughts of the two masters, veritable storehouses of their profound reflections. In Erasmus's case, they addressed doctrinal matters of theology and ecclesiastical abuses, and in that of Voltaire, brought to light his changeful reflections upon the state of Europe, on history, and on the larger issues directing his moral philosophy.

Erasmus and Voltaire each required some external pressures before committing themselves to what they considered a minor genre. After a lapse of nearly twenty years, a well-intended but unauthorized gathering of Erasmus's earlier Latin language lessons travelled by various hands, including those of Beatus Rhenanus, who was later to be Erasmus's biographer, to Froben, the noted printer of Basel, where they were first published in November 1518 as *Familiarum Colloquiorum Formulae*. This edition was copiously reprinted throughout Europe. Erasmus, understandably annoyed, but also pleased by the favourable public reception, had his own edition printed with additions and corrections at Louvain in March 1519. Thus began the whirlwind of activities surrounding what was at first a slender volume. In 1522 Froben brought out two editions, twice as long as the earlier, with emendations and additions, including what is perhaps Erasmus's most accomplished colloquy, 'The Religious Feast.' New editions of the *Colloquies* appeared in Basel in 1523, 1524, 1526, 1527, 1529, 1531 and 1533 (Rummel, *Colloqui di Erasmo da Rotterdam* 17).

Voltaire had been giving private readings of some of his *contes* to the delight of friends. He was a born storyteller (*conteur né;* van den Heuvel 330). As a young blade about town he would regale his hosts and hostesses with stories and anecdotes of Parisian life, always spiced with wit and some sauciness. From the start of the 1730s, his *Lettres philosophiques* and his history of Charles XII reveal his capacity to mingle history with appealing accounts marked by irony, comedy, and caustic wit (331). But he refused to publish his *contes*. Finally persuaded, he did not release *Zadig*, his first published *conte*, until 1747. Even those *contes* he had already committed to paper, the *Micromégas* (finished about 1738), was not published until 1752, and like *Zadig*, from about the same time, it was published under a pseudonym. Eluding or complicit with the watchful authorities, by this expedient he may also have felt that the author of *La Henriade*, *Oedipe*, *Alzire*, and *Mahomet* should not be linked to such drolleries, mere divertissements. He even disavowed authorship of *Candide*. Such things were beneath his true calling. But René Pomeau has neatly turned the question around. Rather than asking how the author of *La Henriade* and *Zaire* could have descended to the level of *Candide*, the question ought to have been, 'Comment l'auteur de *Candide* a-t-il pu se complaire dans les conventions de ce qu'on appelait alors les grands genres?' (How could Voltaire have contented himself within the conventions of what they called then high literature? *De la Cour au jardin* 373).

That both Erasmus and Voltaire began developing this new venture in their early fifties is not without significance. Van den Heuvel may discount as a 'legende tenace' such consignment of the *contes* to that period of Voltaire's life (330), but the fact remains that despite their sources and even 'readings' in the preceding decades, Voltaire did not consent to their publication until his early fifties. At that age, psychologists tell us, the person comes into his own, takes possession of what really pleases him or her; there is a settling in to what actually gives pleasure. A kind of 'rite of passage' occurs (Strauss and Howe 13). More spontaneous joy and a contentedness with what is more natural to one's being (to invoke Yeats's poem used as epigraph) now find their moments. No longer abnegated in the pursuit of higher seriousness, these easier qualities can now reclaim their own reliable positions.

And settle in both Erasmus and Voltaire did. At final count, Erasmus's colloquies total some sixty-two. Voltaire's *contes* will vary in number, depending upon the critic's standards of judgment. This formerly neglected genre grew in such profusion that it actually requires some culling if the best is to be retained. Critical sense calls for such limitations and selectivity. To quote Voltaire from one of his letters, 'Plus on lui ôte, plus il est grand' (The more one takes away, the greater it becomes; *Correspondence*, 43:196). In Voltaire's case, the question is not only one of quality but also of appropriateness. If the one governing criterion of a *conte* or a *roman* is that the nature of the situations and conditions surveyed have some impact on the characters, and bring about some change in their emotional beings, then even such major works as *La Princesse de Babylone*, *L'homme aux quarante écus*, and the *Lettres d'Admetus* require different alignments. In his classic study Jacques van den Heuvel, by way of commentary, provides his own deletions. *La Princesse* and others show a Voltaire who has emptied his bag of tricks.The storyteller has given way to the pamphleteer. Van den Heuvel even questions whether *Quarante écus*, with its accumulation of random facts, should be considered a *conte* at all. But those that remain are a formidable quarry, stretching from early to late in Voltaire's career. Although reduced in number, *Crocheteur borgne* (unpublished in Voltaire's lifetime), *Cosi-Sancta*, *Micromégas*, *Babouc*, *Zadig*, *Memnon*, *Scarmentado*, *Candide*, and the *Ingenu* would still represent the best of Voltaire's 'stories.'

Both genres represent milestones in their authors' careers. They reach backward and stretch forward. *The Colloquies* epitomize the shape of Erasmus's adult career. They provide a synthesis of his thought as well as a genealogy that encapsulates his historical development. We are very much in the debt of Franz Bierlaire who admirably assumed the difficult task of sifting through the various printings and editions (*Érasme et ses Colloques*). From 1522 to 1533 twelve new, expanded editions were published, with more than 100 reprintings of the various editions prior to Erasmus's death in 1536. But what is even more remarkable in that eleven-year period, Erasmus added some forty new colloquies. Obviously the form appealed to his taste. They may have come too easily – in some cases he dashed off three in a day– allowing references to them as *Tischreden*, or table talk. What had begun as lively classroom exercises had obviously become more than an ancillary interest of his life, in fact developing into a large compendium of his thought, opinions, and observations of life and manners. This compendious quality is expressed in the various subtitles later critics have added to their studies of the *Colloquies*, such as Bierlaire's 'le livre d'une vie,' or 'réforme des etudes, réforme des moeurs et réforme de l'Église au XVIe siècle.' An early eighteenth-century translation of *The Colloquies* by Nathan Bailey (the last translation into English of the full corpus of the colloquies prior to that of Craig Thompson in 1965) reminds the reader in its title that it concerns 'Men, Manners and Things.'

In their number and scope these works touch on all of Erasmus's major interests, from his beginnings as a pedagogue, intent on devising skits or playlets to arouse his tutorial students' interests in conversational Latin. Their very genealogy reveals the transforming powers of Renaissance humanism as the conversational lessons giving instruction in various greetings and other forms of polite address expanded into formidable thought-pieces touching all aspects of sixteenth-century religious and social life. As Rummel has indicated there exists a tight bonding between Erasmus's *Colloquies* and his many other outright theological works (*Colloqui* 11–12). They express and rely upon the Christian piety of the *Enchiridion*; they are replete with adages as effective means of getting across a point; in some of the major essays, such as 'Rash Vows' ('De votis temere susceptis,' 1522) they show Folly exerting its supremacy in human affairs; Erasmus himself has undertaken to play the role of the Fool, so that he can better utter unseasonable thoughts. While disclaiming any alliance with Lutheranism, in the full weather of the Lutheran controversy they show little tolerance for indulgences, for the veneration of saints, for auricular confession, for pilgrimages, and the worship of relics. As throughout Erasmus's other works, while their first approach is to the young schoolboy, their greater appeal is to the believing layman, who needs to be told that holiness is not the exclusive property of the monastic life, and that marriage can also be chaste. In all of these matters he becomes more than a teacher; he is, rather, a public intellectual addressing matters of common interest for the adult layman, who is encouraged and instructed in the practice of discernment where human ordinances and church ceremonials are the concern. As Augustijn correctly reminds us, Erasmus's efforts are always directed toward the interests of contemporary life (*Erasmus* 194).

Erasmus's colloquies and Voltaire's *contes* also deserve further comparative attention by reason of their differences in satirical method, the extent of their historical and geographic vistas, and their subject matter. Erasmus's satire is directly situational, where obvious follies and the more grievous faults of a materialized religion are exposed. In his satire the cards read themselves, without too much need of outside assistance: the characters are recognizable, and their practices well-known. The colloquies also provide Erasmus with a mask; like a ventriloquist he could pretend that it was not he speaking but rather his manikin. But this defence proved to be unconvincing. The colloquies are dialogues without a dialectic.

Erasmus was a man of strong and growing opinions, opinions which he wished to propagate, and the *Colloquies* provided him with the proper forum. But he was also a person who worked to conceal himself ('il se derobe,' – he steals himself away; Choma-rat 2:1165).Thus, mixed with the presence of strong advice on the remediation of ecclesiastical practices there exist reformulations and reinstatements, congenial to Erasmus's wavering personal-ity. His rhetoric reveals an Erasmus concerned with inclusive-ness, with synthesis, with conciliation rather than rupture, with prioritizing, and with some scale of proportionate values. This split in his personality results in a fundamental ambivalence, at once wishing to strike yet at the same time concerned to soften the blow. This aspect of Erasmus's personality is condemned by von Hutten who attributes it merely to a fear of giving offence.

Unlike that of Erasmus, Voltaire's satire proceeds by caricature (see the entry 'Satire' in *Dictionnaire Voltaire*): he isolates one in-significant element (whether to enter the church by the left or the right foot, whether to wear red or black) and to the exclusion of all other complexities or conditions reduces the argument to its most absurd. This is the classical art of the satirist and Voltaire's usual practice; by decontextualizing he identifies a sect or a group by that which is trivial, and thus reduces the quarrel to matters of some silliness, offensive to reason. For Voltaire reason and satire are twin prongs of the same fork.

Of necessity Voltaire was bound not to show his hand; thus he resorted to numerous pseudonyms, which, oddly enough, is an imposition Erasmus did not have to endure. The sixteenth-century writers manipulated dramatic personae but normally works were issued under their own names. Voltaire's equivoca-tions depend upon practical concealment and duplicitous ruses that assure deniability. He excelled at the machinations that the accommodating authorities themselves did not find unwelcome. His willingness to 'play their game' shows itself in the false end-ings, obviously meant as only lip-service, coda implausibly at-tached (and this frequently from the persuasions of friends). The protocol of hope that was added to the blistering account of the Lisbon earthquake and the attempts at 'reconciliation' that attend the conclusions of *Zadig* and *L'Ingenu* (turning them into paintings by Greuze) are examples of this device. They are additions from which the internal record of the work recoils. Where Erasmus was given to afterthoughts from the spirit of accommodation, Voltaire resorted to reconsiderations by the instinct of survival, so much more onerous had the power and the oppressive surveillance of the state become. Erasmus's accommodations enter into and qualify the nature of the work; Voltaire's expediencies stand out as exceptional, and by being so only reinforce the original intent of protest or accusation.

Erasmus was a well-travelled, cosmopolitan man, but one who maintained that his library was his home, and books his quarters. Yet he knew and incorporated places like Rotterdam, Louvain, and Basel into his home precincts. But historical geography, so appealing to Voltaire, and so dominant in his *contes*, is largely absent fron Erasmus's intellectual topography. Erasmus can pinpoint very ably the specifics of the cities he knew quite well, but he did not open up the larger vistas of flight and fancy that are part of Voltaire's imaginative world. There is little exoticism in Erasmus's *Colloquies*, while Voltaire exploits the taste for the oriental (while also undermining its very appeal). But even this, as Barthes quite rightly emphasizes, turns into a *jeu*, a spectacular game, where gross extravagances of murder, mayhem, and misadventure have little relation to any quotidian reality. Still his flights contain much more. His *contes*, *Histoire des Voyages de Scarmentado*, and *La Princesse de Babylone* take us on tours that are fantastical but also concern matters of historical record, an accounting of the ways and mores of people in different times and places. With Voltaire, geography and history are so intertwined, geography becoming history, that they provide the materials for some of his most profound meditations.

The two authors also differ as to subject matter. The libido seems indomitable in Voltaire's *contes* but it is not absent in Erasmus's colloquies. The difference lies mainly in tone, with Erasmus attempting to fit sex between married couples within the spirit of a Christian chastity, while Voltaire would frequently find good-humoured acceptance of sexuality as one of the bargaining tools of human society. But sexuality becomes more than a bawdy presence, itself undergoing remarkable changes leading to the most serious moments in *L'Ingenu*. In another major difference with Erasmus, Voltaire never would believe that sexuality can be a part of or lead to chastity.

In Voltaire's *contes* we find another presence and that is Thought: thought deriving from his familiarity with Bacon, Locke, and Newton, his willingness to dispute with Descartes and Pascal, and his long-standing closeness with Mme du Chatelet. The *conte* that most exhibits this quality is *Micromégas*, particularly showing

Voltaire's adherence to the philosophy of Locke and the physics of Newton. It also reflects the sheer excitement caused at Cirey by the expedition of Maupertius (with whom Voltaire would later quarrel), which proved by direct observation that Newton's calculations that the earth was a spheroid flattened at its poles was correct (van den Heuvel's Pléaide notice about these matters is admirable). With the gifted hostess at Cirey Voltaire shared an abiding interest in discussing not only the intricacies of technical science (where she may have been his mentor), but also the more philosophical issues such as necessity and liberty, providence and human freedom. Erasmus, as a scholar, editor, and compiler, was not allergic to some of those issues; nevertheless, they are not part of the defining day-to-day more practical considerations of the *Colloquies*, which are mainly confined to questions of contemporary religious practice and doctrine.

Probably the best way to approach the *Colloquies* is by a selection of them, an expedient many of his later translators would adopt (the one by Craig Thompson is excellent).[2] One is better off savouring the variety of the colloquies before searching more completely throughout their wide and uneven extent. Augustijn addresses four in his brief chapter in *Erasmus*. Of those treating doctrinal matters Erika Rummel discusses four in *Colloqui*: 'The Examination concerning Faith' ('Inquisitio de fide,' 1524), 'The Whole Duty of Youth' ('Confabulatio pia,' 1522), 'A Fish Diet' ('Ichthyophagia,' 1526), and 'The Religious Feast' ('Convivium religiosum, '1522). In another chapter dealing with ecclesiastical abuses, she discusses 'Rash Vows' ('De votis temere susceptis,' 1522), 'Shipwreck' ('Naufragium,' 1523), 'A Pilgrimage for Religion's Sake' ('Peregrinatio religionis ergo,' 1526), and 'The Funeral' ('Funus, '1526). Surveying all of them is Erasmus's elaborate defence against his critics, 'The Usefulness of the Colloquies' ('De utilitate colloquiorum,' 1526).

Franz Bierlaire in a fuller study, *Les Colloques d'Érasme*, also provides short summary guides to reading the *Colloquies*. In his chapter, 'Les *Colloques*: Guide de la vie Chrétienne,' he shows in length as well as some depth the many themes that Erasmus engages, beginning with his thoughts as educator. Given the pressure of time, the limited amount allotted to the person, one cannot begin too soon in instructing the young. In fact, proper formation begins with the mother's good health and is nurtured with her own milk (see 'The New Mother,' ['Puerpera'], CWE 39:590). Renaissance humanism was consumed with the argument of time. Not only must education be begun early but it must be followed rigorously, with a proper scheduling so that not one minute of the day would be lost. An example of this method in practice is provided by Erasmus in describing the routine of young Alexander, the son of the king of Scotland and his own tutorial student (Phillips 105-7). Sleep is thus a waste of time, and the young student as well as the veteran scholar must learn to get by with a minimum of sleep ('Early to Rise' ['Diluculum'], CWE 49:916). True learning must not be an unpleasant chore, however, but rather a happy experience with much time given to play, sport, and diversions. While eminently concerned with the education of youth, the colloquies show Erasmus reaching out to adult laypersons and reincorporating them into the body of the church. Baptism is the great act of entitlement by which the status of holiness is shared. It is no longer the monopoly of the various religious orders, but is a way of life open to all Christians.

This suggests that there are ways of approaching the colloquies other than that of abridgment. One is by arranging thematic clusters, or clubs, of colloquies, such as those devoted to women, their roles in society, to marriage and the alternative possibility of the monastic life, and of course, sexuality. This method is aided by the evidence that in most cases the colloquies lacking a true dialectic are written with points to be made. True, there are some genuine disputes, but on the whole these are overcome by a dominant voice and point of view favoured by the author.This places Erasmus under the requirement of resorting to another method in order to express the nuances that exist in his mind. He does this by juxtapositions of rival colloquies. Thus the four consecutive colloquies where marriage seems to be the natural calling of women (to the detriment of the monastic life) are followed in 'The Soldier and the Carthusian' ('Militis et Carthusiani,' CWE 39:328) by the proper ways of entering the monastery and living the spiritual life there enjoined. And even the marriage colloquies, where the wife has agreed by contract to be a happy homemaker, may be modified by 'The Abbot and the Learned Lady' ('Abbatis et eruditae,' CWE 39:499), where the educated woman knows Latin, much to the disgust of the abbot (who remains in his stolid Archie Bunker mentality, a character of some proportions). The households of More in England and Pirckheimer in Germany provided

Erasmus with striking examples of young women capable of immense learning, to the shame but not the embarrassment of the abbot.

Bierlaire reminds us that 'la femme sort grandie des *Colloques*' (*Les Colloques d'Érasme* 177). While such enhancement of women is advanced for Erasmus's time, there is little approval that he will receive from women in later history. In the colloquy, 'Marriage' ('Coniugium,' CWE 39:306) the successfully married Eulalia instructs the unhappy Xantippe in the widely accepted doctrine of St Paul, that 'a woman's highest praise is to be obedient to her husband' (319). Such obedience may require the patience of Griselda but it also involves the manipulative cunning of the Wife of Bath. In fact, though a perfect homemaker operating in the kitchen and managing a household, the good wife must also prove herself to be adept in the bedroom. Only by being available, skilled, and pleasurable does she tame the fierce virility of her husband The girdle that Vulcan in mythology provided for Venus to make her the goddess of sexual love is the wife's by nature. Xantippe naturally recoils from the outrageous examples of women who actually abet their husbands' womanizing. Nevertheless, Eulalia is dominant in showing Xantippe the ways to regain her husband's affection by adopting a strategy more winning than that of mere shrewishness. Given this 'girl talk' it is somewhat surprising that Erasmus can transform the spiritual maturation of such intercourse into the dimensions of chastity and Christian love. As his editor remarks, '[Erasmus] resolves all questions with the invincible assurance of a confirmed bachelor' (306). Of course he performs this feat by hierarchizing: there are two Venuses, the one of earthly love and the other of a more chaste and spiritual love; the development of the one into the other (which Erasmus believes can happen) inspires mutual respect by the meeting of two minds, like 'perfume in a jewelled box.'

Another cluster of colloquies could be made of those dealing with war and peace. 'The Soldier and the Carthusian' and 'Charon' (CWE 40:818) lend themselves readily, but the theme is so extensive throughout Erasmus's works, that one is obliged to refer to the major expanded *Adages* of 1515 and two independent contemporaneous treatises as well. In fact, the issues of war and peace are given new form and made part of the greater issue of the subversion of Christianity in Erasmus's time. In approaching this subject he reaches across the centuries and through the centuries, touching hands with Dostoevsky in one way but ever more forcefully with Voltaire; their mutual detestation of the damages and human costs of war probably was the strongest cable that brought them together.

Rising above topicality, Erasmus extends his argument to a much more profound philosophical and perennial question: can one in altered times recover the simpler original message of a former epoch? Two great conflicting impulses and gestures affect and disturb this inquiry. One motivates Erasmus himself, who worked with strenuous effort but with dubious success to bring back the message of Christ and the apostles. In the midst of a changing and extremely complex society and against the natural sluggishness of humankind, he advocated the simpler measures of a spiritual renewal. The other, far more striking and resonant with popular acclaim, is more an image than a thought. It is the picture of Pope Julius II entering the conquered city of Bologna with all the splendour of full military trappings: Julius, the warrior pope, the vicar of Christ, exulting in the lust of triumph. The argument is Dantesque, reviving that celebrated Florentine's powerfully argued *De Monarchia*, particularly Book III (as Renaudet 189–90 most fully recognized): Can the head of Christ's church be Peter and Caesar at the same time? Is not the church itself better off when, with Boniface VIII at Anagni in 1304 or Clement VII in the hands of the mercenaries, it is buffeted, bruised, and humiliated, thus better fitting the model provided by its founding spirit? The two conflicting visions might very well summarize the complex involvement of Erasmus in the context of his time.

Mixing the discussion of the *Colloquies* with Erasmus's reflections on peace and war taken from the other works admittedly makes the vision bleak. Yet, if ever so briefly, Erasmus was enthralled by more optimistic prospects. It was thus between 1515 and 1517 that Erasmus's thoughts on matters of peace and war gathered a new momentum, as A.H.T. Levi remarks in his introduction to CWE volumes 27 and 28. It would appear that during these years Erasmus was at his most sanguine about the state of Christendom. In letters to Wolfgang Capito and to Pope Leo X (CWE 4:263–8 and 311) he foresees the coming of a new Golden Age, one where peace, genuine learning, and true piety would thrive. Pope Leo X has almost erased the memory of the bellicose Julius II, the learned Henry VIII had succeeded his father in 1509, Francis I would be instrumental in forming the later Col-

lège de France, and the young Prince Charles, after acceding to
the throne of Spain in 1516 (for which occasion the *Education of a
Christian Prince* was written) was elected Holy Roman Emperor
in 1519. While Erasmus would continue to write panegyrics of
all four (see CWE 27:321) this amounted to somewhat alien and
flattering interventions in his argument, for in reality he was beset by deep concerns. In time, all four, but especially Charles and
Francis, became antagonists vying with one another, either in
Italy or in Hapsburgian Netherlands. And all of this was coin-
cidental with the advent of Luther (against whom Leo's attitude
was far from helpful, culminating in the bull of excommunication, *Exsurge, Domine*, of 1520) and the related counterattacks of
the university theologians. The world had turned topsy-turvy. In
two of the colloquies, 'The New Mother' and 'Charon,' the description of the decline of European Christendom is so intense
that Gloucester's lament in *King Lear* is rightly invoked: 'We have
seen the best of our times,' as Erasmus regrets 'how everything's
gone wrong now' (CWE 27:270). Not only between nations but
within nations anarchy, religious turmoil, and violence seem to
prevail. Eutrapellus in 'The New Mother' gives vent to his despair
(CWE 39:592) and Charon is delighted at the heavy influx of new
boatloads of passengers (CWE 40:821). Later the Peasants' Revolt
in 1425 added to his sense of overall degeneration, which was
only aggravated when the Imperial army attacked Rome in 1527.

Erasmus's premature and ephemeral rejoicing gives way to
lamentation. His disappointment at the failure of the monarchs
whose joined arrival together presaged a new dawn is heart-felt
and intense. In fact the height of his expectations can only be measured by the depths of his despair. Luther was never subjected to
the same disappointment because he never entertained such high
hopes to begin with. While insisting on honourable and just conduct in temporal affairs (and thus not to be compared with Machiavelli), Luther knew the vicissitudes of fortune, the failures of
the best-laid plans, the laws of unintended consequences, the cor-
rupting influences of power, and the inscrutability of God's will
when it came to changing events. The ironies of history did not
escape him (Haile 100–5). For Erasmus, the sack of Rome marked
an ending as well as a different beginning. It brought to an end
the adventure in Italian humanism that helped inspire the work
of the Oxford Reformers and the bright lights of the Northern Renaissance. Erasmus knew well an era, his era and that of his allies

in Italy and in Spain, had ended. He abhorred the desecration of the church and the imprisonment of Pope Clement VII, but unfortunately for him the church proved to be resilient and sagacious in its negotiations and in thirty years' time would resurface as the leader in the Counter-Reformation that would evict Erasmian humanism from Italy and Spain.

To be sure there are inescapable repetitions throughout these works – the colloquies, the adages, and the several treatises, the *Julius Exclusus*, *The Education of a Christian Prince* (*Institutio principis christiani*, 1516), and the *Complaint of Peace* (*Querela Pacis*, 1517) – but such repeat performances do not make his arguments less compelling. Throughout, Erasmus admonishes against the notion of a just war; the topic while practically doctrinal is everywhere treated tentatively, hesitantly, and provisionally by Erasmus, and in the *Bellum*, contemptuously. The sword of Christ – alluded to often – is never a physical sword, but rather the sword of the spirit. His Christianity, like the *silenus* of Alcibiades, is a spiritualized one that is quite alien to popular perception, which is limited to sensory awareness of that which is immediate and corporeal. While the people are the victims of the recourse to war, they themselves are fickle and limited in their awareness. Erasmus applies his belief in a spiritualized Christianity to the affairs of nations. But this 'moralizing' quality should not blind us to the complexities of Erasmus's thought. The deformed practices that now encumber the church did not occur overnight, but crept in slowly, almost unobtrusively, by small additions here and there, until incrementally they became massive.

The *Querela Pacis* (1517) may be regarded as a rhetorical piece, but its intensity, detail, and scope of argument, in addition to supporting remarks from other of Erasmus's works, show it to be more than merely rhetorical in purpose (CWE 27:293–322). Erasmus is most adept and specific in describing the horrors of war. The blood-thirsty slaughters are horrid enough, but the wages of war outlast the war itself; the unforeseen and belated costs and casualties do not end with the war's end. Soldiers' pay comes late and always in damaged form. Those who suffer the most are the common people who have no interest in the war (CWE 27:285). This theme is repeated again and again, thus exempting them from any bellicosity (although jingoism might be as deeply rooted in them as in any belligerent). Erasmus quotes the Ciceronian adage, better an unjust peace than a just war (CWE 27:310–11, 313).

Toward the goal of peace, he makes quite specific recommendations; inter-dynastic marriages which confuse boundaries should
be banned and soldiers should not be buried in consecrated land
nor be honoured as martyrs in churches. And he is particularly
aggrieved by prelates praying to the same God for victory of their
opposing forces. Frequently the original causes of the war are lost
sight of, as in a feud. And enclosed behind the borders of each
state, xenophobic tribal hatreds fester.

Erasmus is better in describing the terrors of war than he is in
prescribing the remedies of peace (but it would seem the disasters
of the former are argument enough). In his descriptions of the
calamities of war, Erasmus is an analyst, but in his remedies for
peace he remains a moralist. The tumult of the times is God's punishment for humankind's waywardness. What is needed is a conversion of heart, an individual benevolence. He argues sincerely
that if his people were all better Christians they would have a
greater opportunity for converting the Turks (CWE 27:314).

One can write even more critically of *The Education of a Christian Prince* that it is an instruction manual filled with unassail-
able precepts that are more like blueprints for a building than an
encounter with the unanticipated complexities in the actual construction: it appears to ignore the real workings of state and the
relations between nations. Indeed, it has become customary to
discount this work (in CWE 27:xxviii, the general editor regards
Erasmus as an 'ideologue' and the volume editors regard it as a
product of 'rigorous ethical intellectualism,' 200). Like the growth
of vines around a tree trunk such criticisms – that Erasmus was
'impatient with political realities' (xxviii) – have become practically inseparable from the moralizing nature of the works themselves. They have entered into its genealogy, become part of the
family tree. But several things need to be said. First, Erasmus's
moral instruction is not as lacking in practical advice, even cunning, as is commonly assumed. The wide range of his contacts
and his experiences at large throughout the cities of the Rhine and
beyond did not deprive him of familiarity with the political realities of the time (see thirty long lines in Renaudet 179 that describe
Erasmus's multifarious and serious involvements). Like Voltaire
he laments the prevalence of idleness, particularly among the
priesthood, but even more among the soldiery. Like Rousseau, he
urges the children of the aristocracy to learn a 'useful occupation.'
Following Aristotle, he more directly advises the prince to have

bad news delivered by a subordinate (*The Education of a Christian Prince* 257) and writes that when change is introduced, such innovations – undesirable as they usually are – should be put forward 'subtly and gradually' (258). Appearance is all-important and on no occasion must the prince be seen to be idle (257); while chary of his public appearances, when he does appear in public he must always be seen to be about some public business (strategic advice that is not unfamiliar to readers of Shakespeare's *Henry IV*). While ten editions of the *Institutio* were published in Erasmus's lifetime and while it was quickly translated into the various vernaculars, its messages went largely unheeded. In this and many other regards it contrasts starkly with the very contemporaneous work, Machiavelli's *Il Principe* (*The Prince*). In some of the best pages ever written about Machiavelli (here Renaudet's complete comparisons between the two might also be included, 178–86), Ernst Cassirer, in *The Myth of the State*, enrolls *The Prince* like *The Education of the Christian Prince* in the long-standing genre of treatises concerned with moral instruction in the office of rule. But in its concern with the technique of politics Machiavelli's *Prince* outstrips its forerunners and, in fact, breaks new ground by reason of its substance. Cassirer quotes Napoleon to the effect that only Machiavelli's *Prince* is worth reading, and then asks rhetorically: 'Can we think of a Richelieu, a Caterina de' Medici, a Napoleon Bonaparte as enthusiastic students of works such as Thomas Aquinas' *De regimine principum*, Erasmus's *Institutio principis Christiani*, or Fénélon's *Télémaque*' (152)? While these leaders are hardly endeared to us as models they at least knew the world and the manners and habits of people. At first glance it might appear that Erasmus, unlike them, was confusing cause and effect, that evil was the product of war, and what with the use of mercenaries and the moral degeneration which the long continuation of any war induces, this might in part be true. But he is not lacking in another view, however alien it might be to his ameliorist educational ethic, that war is the product of some 'fatal malady of human nature' (CWE 27:314). But if Erasmus's efforts at peacemaking were lacking in the pragmatic policies that would appeal to a governing monarch, and were more of a plea than a program, it can be said of them what Lezhnev said of Rudin in Ivan Turgenev's novel of that name, 'At least his words are good.' In fact, as one grows older it appears that Erasmus's moralizing is far from irrelevant.

The *Adages* are underrepresented here because they bear little convergence with any works of Voltaire (with the possible exception of the *Dictionnaire philosophique*). Beginning with the potboiler first version, the *Adagiorum Collectanea* (1500), and then the expanded *Adagiorun Chiliades* (1508), and proceeding down to the even larger *Adagiorum Chilides* (1515) Erasmus brought out many separate editions of *each*, and after 1515 inserted many additions, usually of a mollifying nature. Unlike what happened with his 'rediscovery' of the colloquies he did not take to the adages eagerly, and constantly sought to escape from the tiring and tiresome scholarly research they required. Somewhat self-pityingly he describes the burdens of editing and compiling, the difficulties of bringing disparate texts together from four languages (he added the Aramaic), some mangled or garbled, only to be met by nitpicking quibbles on the part of critics. In *Festina lente* (*Make Haste Slowly*, 1508) and *Herculei labores* (*The Labours of Hercules*, 1508) he bemoans the detailed research such works have imposed, and seeks a wider field for the full expression of his thought, his abiding interest in the 'amendment of life' and a 'plan for living' (*Adages*. 201, 296). One does not search through the more than 5,000 *Adages* for a consistent point of view, just as one would not seek a *Weltanschauung* in a thesaurus; still, from among the thousands of catchy phrases, some grew into full-blown essays. In the 1515 edition of the *Adages*, there appeared in enlarged form some of the most famous, such as *Dulce bellum inexpertis* (*War Is Only Sweet for Those Who Haven't Been There*) or *Spartam nactus es, hanc orna* (*You Have Obtained Sparta, Now Enhance Her* – with several other variant translations possible, such as You have Sparta, now do the best with her, meaning 'Stick to your knitting'), *Scarabeus aquilam quaerit* (*The Beetle Takes On the Eagle*), and the *Sileni Alcibiades*, which have had long-lasting appeal and special relevance. It was almost natural that Erasmus would grow tired of the onerous tracking of variant readings and examples of his now over 5000 adages, and that his speculative wings would need to take flight. The expanded adages – now full essays – provided him with this opportunity.

The *Adages* express even more fully the dilemma in Erasmus's thought that is becoming painfully clear, and that is the discrepancy between his life-long quest as a Christian humanist for a spiritual ordering of society and the resistant nature of the world he encounters. Not all his mollifying, accommodating rhetoric could

resolve this essential divergence. While involving all sectors of society, this dire discrepancy can be located more specifically as existing between the teachings of Christ, the examples of Peter and
Paul, and the current church leadership. The bellicose activities of
Julius II entered deeply into his thought causing much consterna-
tion. In perhaps his most summary adage, the *Sileni of Alcibiades*,
the entire scheme of Christian values is described as being turned
upside down, or inside out. Here, deriving from *Praise of Folly*, as
will be discussed below (chapter 5), there seems to be an interminable warfare between popular and widespread values and those
that should be chief in the hearts of princes and church leaders.
Christ has become unrecognized by his modern descendants. One
could say that Erasmus was writing Dostoevsky's remarkable
Grand Inquisitor episode before Dostoevsky did. Not only is the
message of Christ unheeded, it is unwanted as interfering in the
new order of the day. The modern church has been refashioned
into a grander, more powerful institution, as 'his' Julius argues.

Even if we discount *Julius Exclusus*, whose single authorship
by Erasmus is much disputed (see note 6 below), the same story
is told throughout the fully developed *Adages*. Where Dostoevsky
relies on the later concept of absolute freedom, the time of Erasmus's story is that of the early sixteenth century when the freedom
brought by Christ is that of Christian liberty, a principle so very
basic to the thinking of both Erasmus and Luther. It appears most
appropriately in the convivial colloquies (to which must be added
the 'Fish Diet'). Dietary restriction such as fasting and meatless
Fridays and other days of abstinence naturally offended both the
scrupulous mind and the tender physique of Erasmus. He found
no justification for such prohibitions in scripture, but instead the
opposite, the summary conclusion expressed by Christ again and
again: 'For the son of man is Lord even on the Sabbath day' (Matthew 12:8). And the reference quoted by one of the characters in
'The Profane Feast' makes a similar point by quoting Mark 3:4: 'Is
it lawful to do good on the Sabbath days, or to do evil? To save
life, or to kill?' Subsuming and controlling the multitude of similar expressions are Jesus's own better-known words: 'The Sabbath
was made for man, and not man for the Sabbath' (Mark 2:27). It is
Christian liberty that bestows on the adult Christian the freedom
to adhere to or not to adhere to what are merely human ordinances which have no warrant in scripture. Implicitly or explicitly, this
is the doctrine that the new 'tyrants' of the church, defending the

divergent needs of the present day, the present time, would deny. Christ is no longer relevant. It is against this travesty, represented as descending down from the example of Julius, through the bishops, to the priests and the common folk, that Erasmus militates. It is hardly surprising that Erasmus's call found meagre response among the majority of the people of his day. But it was an appeal that would elevate expectations, even heighten discourse, and one that would in time, perhaps by simple seepage, win a broad measure of accord.

Turning again to the *Colloquies*, Erasmus's role as an educator for the common good, a public intellectual, also brought down on his head unrelenting criticism. What is remarkable is not so much the defensiveness (or even the arguments of defence) but rather his persistence in enlarging and adding to the collection. This even in the time when, as other writings and his letters indicate, he came to deeply regret, even recant, his role in the spread of reformist ideas (see chapter 6 below). While all of his opinions are conciliatory and modulated by the typical Erasmian rhetoric of reconsideration and inclusiveness, it is notable that they were expressed in the full season of the controversy with Luther after 1518, and even more fully between 1526 and 1533. This is one of the reasons their genealogy is still so attractive to scholars. In spite of everything, Erasmus continued to print and enlarge upon his colloquies, now become minor dramatic essays in their own right. Part of the reason for this controversy is not only the nuanced complexity of Erasmus's views but also his taste for paradox, for exploiting sensational topics, such as the 'lunacy' of the truly Christian way. The conclusion of *The Praise of Folly* thus finds its corollary in the last of the printed colloquies, 'The Epicurean' ('Epicureus,' CWE 40:1070). If folly can be the way of the saint, then Epicureanism, that is, genuine, lasting pleasure, can only be the result of Christian faith and righteousness. Such turnabouts obviously are intended to send heads spinning and tongues wagging, but they also produce two of Erasmus's grandest works.

The severe criticisms and attacks prompted by the *Colloquies* were even more intense than those contained in Dorp's letters of complaint. Where the earlier critics were concerned with philological and textual readings and thus were contested with confidence and some aplomb on Erasmus's part, the later critics, coming from Paris as well as Louvain, were distressed by theological implications, those issues that were aroused by the onset of Luther's highly charged doctrines. Thus Erasmus's *Colloquies* were attacked at the University of Paris on sixty-one points, some deemed heretical. The book was later forbidden. The new band of critics necessitated Erasmus's lengthy response of self-defence, 'The Usefulness of the *Colloquies*,' which was too long and too itemized (he actually refers to thirty-seven colloquies). Yet it critically adds to our understanding of his understanding of the *Colloquies*. In answering his critics he is defining, even refining, his purposes, and in several remarkable statements he makes them clear. He recounts the arguments of 'A Fish Diet,' where he advocates moderation in regard to 'human ordinances,' but at the same time blaming 'the ridiculous human judgments the world has been filled with; noting also what has caused all this present uproar in the world' (CWE 40:1104). Such issues are the required focus of the colloquies. There is no need to condemn flagrant vices; they are deplored as soon as known. 'The danger to true godliness comes from evils that are not perceived or that entice in the guise of righteousness' (1104). This one sentence clarifies the uproar that not only the *Colloquies* but Erasmus's other works provoked. His purpose is to undo the false masks of righteousness, the self-assured and confident Phariseeism that holiness may be attained by simply observing the ceremonies of the church, even where the true living spirit of belief or conviction may be lacking. What eventually causes the Butcher and the Fishmonger to sing in unison (and this for ten pages) is their disgust at chidings and punishments people receive for minor infractions of codes of dress or fasting ordinances while grosser more cardinal deficiencies are condoned or overlooked. Erasmus will raise the same point in his defence: why am I being attacked for correcting abuses while the abuses themselves, gross sins of dereliction or worse, are ignored. Two answers come readily. Erasmus's criticisms were thought to be levelled at the totality of doctrine when he thought he was attacking their excesses and abuses. Erasmus is also warring with human nature. His call is to a spiritualized Christianity that the mass of humanity cannot endure. In Dostoevsky's hands Erasmus might well have become the disappointed idealist Ivan, who finally assigns painful victory to the Grand Inquisitor because humankind cannot sustain its freedom, or Christian liberty.

Erasmus could rightly accuse his opponents of being dim-witted and tone deaf, of not being sensitive to humour and light-hearted banter. Moreover they were captious, intent on nit-picking, if not gross misreading. They missed the qualifications, the rhetoric of modulation and reconsideration, his evident respect for the customs that have accumulated, and his unwillingness, after Paul, to give scandal to the weak. In fact, he repeats from 'The Fish Diet' his admonition: 'I myself believe the laws of our forefathers ought to be reverently received and dutifully obeyed, as though they came from God. It is neither safe nor right to sow harmful suspicion concerning public authority' (CWE 40:1108). Erasmus's rhetoric is part of his personality and experience. An impoverished, orphaned scholarship student, he learned well the art of pleasing. A man who had to work his way to the top, he learned the skills of circumspection, of not resorting to outright exclusion, but rather finding ways of inclusion. Augustijn writes that Erasmus 'shrinks' from any complete rejection of earthly things (*Erasmus* 47). His rhetoric is incorporative: the mandates of the church, honourable traditions, and pious customs are not to be rejected as they are necessary for the weak and observed by the strong so as not to give offence. Consequently even his hardest positions involve qualifications. The rhetoric has the added importance of indicating that there should have been no shock or surprise at Erasmus's later recanting: the preparation for it was there all the while in the crucial manner of presentation, the mode of qualification.

Practising a fine discernment, Erasmus caught it now from both sides, from reformers as well as conservative theologians and churchmen. The times had changed but so had Erasmus (Rummel, *Erasmus and His Catholic Critics* 151). The storm unleashed by Luther caught Erasmus in its path. At first, there was an equivalency: opponents could quip that either Luther 'erasmianized' or Erasmus 'lutheranized,' so similar were their doctrines. But there were also charges of causation. Erasmus laid the egg that Luther hatched. Luther reaped what Erasmus had sown. Even when Erasmus tried to prove his credentials by attacking Luther on the freedom of the will, this was deemed too little too late, or seen as secretly supporting the Lutheran cause by the ineffectiveness of its arguments, or showing the typical Erasmian slippery equivocations rather than a forthright defence. All of this had its effect on Erasmus: he was, against his will, drawn into interminable polemics that seemed to spring up everywhere. A noted classicist could not avoid comparisons with Hercules and the ever-renewing Anteus. Moreover, Erasmus's star seemed to have waned as the younger intellectuals who had once gathered about him shifted their allegiances to new leaders, primarily Luther. Erasmus himself seemed to have lost his grip (ibid. 153). He was understandably miffed by the charge that he was old hat, lacking in spirit, someone who had taken the troops as far as he could but must now relinquish leadership to those of better account.

One concern troubled Erasmus throughout: why were they attacking him rather than Luther? Even under the guise of naming Luther, the real target of the subtext remains Erasmus and what he was most sensitive to and concerned about, the new humanistic education that he fostered. Psychologically, of course, the most feared and hated enemy is the one closest to you. There is a known and noted directness in Luther's opposition, but Erasmus could be condemned as a 'false Catholic' (Rummel, *Erasmus and His Catholic Critics* 102) and hence be considered more insidiously appealing in his arguments. To open the door if only a crack is to invite the deluge. A Trojan horse can do more damage than an outright siege. It was such accusations and attacks (frequently veiled but nevertheless clear in intent) that prompted Erasmus's responses that sound like whining and which are most audible in the two installments of the *Hyperaspistes*, where he could not rise above wondering why his obviously well-intended discourse on the freedom of the will drew such vehement personal denunciation from Luther. Why must his clearly good intentions be so wrongly abused?

His Catholic critics were beating him with the same rods that Luther had employed; the irreverent and facile humour, the slipperiness of his arguments, and his equivocations. One does not know where to pin him down. His ambivalences lead to no effective action or firmness of position. This despite the fact that, with all his reformist tendencies, he made abundantly clear in statement and by rhetoric that he could never belong to the Lutheran camp. He obviously shows his differences with Luther (CWE 40:1108) and others (although in 'The Inquiry Concerning Faith,' he tries to placate both sides by showing that on essential matters of faith, there was little difference between them). He defends 'The Whole Duty of Youth,' where the proper method of hearing of mass is described, as are the means for confession before communion. He argues for the retention of certain Christian customs even though they might have no justification in scriptures. In 'The Profane Feast' participants are taught to comply with pontifical orders rather than the advice of physicians. But even those favourably disposed failed to make the distinctions Erasmus thought he was making concerning fasting, ceremonies, pilgrimages, the invocations of saints, monastic vows, but most important, the extreme importance attached to human ordinances that found no validation in scriptures. This may have been because the changes Erasmus recommended would have necessitated wholesale alterations in almost all aspects of daily life. It was not so much the individual variations as the totality of them when gathered together that prompted fear. That these were presented with modulation and circumspection, as the *Colloquies* show, did not alter the essential call for change, change that appeared to ally itself with the more aggressive Lutheran pronouncements.

Throughout the bitter exchanges and the attacks, Erasmus always suspected that whether they were attacking Luther directly or himself indirectly, the real target was the program of studies he fostered, the *studia humanitatis*. Of course in the academy all *Kulturkampf* is a turf war, and as noted earlier, Erasmus's attempts, largely successful, to implement the *Collegium trilingue* in Louvain posed a threat to the methods and the positions of those in power (although the special colleges were separate from the universities). The real argument is with the humanities and the use of Greek, Hebrew, and Latin in the exegesis of sacred scriptures. The *studia humanitatis* triumphed over the longer run, because knowingly or unknowingly its beneficiaries imbibed this sense of thought at its best, at its most thorough and eloquent. What the early humanists promoted was more than subject matter; it was an attitude, a spirit of discovery, an earnestness in searching out basic principles, and a willingness to accept change. And in advancing these qualities Erasmus, joined by Thomas More and others, represented the advanced stages of European thought, to the detriment of their conservative critics who, while earning the title of 'modern' in their own minds, were too concerned with turf and authority. In time, of course, the educational system that Erasmus had promoted itself became stalled. By emphasizing its own authorities in the Greek and Latin classics this education had eventually acquired something of a posture if not a pose. I have argued in the epilogue to *Dualisms* that the humanities thrive when rooted in new attitudes. This principle is represented by Erasmus to the fullest in his openness to change, his wide-ranging advocacy and acceptance of what were new sources of true knowledge. With all his backsliding and cautions, his thin-skinned defensiveness, his need to collect authorities to support his arguments, his avid self-promotion and self-protectiveness, Erasmus, if he does not exactly stand like a tower, can still shine like a beacon. Within severe constraints, he continued to move forward and argue cogently as a public intellectual concerned with the best interests of his society. And in so doing he has attained, as his *Colloquies* and his enlarged essays from among the *Adages* attest, a persistent relevancy.

No single strand of interpretation can encompass the variety and quality of Voltaire's *contes*. They range from the culture of mundanity to the higher aspirations of Thought, elevated by Locke and Newton and enshrined at Cirey, from the vindication of the just man to the inconsolable death of a young woman killed by shame, and from the abysses of theocratic blackguardism to the possibilities of some improvements represented by the development of a Protestantizing European North. Even when assigned to thematic clusters divergences occur. This might be because of the different times in which they were written. As van den Heuvel has shown the *contes* are direct responses to the crucial events and changing episodes of Voltaire's life. But such biographical indebtedness has its obvious limitations: events do not control Voltaire's creativity; rather, his spirit bends events to fit the contours of his mind. We must acknowledge the ulterior ways of creativity, which follow their own channels and purposes. This means that these 'tales' are not all of the same quality. Even *Candide* must come in for some reconsideration and can no longer qualify as a stand-alone masterpiece; or, at least, it may be in need of supplementation.

More so than the *Colloquies* (where there was nearly a twenty-year hiatus between the earlier *formulae* and their later expanded republication), the *contes philosophiques* tell the story of a life and show the stages of Voltaire's intellectual development. Reaching back perhaps to the period of 1715–16 (that of *Oedipe*) they reflect, along with Voltaire's consistent preoccupations, the new interventions of science, industry, and commerce. They record significant phases of his experience, the polemics along the way, culminating in the personal defence contained in *Zadig*, whose hero commentators cannot resist referring to as Zadig-Voltaire. There was something easy about the *contes*, something that appealed to Voltaire's 'naturel.' He felt liberated and was able to write without restrictions of language, plot, or sentiment. From this derives their immense appeal, one that surprised Voltaire himself (Billaz, *Dictionnaire Voltaire* 244). As noted earlier, they offered possibilities that eluded the strict enforcement of rules and that were rich with exoticism and practicality, with some adventure and philosophy, with banter and profundity – in short a form and style that appealed to his playful, satiric, and serious nature. The genre itself was different from the revered obligations of the stage. But, while intended as amusements, the *conte philosophique* was a *pensum*, that is, a way of weighing and considering serious matters. And while reflecting new stages of Voltaire's intellectual development, these narratives also preserve and reveal the more enduring qualities of Voltaire's mind.

Le Crocheteur (RC 3–8) has been called a small chef-d'oeuvre and so it is, lending itself to modern sexual interpretations that have newly become attached to fairy tales. The *crocheteur*, a heavy-duty porter, without our being aware, subsides into a dream where he saves a beautiful woman from her runaway train of horses. Delicately dressed, she is ill-equipped to master the rocky terrain on foot. She falls and in attempting to rise reveals more of her body, sending Mesrour even more madly into the transports of love. He forgets that he is dirty, a porter, one-eyed and lacking all the gallantries of love (which, Voltaire adds, contributes to its *ennuis*), and makes use of the animal strength with which his work has endowed him. 'He was brutal and happy.' The princess, for surely she was one, may have fainted, but nevertheless groaning through her fate, marvels that such misfortune could culminate in so happy a conclusion. The *crocheteur* was a perfect lover, responding to 'faiblesses' on the part of the princess with renewed force. At the break of day, she was astonished to find instead of the dirty carrier, a young prince charming, such are the transforming powers of love, as even the medieval fabliaux tell us. We find the same transformations in Shakespeare's *A Midsummer Night's Dream*, where Titania loves Botttom, in one of the many versions of the grand theme of the queen and the gardener, and again in *Lady Chatterley's Lover*. In Shakespeare and Voltaire, the dream forms the substance of the story. Nor is the validity of the dream undone when the *crocheteur* is rudely awakened from this dream of male mastery and female submission, the power of sexual domination, to discover it was only a fantasy. The dream world lingers, as the mysterious story of Beauty and the Beast is told again with wit and verve.

The 'femme' does not universally emerge 'grandie' from the *contes* of Voltaire (unlike what Bierlaire finds to be true in the *Colloquies*). With only rare exceptions (and they are notable) 'she' seems committed to a sexual polyphony, or is willingly or forcibly obliged to barter her favours for some advantage (not totally unknown to our modern times, as this forms one of the themes of the film *Casablanca*). Thus the heroine of *Cosi-Sancta* (a tale, like the *Crocheteur borgne*, having its source in the period of 1715–16) is obliged to venture her sexual favours in order to save the lives of her husband, her son, and her brother. Thus she is saintly, after her fashion. The tale is highly ironic, the author concluding: 'Ainsi, Cosi-Sancta, pour avoir été trop sage, fit perir son gallant et condemner a mort son mari, et, pour avoir été complaisante, conserva les jours de son frère, de son fils, et de son mari' (RC 14). The flippancy of the sexual complaisance is highlighted by the finalizing motto: 'Un petit mal pour un grand bien' (A small wrong for the sake of a greater good). In his excellent notation, Frédéric Deloffre argues that this early work shows that the 'irrévérence et ce qu'on appelle "l'esprit voltairien" font bien partie chez Voltaire d'un fonds très ancien' (RC 685). But the lethal effects of such bartering will account for the most impassioned *Voltairien* outbursts of *L'Ingenu*.

Such sexual complaisance inheres in Voltaire's culture of mundanity, which he elaborated in the two instalments of *Le Mondain* in 1735–6, and which is expressed in two of his best known *contes*, *Babouc, ou Le monde comme il va*, and *Memnon, ou la Sagessse*. But just as all sexual bartering is not alike, so not all *ingenus* are similar. Some need to lower their sights, while others need to raise theirs. First appearing in 1748, the idea for *Babouc* reaches back into the late 1730s. Babouc is a young emissary inspector sent from the regions of Scythia to see if the badly reputed city of Persepolis should be preserved or destroyed. He is the innocent observer who is at first disgusted by the vices of the city. But it is he, the moral rigorist, who is out of step, who needs to be initiated into the ways of the world. While judgeships are bought and sold, the young judge renders decisions based on the rules of reason and common sense; while married partners each have their paramours, they themselves remain the best of friends and would do anything to help their spouse. It is Babouc, the moralist, who must acquire full comprehension of the workings of a complex society before he is able to pass judgment. Finally, being more fully apprised, he can conclude with another *Voltairien* motto: 'Si tout n'est pas bien, tout est passable.' The world such as it is, if not of the best, is still acceptable. Or put another way, what appears to be irrational might not be unreasonable.

Two interests of Voltaire emerge. One is impatience with the abstract moralist – more an escapee from arrested adolescence – who does not understand the real cohesive and organizing powers of an extremely complex society and thus tends to render superficial judgments based upon the limited knowledge of first impressions. The second, stemming from his culture of mundanity, is the need to immerse himself in the society and ways of his world. There is a third element that attaches to this story in particular, and makes criticism part of its genealogy. Unlike other works of this period with similar accommodating conclusions, *Babouc* triggers disbelief among contemporaneous as well as more modern critics, a willingness to contest its conclusions, or an unwillingness to suspend disbelief. They are not arguing with any insincerity or aesthetic failure, but rather with its aesthetic success. There is something about this story that ignites opposition to its message of accommodation, almost as if hovering over the *conte*, still some forty years in the future, would be the cataclysmic event that would bring down with wrath upon society Babouc's severe judgments. Future history enters into the story rendering its delicate equilibrium, like all equilibriums, fragile and precarious.

Memnon, with its subtitle, *ou la Sagesse*, is of the same camp and time as *Babouc*. The eponymous hero attempts to put into practice the Stoic mantra that both Voltaire and Mme du Châtelet adopted – the doctrine of abstention, or separation from the entanglements of the world. So Memnon determines to be perfectly 'sage' by a moral isolationism, by avoiding the passions of women, the intoxications of wine, and dependence upon others. Within twenty-four hours he fails miserably in all three 'sots projets.' Advised by an administering angel, he learns that angels can be perfect because they are totally wanting in passions, and that in comparison with other worlds, that of the earth is way down on any scale of values. But Memnon is urged to raise his sights and to see the earth in a universal perspective, one orchestrating the final arrangement of things. He is advised to curtail his expectations. From such a heightened universal perspective, which concludes that 'tout est bien,' Memnon, who has been physically and financially wasted by the difference between the world and his Stoic philosophy, can only reply that he will believe that when he regains the eye lost in his misfortunes. The fault, however, lies in the original philosophy of separation. For Voltaire, immersion in the world with all its passions and their hazards is an unavoidable part of being human. For Erasmus, the same is true for young women who seem unwilling to accept the risks of marriage. The one in 'Courtship' ('Proci et puellae') is in actuality only coyly pretending, but her suitor advises her that 'one who refuses to run the risk of human life,' ought to give up life altogether (CWE 39:266). Another in 'The Girl with No Interest in Marriage' ('Virgo misogamos'), enticed by the trappings of a nun (from which she quickly recoils) and chagrined by the ribaldry of dinner parties, is advised that 'the person who tries to avoid any embarrassment whatever had better quit this life' (CWE 39:289).

With Erasmus it is clear that the message of Christian liberty involves its hazards as well, but how can we account for Voltaire's stories? Are they simply jeux d'esprit, gambols of wit, or overly serious, overly obvious sketches of a philosophy. Combining both aspects, we can see them as condensations of a lived experience but treated at some distance, which accounts for their element of witty disenchantment, their inescapable taste of irony. Voltaire's decade-long involvement with Mme du Châtelet was one that involved active intellectual seriousness. Not only did the two (actually it was a *ménage à trois*) study philosophy (as well as many other things), but they attempted to forge a guiding philosophy of life. Their Stoic philosophy falls apart in *Memnon*. Interestingly enough, that perfect man, the Stoic, was deplored in Erasmus's *The Praise of Folly*. Voltaire was cautious enough, sceptical enough to know that when tested by life itself, such 'philosophies,' like New Year's resolutions, tend to crumble at first contact. Life is too multiform, too opaque, too resistant to be plied by such singular intellectual determinations. Yet Voltaire and his companion were intellectually serious enough to attempt to formulate such rules for living, naive enough to believe in or to search for a philosophy of life. Nevertheless the stories extend the suspicion that all such theories fail in the end. From within the bounds of his own experience, Voltaire thus came to appreciate the futility of arranged schemes of life that do not allow for the upsurge of raw experience. He came to realize that his commitments must be kept within the more limited region of known certainties, the so-called logic of facts. The discord between the two – a need for a philosophical basis to existence and the obvious contradictions presented by the raw facts of existence – are the conflicts that inhere in all the subsequent major stories.

Even more extensively, in this crisis in Voltaire's life we can discern the beginning of the spreading crack in the floor of modern thought. The hope persisted that like Newtonian science a large, systematic philosophy of life could be found that would solve the mazes of existence to the satisfaction of the thinking human being, or that if it could not fill in the empty spaces left void by the slippage of the Christian calendar, it could still offer a positive resolution of philosophy and religion. But Newtonian science was verifiable, confirmed in the every day world, while the new philosophies were contradicted by the elementary facts of existence. Their collapse was caused by observation and common sense.[3] At this depiction of the clashing battle ground of theory and practice Voltaire excelled. But such restrictive exercise of critical thought (not to be confused with anti-intellectualism) does not tell the whole *Voltairien* story; he has his own small faiths and a sense of justice that take us beyond the limits of a sterile 'facts only' positivism.

Zadig, the most personalized among the *contes* of Voltaire, was originally entitled *Memnon* when it appeared in 1747, but when republished in the following year acquired its current title. It brings together many of the disparate motifs of the other stories of this time, summarizing Voltaire's own quest for faith and justice, for what is worthy of belief. Unlike *Babouc* or *Memnon*, Zadig must not lower his sights or reduce his aims, but rather raise them so that he can see the true itinerary of his life. Leibnizian this heightened perspective might be, but always meeting with Voltaire's customary qualms and questioning. This story burns deeper into Voltaire's bones; it is a story of his own self-justification, of his own setbacks and it asks the question simmering in his heart as to why the just man, the talented man, the man of rectitude must suffer. One can see why van den Heuvel wishes to attribute to Voltaire's stories an immediate context in his life.

If we cannot fathom cosmic intentions, we can respond with vigour and clarity to what affects us personally, what is alive and visible before our eyes. Voltaire had the sense – despite his good humour – of being ill-used, even abused. He had already met the frontal brutality of Rohan, and afterwards the other brutality of his degrading detention in Frankfurt following his attempt to abandon the court of Frederick.[4] And all along the way he had been met by envious slander, forcing his many retreats. Yet, somehow he was resilient, talented, and reasonable enough to extricate himself from the scrapes that sometimes he invited and sometimes came uncalled. *Zadig* is a story of Voltaire's own heroic survival, and of faith in his own good faith being rewarded. This was not a philosophy but rather a living trust. He was *embastillé* after the Rohan affair, but that led to two gloriously decisive years in England; he was an émigré after Prussia, but that led to Les Delices and Ferney. Perhaps there is a higher purpose, or some destiny governing human affairs. In the final arrangement of things, as it so happens in the Hollywood ending of *Zadig*, virtue will be triumphant and all rewarded. But this conventional gathering up of the story, while not convincing, does not detract from the genuine appeal of a young man of talent and probity and rational powers seeking to escape from the many roadblocks, the traps, and the slander that the back-stabbers, the simply evil, or those mad with envy or jealousy, the plagiarists, and certainly the less talented, placed in his way. Personally indulgent, to be sure, but it is Voltaire's story nonetheless, one that through its many twists and turns finally met with palpable and enduring success.

Not only is Zadig well-formed and of an excellent character (a person who, unlike Voltaire, knows how to keep his reserve), but he is also a natural scientist, moving from observable evidence to warranted deductions. For example, he is capable of knowing by her tracks that a *chienne*, who had recently borne pups, had passed by, and by the same methods, of determining the height and nature of the missing horse. Thus he is a Sherlock Holmes as derived from the experimental school of Locke. And like the biblical Joseph, he is an able and dedicated administrator, who must suffer for his abilities. In the dramatic gallery of Voltaire's works, he also recalls Philoctète, who must endure the insult of accusation. Voltaire's exposition of characters frequently invites such larger associations.

Along the way of his many adventures he finally meets up with a venerable hermit, who turns out to be the angel Jesrad, who is quite willing to explain to the rightly questioning Zadig the eternal order of things. Why should there be crimes and troubles ('malheurs') and why should the 'malheurs' fall mainly upon the good? Jesrad responds that if the troubles of the good are sporadic, the 'mechants,' or evil people, are, by their natures, always unhappy. You would not want to live in their minds. The purpose of 'malheurs' in the world is to 'éprouver' (that is, to test, or to bring out the best in) the small number of the just. He reaches another apothegmatic conclusion: 'Il n'y a point de mal dont il ne naisse un bien' (There is not a jot of evil in the world from which some good is not born). But here again, Zadig interjects his 'mais.' What if there were no evil in the world? Then it would be another world, is the angel's reply. Whether one must raise one's sights (Zadig) or lower them (Babouc and Memnon) the answer is the same: this is the only world you have, and you are enmeshed in it, so you had better accept its conditions. This is a long way from saying it is the best of all possible worlds (unless we attribute extraordinary elasticity to the word 'possible'), even if it is the only one that is possible. If all worlds are unlike each other, and this world is the only one of its kind, then to say it is the best is like declaring it a winner in a one-horse race. Because it is the only possible one does not mean all that happens is for the good, that all events are part of a vast providential plan of happenings. This kind of argument is not exempt from the tautology that what happens happens, and that because it happens and that consequently it is the only thing that could be happening, it must be for the good, somewhere or other down the line. All things have their reasons but that does not mean that they are right. One could see why this earlier Leibnizian adoption (and a partial one at that) on the part of Voltaire would collapse like a house of cards at its first true encounter with a shattering challenge.

But if we are enmeshed in the world, and we must make the best of it, and the evils are there to 'prove' or test the just, then history has its own dialectic, and this is what Jacques van den Heuvel argues in his notice to *Zadig* (RC 736–53). Zadig becomes more than himself: 'La lutte qu'il mène contre les forces obscures dépasse de beaucoup le plan de son existence personelle' (The fight that he conducts against the obscure forces goes far beyond the level of his personal existence; 746). It is in the name of humanity itself that he fights. This extra dimension attributed to Zadig coincides with Voltaire's own historical researches at the time, researches that have brought him to a remarkably staying conclusion: 'L'histoire de l'humanité est celle d'un cheminement de la conscience à travers tous les obstacles qui s'opposent à son épanouissement' (The history of humanity is that of a constant struggle of consciousness against the obstacles that hinder its blossoming; 746). Oddly enough, by a strange and mixed itinerary, through his emblematic Zadig, Voltaire has brought us back to one of his personal keys, surpassing the culture of mundanity by his admiration of the number of the just who are few but who nevertheless expand the domains of culture and civilization. Such aspiration toward and admiration for such great figures would always be part of any *Voltairien* academy. Historical dialectic seems to be more in keeping with the *Voltairien* spirit than the adoration that Jesrad the angel requires, particularly when based upon such entangled ideas as those proposed.

The last works of Voltaire have been generally disparaged, most notably by Jacques van den Heuvel, as leading to mere pamphleteering, where the strong emotive principles of his personal life no longer become the matter of the *contes*. 'Alors le conte voltairien se perd dans la multitude des dialogues et des pamphlets' (Thus the *Voltairien* conte loses its way among the multitude of dialogues and pamphlets; 319). For instance, *La Princesse de Babylone* unrolls on a split screen, and while the two lovers eventually are reunited in forgiveness, they are more like aerial photographers, untouched by what they observe. That is, they are unlike true characters from the *contes* who undergo changes in character according to what their varied sightings and experiences bring them. Their surveillance of the states of Europe has little effect on their search for each other. The *Homme aux quarante écus* is such a mass of disparate information and statistics that its narrative would better qualify as a pot-pourri. But there is one late work that escapes these censures and might well rival *Candide* for primacy of place in the canons of *Voltairien* fiction, and that is *L'Ingenu* (1767). While some of Voltaire's *ingenus* are in need of initiation in the moral structure of their society, the Huron who comes to France is far from myopic, and indeed is striking in the clarity of his vision and his native good sense. He turns out to be a willing young Protestant, judging all practices that are urged upon him by their justification in scripture (which he has been taught to absorb).Voltaire goes 'funning' as the Huron now judges all ordinances by scriptural precedent. Thus, citing lack of scriptural support, he protests against his hosts' insistence that he must be circumcised, much to the chagrin and fears of the ladies who have surreptitiously admired his body (RC 295). He will confess his sins only if his confessor does the same (296). He will only be baptized in a river, because that was the only source of baptism in the Bible (298). He is only made amenable by the gentle reasoning of his sponsors, the people of Basse-Bretagne, and particularly by the interposition of Mlle Saint-Yves, whom he wishes to marry. He fails to understand why this marriage requires consent of witnesses, nor why he cannot marry his *marraine*, Mille Saint-Yves, who is also tenderly in love with him (300). Nor can he tolerate the convent to which she has been committed in order to prevent the marriage. He does not understand the nature of the pope (301) since there is no such office in scriptures, nor does he understand why the Huguenots have been expelled with the revocation of the Edict of Nantes, thus depriving the country of hundreds of thousands of productive citizens (308). Like the Quakers, these equally persecuted, industrious, skilled workers, forced to leave their country, the Huguenots find a sympathetic and favouring advocate in Voltaire. With the clarity of his vision and untrammelled understanding the *Ingenu* more seriously represents one of Voltaire's great negative educational principles: never learn anything that you will later be obliged to unlearn (325).

Like other Voltaire works, *Candide* included, *L'Ingenu* pivots in the middle, when the scene shifts to Versailles and the Bastille, when discussion is between the Huron and the Jansenist Gordon, and when with exemplary courage Mlle Saint-Yves, having found her lost lover, submits to the shameful act that will effect his release. It becomes Voltaire's most devastating and uncompromising portrait of the times, where the stench of corruption stretches from the layered bureaucracies and the exacting ministries of the mendacious court to the unjust confinement of victims in the Bastille. Voltaire turns his back on the earlier works of mundanity. The moral of *Cosi-Sancta* – where one is encouraged to forgive a few pecadillos for the sake of a greater good – is explicitly invoked and repudiated (RC 330–1) and so too is the accommodating code of *Babouc*. Even the rehabilitation that Zadig achieves is waylaid. Falling under the tutelary casuistry of a Jesuit, Mlle Saint-Ives sleeps with a powerful minister, Pouange (whose name brings together 'louse' and 'angel'), in order to ransom her 'husband.' And from the shame of this act she eventually dies. One can, with van den Heuvel (RC 981), find that the *roman* offers the possibilities of reconciliation, but this is all illusory. In *L'Ingenu* Voltaire shows his refusal to be comforted. Rarely has his fictional fervour reached so high a pitch. More powerfully than *Candide* (a work strangely lacking in affect), *L'Ingenu* reaches back to the *Poème sur le désastre de Lisbonne* and Voltaire's earlier expression of horror at the devastation and ruin of that disaster. When the overly eager 'amie' and false 'confidante' of Mlle Saint-Yves bounces into the sick-room scene, returning the bejewelled earrings that the suffering woman had so regally rejected, rather than earning recompense she hears the fatal words: 'Vous m'avez perdue! Vous me donnez la mort!' (You have undone me. You have brought my death; 338). The *Ingenu* finally understands at what cost his liberty and that of his friend, Gordon, were obtained.

In the most heart-felt and searing pages that Voltaire has ever written, he rebuts the commonplaces that human beings invoke to console themselves with death. Here everything rings with the need for the direct expression of genuine human emotion, and not only that, but with the justification of these expressions. Voltaire, who closed the eyes of the great Adrienne Lecouvreur and who never forgave her ignominious burial, is at his best when enflamed with indignation. He rejects the 'fastueuse' (pompous) means of consolation, such as saying that the dying person expired with courage. How could this be the case when a twenty-year old dying woman sees her love, her life, and her honour all torn away from her? Certainly her regrets and torments are justified, unless of course age or the extent of the illness has rendered one's organs 'insensible.' Then one is not human but rather simply an animal. Hers is a human death, one devoid of the pompous expressions of those seeking to console. 'Quiconque fait une grande perte a de grand regrets; s'il les étouffe, c'est qu'il porte la vanité jusques dans les bras de la mort.' To regret nothing is to carry vanity right into the arms of death; such a vaunt is reserved only in the bravura of popular song. And above all, as in *Poème sur le désastre de Lisbonne*, Voltaire is justifying real expressions of human emotion as against the consolatory writs of the proponents of theodicy. There are some losses that are inconsolable, and sadly in real life these have to do most painfully with the death of young women, Voltaire's beloved sister Mme Mignot and, of course, Mme du Châtelet.

Such direct confrontation with the realities of life does not end there. In prison the *Ingenu* was able to change the rigorous ideas of his Jansenist cellmate by changing his heart, by speaking of the tender emotions of love that he felt for Mlle Saint-Yves. From a stringent Jansenist, Gordon has become a sympathetic human being. And while he and others, aware of the *Ingenu*'s greatness of soul, fear suicide and thus have removed all possible weapons and have kept a watchful control over his actions, to the *Ingenu*'s question of whether anyone has the right to prevent him from taking his own life, the newly transformed Gordon refrains from responding with the usual arguments, such as a soldier must not leave his post, or on a higher level of theodicy, whether it mattered to the 'Being of beings' what afflictions humans must endure. These are the 'raisons impuissantes' that a resolute soul scorns and to which, like Cato, he responds with the fatal knife.

Such are the impassioned thoughts of Voltaire before the final rounding out of the story, which critics see as leading toward reconciliation. But these three paragraphs overrule such a conclusion. In his many discussions with Gordon in prison, the *Ingenu* reaches the telling point of the *Voltairien* ethic. As in the case of Erasmus's quarrel with Luther, it concerns the nature of God and humankind's relations to such a Being. Like Erasmus, a confirmed ethicist, Voltaire has little patience with the notion of hidden truths, or a hidden God. His God is a justifying presence. 'C'est un outrage au genre humain, c'est un attentat contre l'Être infini et suprême de dire: "Il y a une verité essentielle à l'homme, et Dieu l'a caché"' (It's an outrage against the human spirit, it's an offence against the supreme and infinite Being, to say: 'There is a truth essential to humankind and God has hidden it'; RC 325). To the contrary, for Voltaire God is the protector of the truths that humans have discovered, of the emotions of rage that they have expressed. The notion of a God is the warrant of the human sense of justice, or righteous anger. Voltaire makes this quite explicit: 'Sitôt que les hommes sont rassemblés, Dieu se manifeste à leur raison: ils ont besoin de justice, ils adorent en lui le principe de toute justice' (As soon as humans gather together, their notion of God becomes manifest to their reason: they have need of justice and they adore in him the principal of all justice; 'Questions de Zapata,' *Melanges* 947–8). This relatively late assertion (1767) complies with 'Poème sur la loi naturelle,' the response to LaMettrie's materialistic relativism. Christiane Mervaud is correct in her assertion that it was already in Berlin around 1752 that Voltaire launched his first campaign against a doctrine he found pernicious (Pomeau, *De la Cour au jardin* 88). Voltaire's moral universe does not depend upon the absence of God, but rather upon its presence. Without a sense of moral justice the way is open to nihilism, the notion that all things are of equal value and equally disposable. A God who sustains the reality of things, an objective reality where there is good and evil, right and wrong, and even more important, genuine expressions of human emotion, whether of rage or of pity, of anger or of consolation, is essential to Voltaire's moral universe.

At this point we enter into the true complexity of Voltaire's thought, the Voltaire who transcends by far the witty epithets designating him as 'le maitre à penser de l'homme moyen' (Pomeau, *On a voulu l'enterrer* 425). There are greater extremes in Voltaire's mental makeup and emotional needs. And here he was truly, like Rousseau, in fulfilling his personal needs responding to the needs of his time, near the top of which stood the quest for a 'second Reformation.' If the people of the sixteenth century were God-hungry and in search of authority, those of the eighteenth century suffered from religion-weariness and authority-fatigue. As Erasmus had predicted in his *On Mending [Restoring] the Peace of the World*, if nothing else it will be sheer 'exhaustion' that puts an end to strife (Dolan 389). A renovation of religion and other changes were on the horizon – a second Reform. Thus, as earlier indicated, Erasmus was reborn as the patron saint of this new religion, but one whose newly adopted philosophy was tempered with some moderation (a trait appealing to Gibbon and Voltaire alike). As Cassirer notably remarked , it was as if the contest between Erasmus and Luther were being waged all over again, but this time, it was Erasmus who emerged the victor (Cassirer, *The Question of Jean-Jacques Rousseau* 160). If Erasmus figured in this famous second Reformation by being remade, Voltaire did so directly by the fullness of his active sensibility. His God was the sun-God, Apollo, not the man-God, Christ. This God by his very presence denied that all things were permitted, and affirmed that there was such a thing as intellectual justice, and there this deity was essential to society not as a kind of warden but as a warrant of the sense of right and wrong. As a moral principle or a physical presence this God was as alive for Voltaire as was the rising sun. There are episodes recounted by Pomeau of Voltaire's rhapsodizing over the first glimmers of daylight, of his delight in the powerful rebirth of the day and of life itself. This God was the God of all peoples but subject to no single religion's claim. After one powerful episode where he practically sings hymns to the Eternal Being, he dryly recomposes himself and with typical wit adds: 'Quant à Monsieur le Fils, et à Madame sa Mere, c'est une autre affaire' (But when it comes to Master the Son or Madame his mother – that's an entirely different story; Pomeau, *La Religion de Voltaire* 417). Voltaire was willing to provide what a reborn and reconfigured Erasmus would offer and that was a religion without puzzling theological encumbrances. As soon as one introduces the Son, Trinitarian and anti-Trinitarian questions are the least of the vexing problems for theologians. Voltaire, like Erasmus, would put the theologians out of work. The same sort of unanswerable questions attend the presence of Mary. This was an age that countered its weariness over such theological questioning with a heady dose of scepticism. Into the vacuum left by the decline of traditional religion, rushed the adherents of another reformation, providing a more comforting religion, one suitable for the 'honnête homme.' In his *Sermon des Cinquante* Voltaire distinctly saw himself as the 'successor' to Luther and Calvin (Pomeau, *La Religion de Voltaire* 428, 430, 432, 436, 482).

Voltaire was an intellectual leader here, providing a sense (in the real meaning of the word) of religion against the newly found enemies represented by the atheism of Diderot and d'Holbach and yet slamming the door in the face of 'unintelligible' philosophical or theological speculations. The two opposing positions in fact go together, despair caused by the demolished defects of superstitious and literal belief easily carrying over to an equally harmful disbelief. Yet he met the needs of the age in other ways as well. He was an advocate of commerce and industry (not a pressing issue with Erasmus), of art and culture, and finally of civilization itself. And yet his *Essai sur les moeurs* is one long recounting of the horrors perpetrated by humans against their kind, of the corruptions of power and of the perversions that attached themselves to the original religious impulse. Finally he is brought to admit the great abyss that exists between God and humankind. Here his disgust with humans in their physical beings and their mortal ends borders on the abhorrent: they are bags of gas, they perish like worms in a world of which they understand little. Their words and high-sounding theories finally signify nothing. The manifold realities of life and the different levels of existence that Voltaire takes into his embrace are simply astounding and separate him from facile comparisons with Pascal.

The later *contes* and *romans* have been widely discredited, but this is not to say that they are without value and devoid of illuminating moments. Two works should be brought together in this regard: *Histoire des voyages de Scarmentado* and *La Princesse de Baby-*

lone. The first surveys the known world in the years following 1600 – a historic low point for Voltaire – and finds only horror and desolation, theocratic ruin and civil wars. Moreover, it is the Age of the Assassins, where regicide had been actively promoted and defended by the Jesuits. But this same epoch also saw the beginnings of some restoration of order. In his still useful study, *Europe in the 17th Century* (which in the course of twenty-five years went through at least six editions), David Ogg maintained that the seventeenth century was a period of increasing absolutism in government and of revolutionary progress in scientific and philosophic thought (515). In Voltaire's life and thought we can see how the latter served to modulate the former. That was when the work of the *philosophes* and their forerunners began to have some effect. Voltaire may be accorded some credit in modifying the positions of both monarchs and philosophers.

I have already expressed some uneasiness with *La Princesse de Babylone.* But that the two separated lovers seem relatively untouched by what they see does not diminish the value of what they see. And what they see is a totally remade map of Europe. Formerly Voltaire's historical geography, his 'geographie symbolique,' was built along an East-West axis (even the Seven Years War was conducted along that line). *Candide* stretches from Eldorado to Constantinople. But with the *Princesse* this alignment is profoundly and materially altered into a North-South axis, that is, the enlightened, mainly protestant North versus the backward Catholic South. Voltaire may not have been the first – in the elusiveness of historical diachronics, where shall we ever find 'the first,' there always being 'firsts' before 'the first' and antecedent reformations before The Reformation. But as with his introduction of Shakespeare to France, he was among the most prominent to take fully to heart, to make central to his thought, the great transformations that had begun to form the new radical division in Europe, and he did so not only on the basis of psychology, but in relation to enlightened government, religious and civil freedoms, and economic progress.[5] In his time, as the overflight of the *Princesse* shows, in the northern tier of Europe, from the Russia of Catherine (RC 384), to Poland (386) and Denmark and Sweden, where the one despite its government is good and the second is better (385) and across by way of the United Provinces to Great Britain (387–94) people lived under enlightened despots (or in an oligarchic republic), who favoured religious tolerance, habeas corpus, and did not exercise absolute power. By this time, of course, after the defeat of the second Spanish Armada by the Dutch, and the defeat of the Dutch by the English gunboats, Britannia ruled the waves (Hobsbawm 57; Ogg 41). But she also set the model for a parliamentary system of monarchy. Drawing upon the lessons that could have gained from Shakespeare's dramas of power, from *Richard II* to *King Lear*, her people learned that the aspirations toward permanence must be separated from the quest for power. One body cannot have both permanence and power. Either one seeks permanence under a hereditary monarchy that has relinquished most claims on power, or one seeks power through the various Houses of the legislature that know they cannot attain permanence. The English solution in this most profound psychological sense, recognized this divergence between rule and power and accepted the necessary separation. Royalty has permanence, while the Houses vie for power. Although he might not have used this language, for Voltaire, through its historical travails and trials, the emergent United Kingdom had established the psychological conquest necessary for the emergence of the early modern state.

Reason and philosophy are celebrated in the north. Thus two Voltairian principles emerge from this overview. The first, pertaining to Catherine, who 'perfected' the work begun by Peter, establishes the importance of openness and toleration. He argues that Catherine, 'whose name will be immortal,' made the first law . of the code of laws she provided for her country that of 'universal toleration' (Besterman, *Voltaire* 661). (Unfortunately, Voltaire in pursuit of several favourite principles, turned a blind eye to many of Catherine's blemishes, which might be more than that.) Voltaire believed fervently that when a country shuts down its borders it is closing its mind, and will hide its ignorance behind a self-satisfied wall of imagined exclusivity. Both Peter and Catherine fulfilled his more positive goals by not only opening Russia to the West but also by attracting Western intellectuals to their country. The second principle, not unrelated to the first, is Voltaire's distinction between 'la morale universelle' and a cult. Acknowledgment of the first invites tolerance while adhering to the second magnifies differences that can lead to prejudice and worse. All the northern countries differ specifically from the southern in that they have banished convents and monasteries, with the quite earthy understanding 'que si l'on voulait avoir des haras il ne fallait pas separer les plus forts chevaux des cavales' (that if one wanted a stud farm one should not separate the stallions from the mares; 386). They have also done away with practices no less bizarre and pernicious. Here the people have no fear of being reasonable, while 'elsewhere' one believed that government was only possible over 'imbeciles.' Once again Dostoevsky's Grand Inquisitor emerges well before his time as the constant enemy of an enlightened faith in human advancement.

These reigns of some reason and welcoming tolerance, as Voltaire argued, depend upon a continuity of enlightened monarchs. Before Catherine there was Peter, who was outgoing, enterprising, seeking to open his closed country to international influence and to bring back from the West whatever was useful. Catherine herself was well travelled but also became a magnetic draw, attracting scholars of note to her court, in fact, providing a large stipend for Diderot and offering d'Alembert a huge salary for the education of her sons, which offer he was obliged to turn down (Besterman, *Voltaire* 667). Here the supreme model was Louis XIV, who offered stipends to foreign scholars and invited to his court at Versailles the best minds of Europe. The same could be said of Frederick II of Prussia, omitted in Voltaire's passage across the northern states but abundantly present in Voltaire's imagination. He had a notable predecessor in Frederick Wilhelm, who, however detested his son, regarding his interest in poetry and French literature as 'effeminate,' did establish a capital that exerted the same attraction on persons of note that all established courts should do. These enlightened monarchs all provided safe harbour for various dissidents. Such opening up of their borders to the ingress of foreign influences and the broad exercise of religious tolerance for Voltaire are indications of a healthy thriving organism and contrariwise might explain in part why it was that beyond naval and other military disasters Spain declined. 'There was a gradual separation of Hapsburg Spain from the mainstream of European intellectual development. Early sixteenth-century Spain was Erasmian Spain ... From the 1550s there was a chilling change in the cultural climate' (Elliott 198). The country was hermetically sealed to every spiritual influence from without (Ogg 379). Attitudes toward Erasmus seem to be a touchstone here: after 1559 the Dutch intellectual's works were foreclosed in Italy, with similar import for the intellectual health of that country as well.[6]

Whether Voltaire was the first to indicate the crucial importance of this new alignment I do not know (Landes refers to other
such north-south theses in the eighteenth century but offers no
examples);7 nevertheless he did it with remarkable force and per-
spicacity. In reality he witnessed the kinds of worlds and transformations that Erasmus had only envisioned (and this primarily
in moral and religious vocabularies). The new alignment of European countries along a north-south bias, with all of its individual
changes, regressions, and restorations which Voltaire would have
comprehended, was to last in its most basic format for more than
two hundred years and to be the mastering destiny of Europe's
social and economic map. One twentieth-century attempt to make
a north-south axis failed catastrophically with the Second World
War. Only the European Union has now succeeded in overcoming the gap that was opened between the two divergent poles.

All these heartening improvements did not happen overnight.
There were national traumas of bitter warfare, civil wars from
which eventually better graces evolved. Voltaire goes to great
pains to describe the centuries of war and civil strife that had
to be undergone in Russia (*La Princesees de Babylone* 385) and in
England (ibid. 391) before these more advanced stages could be
reached. In a small gem of an essay, *Éloge historique de la raison*,
perhaps best summarizing Voltaire's ideals as well as his realization of the difficult paths of gradual evolution, Reason explains
to her daughter Truth: 'Vous voyez que tout vient tard: il fallait
passer par les tenebres de l'ignorance et du mensonge avant de
rentrer dans votre palais de lumières' (You see that everything
happens tardily: it was first necessary to pass through the shadows of ignorance and lies before returning to your palace of
Light; RC 570). It might appear that in Voltaire's thought not only
'tenebres' but rivers of blood must be crossed before reason and
reflection find their rightful seats in the congress of humankind.
Palaces of light crumble and fall, stones thrown have a way of
being returned in fire. It is fitting then that Voltaire should end
his very complex picture of human advancement by the triumphs
of individuals (Galileo, Copernicus, and Newton), who serve as
warrants for the eventual advancements of their kind – however
large the obstacles and perverse the regressions. Barthes' arguments (*Essais critiques* 96–9) that history for Voltaire is 'immobile,'
that is, it lacks 'epaisseur,' that it is simply chronology, and that
there is no evolution can be jettisoned without much hesitation.

FIVE

The Survivors: *Praise of Folly* and *Candide*

Satire is a lesser genre. It is to the great credit of both *The Praise of Folly* and *Candide* that they triumph over satire. Satire depends upon the debasement of an object, a practice, or a person. It objectifies and separates the author from his target. Erasmus's satire derives from situation, where the derelictions are very obvious and dependent upon our awareness of an implied or distinctly stated code of values. The code of values for *Praise of Folly* had been provided by the Christian doctrine of the *Enchiridion*. Quite different in method Voltaire's satire proceeds by caricature. He decontextualizes, or isolates, a practice or other particularities, and removing from them all sense, reduces them to their absurd external manifestations. The larger relevancy of symbols as trip-wires is ignored. The enemy is well recognized by a simple name (legitimate or mocked), while the author roams relatively freely, present only by his moving hand. While such moments have their modest appeal, *The Praise of Folly* and *Candide* would not be classics on the basis of their satire alone. Their greatness emerges when their authors enter into the works and themselves become players and victims among the rest. They themselves acquire an identity, are objectified, and their work acquires a dialectic. But that is a very drab phrase to describe what happens when an author submits the limits and liabilities of his own cherished commitments to critical scrutiny, when in the operations of solitude he becomes two-in-one, that is, he becomes a thinking person. Then he ceases to be the satiric manipulator but rather he becomes a player himself. He breaks out of the conventional mode of giving the enemy a face and a name and discovers that he too harbours the face of an enemy.

There are other related reasons why *The Praise of Folly* and *Candide* have survived in the historical memory. Such preservation represents something of an anomaly, because in their basic principles – the reasons for their preeminence – they contain much that runs counter to Erasmian or *Voltairien* values. They do not prioritize, they present no scale of proportionate values; they are not accommodating. Rather they present contests of values, agons, clashes of principles and values. And by such dialectic they have endured and found their constant appeal. This is not a question of complexity versus simplicity (for as Shakespeare reminds us, there is such a thing as simple truth that might be miscalled simplicity; see Sonnet 66), but rather of what emerges when an author engages in debate with himself, presenting the most stringent of auto-critiques. His most cherished opinions and activities are called into question, challenged at their core. In such moments of self-impressment, he has taken himself prisoner. In such a magnificent and rare encounter the writer (or artist) manages to bring out the neglected or invisible self, one that had been recognized but never acknowledged in the public face of the author. The whoreson must be acknowledged. This is a true 'overcoming,' or *'dépassement'* and revels in the presentation of a more superior confrontation, not with the other, the common enemy with names, the 'sophists,' the Jesuits, the Jansenists, and others, but with that unnamed part of the self that had been so elusive but now is brought forward, unmasked in stupendous recognition and admission.

The Praise of Folly is a genuine masterpiece. Yet Erasmus, with his customary deprecatory (and self-defensive) tic, dismisses it as being tossed off in a matter of weeks when he was ill in Thomas More's house.[1] The ease of its coming should not belie its profundity, nor Erasmus's receptivity. In discounting it, he had adopted something of a labour theory of value, neglecting the years of keen observation, the convictions born of personal experience, and the diligent study that went into its making. Ease of composition does not indicate slackness in conception or flabbiness of information. Like all good satire, *The Praise of Folly* has a firm moral grounding that extends back to his much earlier *Enchiridion*, where Erasmus first postulates his *philosophia Christi* and his spiritual hermeneutics. But *The Praise of Folly* achieves its measure of greatness by the wider extent of its pitch, by the rapid-fire mobility of its thought, by the fullness of detail and thought. The Erasmian profile is very

present in the work, despite the persona of Folly. Acts of denunciation do not hide the maker's hand. Erasmus knew what he was
talking about, and covered familiar terrain when he attacked the
number of superstitions that attend any popular adherence to a
materialized religion. And this is further witnessed in his satiric
roll-call of the professions, with its detailed description – with one
thought following rapidly upon another – of the derelictions of
those who should be better leaders of the people. But in two areas
Erasmus outdoes himself. The first is a self-portrait of the weaknesses and fallibilities of the wise, who fall victim to what could
be called the tragedy of Nature. The second occurs near the end,
where Erasmus, for the moment loosening his normal sense of
preferring the spiritual over the corporeal, admits to an 'irreconcilable warfare,' a profound difference of parts that can no longer
be subordinated but rather exist in inveterate unending lateral
opposition.

Superstition is always present in the popular imagination. In
the early sixteenth century Erasmus subjected it to particularly
strenuous review. Not that he had to, as others were only too
willing to pronounce against its deviations. Many of the issues
that Luther would later denounce, such as indulgences, masses
for the dead, and the human ordinances that have no basis in
scripture, Erasmus had already demeaned. But he shows a special hostility to those practices that inspire a false confidence and
that interfere with a direct worship of Christ. Icons and images,
stained-glass windows and murals might well be the 'Bible of
the people,' or, as later, 'silent poetry.' But that is one thing; it
is totally another, and quite misleading, to allow them to be the
objects of religious veneration on the part of the people. Against
this latter transposition Erasmus wars decisively with all the tools
of his rational theology. Such unbecoming substitution results in
the veneration of saints, even of Mary herself, the adoration of
icons and pilgrimages to faraway places to bow before and kiss
dubious relics (CWE 27:122). These are the same critical qualities
that show themselves in the *Colloquies* such as 'Shipwreck' and 'A
Pilgrimage for Religion's Sake,' among the most prominent. More
than intermediaries such poetical and legendary saints as George,
Christopher, and Barbara stand in lieu of a faith in Christ, sur-
rogates to whom one turns for grants of their specialized favours
(114). The inclusion of Mary is somewhat surprising, when one
considers her restitution as the Mother of Christ so beautifully

invoked in 'A Pilgrimage for Religion's Sake.' But just as to the pseudosaints who have their particular wares, so people turn to her for many things, her, the Virgin Mother, 'to whom the common people do in a manner attribute more than to the Son' (115). But Erasmus is quick to indicate the proper meaning of Mary in Christian thought: 'How many are there that burn candles to the Virgin Mother, and that too at noonday when there's no need of them! But how few are there that study to imitate her in pureness of life, humility, and love of heavenly things, which is the true worship and most acceptable to heaven!' (120).

The ways of the common people differ in their simplicity from those of the learned. If the first follow docilely and unthinkingly, the second are guilty of overly subtle disputatious turns to debate and definition. Yet, they are joined together, as each is ignorant of or ignores the teachings of Christ, the Gospels and apostles, and the early church fathers, all those that form the basis of Erasmus's Christian formation and practice. A large portion of *The Praise of Folly* is made up of portraits of the so-called leaders of the Christian society; these depictions comprise a veritable rogue's gallery, a mustering of the professions, and in their massive detail and keen insights they are examples of Erasmus at his satiric best.

While there are nine such portrayals, three of the longest and the most discerning are those, understandably enough, devoted to the grammarians, the theologians, and the monks. In his objections to Erasmus's treatment of the theologians, Maarten van Dorp obviously could not have had in mind Erasmus's dire portraits of the grammarians – which may have been added later. The latter are pedants in their work and tyrants in their classrooms. Merged with school teachers they are kings of the kids (and of their doting parents as well). Their scholarship is devoted to petty trifles, over which they crow if they discover any new phrase. Their comings and goings are devoted to punctuation and to parts of speech, and woe to any person who manages to make a small mistake. 'What uproars, what bickering, what taunts, what invectives!' One specific culprit, who spent twenty years sorting out the parts of speech, makes it a matter for the sword if someone makes a conjunction out of a preposition. Then there are the pluckier ones who simply steal others' works, and in the tangled publication industry of the time, pass off the pirated work as their own (the same outcry heard from Voltaire in his letter to Rousseau). They have the effrontery to adopt classical names (and here

Erasmus is cutting close to home), and as a form of defensiveness against bad reviews resort to an inbred, incestuous chumminess with their fellow grammarians, each engaging in mutual back-scratching (CWE 27:123–5). The portrait is far from limited to Erasmus's own time.

The theologians (CWE 27:126ff)) have a heavy weapon at hand to persuade their opponents, the charge of heresy. Otherwise their lives are spent in the pursuit of 'subtle trifles,' of pretending to answer questions that no sensible person would ever think of asking, such as 'whether it was possible that Christ could have taken upon Him the likeness of a woman, or of the devil, or of an ass, or of a stone, or of a gourd.' And then, throughout these novel transformations, whether he could have performed the miracles and died on the cross (127)? Obviously this is a generation and a profession, which through specialized training, run-away speculative imaginations, and a forward tendency to dispute and debate, along with professional pressures to make a mark, has lost its bearings, its compass of centred direction. What they have lost is direct contact with Christ, the Gospels, the apostles and the church fathers. Paul knew what faith and charity were but his understanding was far from the definitions of the scholastics, with all the subclassifications and distinctions (127). The urge to define has violated two codes essential to Erasmus: respect for the mysteries and obscurities of the world and the need for direct experience. There are questions beyond our knowing and there are experiences within our telling. The apostles were able devoutly to consecrate the Eucharist, but they had no need of the terminologies and specific processes of transubstantiation (127). They knew the mother of Jesus, but had no need to prove her preserved from original sin (128). They baptized but did not need the support of further argumentation. They do not search out the various compartments of hell (130). In all of this not only do the current theologians fall short of the apostles, but they even refrain from reading the Gospels or Paul's epistles. They pay even less heed to the early church fathers, including Jerome. And yet – here we must understand the immensity of Folly's indictments – these are the people with their abstruse intellectual convolutions who control the thought of the church. They believe that their certainly more subtle and rarified questionings and procedures have raised theology to the level of a higher physics, to which not everyone is entitled to ascend. But Erasmus and his numerous cohorts, including Luther, regarded their obfuscations as nothing more than gibberish. Erasmus is particularly attuned to their errors in speech and their inelegant, if not barbarous, Latin. A tonic for its time, a chronicle of generational warfare, Erasmian satire at its most potent steps out of its time and continues, even in its specifics, to resonate down to the cultural wars of our own day.

Just as Erasmus discovered early his distaste for the 'modern' theology, so too he discovered quickly and decisively his aversion to the monastic life. But in the latter case it came after he had already entered the monastery at Steyn, and thus much of the efforts of his later life were devoted to fruitful attempts to free himself from that first misstep. Very early he announced in the *Enchiridion* that the monastic life has no monopoly on piety, that one can as a layperson lead a fully Christian life. In fact, Erasmus's intellectual efforts might be summarized by that belief and by his efforts to reach out and persuade eminent laity of that possibility. Yet monks and their cohort friars exercise a strong hold on the susceptible popular imagination. Like the theologians they wield threatening powers: the charge of heresy, excommunication, and worse. And the friars, who hear confessions, have access to people's innermost secrets (thus he urges that confession, when necessary, be heard by the parish priest). The two are further bound together by a heavy regimen of rules and by intra- and extramural rivalries. The rules extend to petty trifles, which are however treated with the exactitude of mathematics, and the rivalries accumulate both within and without the various orders, with all their pullulating new crop of subdivisions and breakaway reorganizations (CWE 27:131). But what most galls Erasmus is that along with literal-mindedness there is often joined illiteracy, a fumbling intonation of Latin phrases meant to impress and entrance the populace. Folly is amused that these people 'with their petty ceremonies, ridiculous trifles and noise exercise a kind of tyranny among mankind' (ibid.).

If this is what we were to be left with from *The Praise of Folly* – a theology derived from the *Enchiridion*, the satiric roll-call of the professions – then we would have a remarkable record of the times, even in several cases extending beyond the times to recurrent issues in Western culture, but we would not have a world classic. Nor would we have an Erasmus whose insights suggest comparison with Montaigne or one whose arguments and figures are recognizable in some of Shakespeare's greatest plays. This

Erasmus we get when in the very same *Praise of Folly* he reaches both beyond himself and within himself, exposing the tragic imbalance of the intellect and Nature, the obscurities of existence, and the paradoxes and conflicts inherent in the human condition. This is not only an Erasmus of some relevancy but an Erasmus who is profoundly perennial.

At length realizing that she has produced more of a satire than an 'oratio,' the chagrined Folly (Erasmus) abandons this task. These pages, constituting almost one third of the volume, are concerned with the perversions and violations of true knowledge. The earlier portion, to my mind the most important section, amounting to a bit more than one fifth of the volume is devoted to the liabilities of learning. In the one instance Erasmus calls for the restitution of good learning and true piety, based upon the imitation of Christ and familiarity with the Gospels, the works of the apostles, and those early church fathers. In the other instance it is learning itself that is out of step with Nature, with the regular workings of society, and with the general condition of humankind. In the first he rebukes deviations from essential guides to life; in the second he records the painful lesson that learning may be ill-suited to the requirements of existence. The first deviation suffers from the mania of definition and debate as well as intellectual hubris; the second disjunction from modesty and fear.

The earlier section could be called a defence of ignorance and opens a clear path to Montaigne and eventually to Rousseau's first *Discours*. It is based upon three under-emphasized components of Erasmian thought. The first is his deeply held sense of the obscurity of things. In his letter to Marcus Laurinus of 1523 he addresses his apparent lack of spiritual conviction: he knows so little of himself, he writes, how can he bring any certain judgment to the motivations of others and their springs of action? Then there is the famous Silenus head of Alcibiades (102–3) suggesting the great difference between appearance and reality. But more important and finally all things are ruled by the principle of dissimilarity (Silenus's two faces are 'dissimiles'), thus generating difference and conflict, which becomes an operating rule in human life. Intellect and Nature are dissimilar: where mind is complex, Nature is simple; where intelligence is sharp, Nature is blunt, which makes it so that intelligence or learning is a great inconvenience in all normal human dealings.

Thus the 'fool' has an advantage. At this point, Erasmus, whom we can designate as one of the founders of the modern *studia humanitatis* (not forgetting his Italian predecessors), exposes the hazards of such learning itself. The wise man has recourse to the books of the ancients, and from them picks nothing but verbal subtleties (CWE 27:102). The liabilities of modesty and fear fill the wise man with unwarranted anticipations, the hesitations that hinder any call to action. But the foolish person (now become audacious) suffers none of these inhibitions, from which folly sufficiently frees us. 'Few mortals realize how many other advantages follow from being free from scruples and ready to venture anything ' (102), which the older Wilson translation renders more succinctly, 'Few there are that rightly understand of what great advantage it is to blush at nothing and attempt everything' (42–3). These are searing insights of self-recognition where Erasmus sees in himself the deficiencies of the overly-compunctious learning that he laboured so sedulously to establish. The century that witnessed the tragic transformations of humanism was marked at its early beginning by *Praise of Folly* and at its later ending by *Hamlet*.

Delusion, like folly, is of immense value, for it conceals or overlooks the ugliness of existence, the processes of aging and finally dances in the face of death itself. If one were to look at life squarely, at the thing itself, who would not be justified in committing suicide (CWE 27:105)? But from these terrible truths delusion spares us. The old man marries a young wench; the old woman still uses cosmetics to preserve appearances (105–6). But these are more than appearances; they represent attempts to keep hold of identity and to fight off the inevitable nothingness that awaits in the wings. Shakespeare's Richard II, captive in the crushing reality of the thick prison walls, still sends up flashes of imaginary beings: 'Nor I, nor any man that but man is,/ With nothing shall be pleased, till he be eased/ With being nothing' (V.v.39–41). Life is a play and we are merely players: we change into many costumes along the way, until the 'property manager' calls upon us to return our dress. 'Thus are all things ruled by counterfeit, and yet without this there were no living' (Wilson 44).

The scholar, who had demystified so many saints, now has recourse to fable and to myth. It is not the precepts of Plato or Aristotle that hold cities together, but rather the fetching tales and symbols of myth and mythology (Wilson 40). All the silly parades and the added paddings of names of honour for the victors may be mocked, 'and yet from this source sprang deeds of valiant heroes which the pens of so many eloquent men have extolled to the skies' (CWE 27:102, Wilson 41).

As in Shakespeare, the allowed fools are able to utter truths without censure (Wilson 56–60). Like the lilies of the field, they neither spin nor weave, harbour no fearful anticipations nor wish for future good. They exist totally in the innocent nonchalance of the present, and for this their company is sought out and embraced by all. Contrast this with the lucubrations of the wise man, one 'who has frittered away all his boyhood and youth in acquiring learning, has lost the happiest part of his life in endless wakeful nights, toil, and care, and never tastes a single drop of pleasure even in what's left to him. He's always thrifty, impoverished, miserable, grumpy, and harsh to himself, disagreeable and unpopular with his fellows, pale and thin, sickly and bleary-eyed, prematurely white-haired and senile, worn out and dying before his time. Though what difference does it make when a man like that dies? He's never been alive. There you have a splendid picture of a wise man' (CWE 27:110, Wilson 60) – and a self-portrait of Erasmus himself.

One can well imagine Erasmus's pained grimace as he draws that curriculum vitae. The 'great wise man' has his true complement in the most perfect of men, the Stoic. Each is a born party-killer. The first poisons either by morose silence or screeching argumentation, the other with a deadly eye scrutinizes all human festivities. Which city would choose him as a governor, what wife as a husband? Better to stay with 'boon companions,' as one who thinks nothing human to be alien (CWE 27:103–5).

Two recurrent points of reference underlie the value scheme of this remarkable part of *The Praise of Folly*. They are the bounds and limits of Nature herself, and the regularity of ordinary life. While all other creatures are content to exist within those boundaries that Nature has set for them, only humankind has the effrontery to try to exceed them (CWE 27:108). It is Nature that establishes 'the common lot of all mankind. There's no misery about remaining true to type' (106). Such commonality extends to the social order as well, with which the wise man is similarly out of sync. The wise man's learning has rendered him incapable of carrying on the normal businesses of life, 'and all because he is wholly ignorant of ordinary matters and far removed from any common way of thinking and current practice. And so inevitably he is disliked, doubtless because of the great dissimilarity in mentality and way of life' (propterea quod communium rerum sit imperitus, et a populari opinione, vulgaribusque institutis longe lateque discrepit; 101. Wilson 54). But the main reason he attracts such odium is that there is such a great 'dissimilitudinem' existing between them in both their 'lives and souls.' The word *dissimilitudo* recalls the 'dissimilar' parts of the Silenus head. Such difference means opposition; such 'unlikes,' as Coleridge tells us, cannot but end in dislikes.

The sublime conclusion of *The Praise of Folly* invokes the numerous connections between folly and the religious life, particularly the affinities between folly and Christianity: 'the foolishness of the cross,' 'let us be fools for Christ's sake.' As a scholiast, a concordance compiler, Erasmus evidenced a pedantic passion in this multiplication of citations. But the true function of the finale is to bring together in confrontation the two codes of values that have thus far been exemplary. In the earlier section it is natural wisdom, what Huizinga calls 'spontaneous energy' (71), the teachings of nature, and the ways of the ordinary world that prevail. In the longer more satiric survey of the professions, it is imitation of Christ, immersion in the Gospels, and the authority of the apostles and the early church fathers that matters. The quarrel is between Nature and holiness. How can these two be reconciled? In fact, Erasmus tells us, they cannot. There exists an 'irreconcilable enmity' (irreconciliabile bellum; Wilson 145, CWE 27:204) between them. The one is attached to the corporeal, the material; the other to the spiritual, the invisible. Each takes on the colour of his mental attachments, and so where the one is competent the other a blockhead, and where the one finds his habitat the other lives in the shadows. Hence it follows that there is 'so great [contrarity] of opinion between them, and that too in everything' (Wilson 147, 206). Erasmus's phrase is actually 'dissension,' rendered in the CWE translation as 'disagreement.' But John Wilson in his translation from 1668, to which I have been attached, is intuitively right in that throughout this episode Erasmus proceeds by contrast, starting many a sentence with the word 'contra,' or, 'contrariwise,' as if he were setting up a table of oppositions, emphasizing rhetorically the non-alignment, the inherent disagreement or 'dissensio' between the two dominant ways of viewing the world as if they must always exist in a state of mutually uncomprehending difference, if not warfare.

But what is most remarkable here is how at odds this description of eternal warfare, or lateral opposition, is to Erasmus's normal rhetorical procedures and his ways of viewing the world and resolving conflicts. Rhetorically Erasmus has been given to defusing differences, to finding ways of incorporation and of amelioration. Normally he does this by prioritizing, as Chomarat has indicated. The one kind of assertion or procedure might be of lesser importance but still it figures as having some merit in any proportionate scale of values. This is just one of the rhetorical devices employed by Erasmus in order to bridge difference. Yet here for page after page Erasmus, as he did in the earlier sections, emphasizes 'dissensio,' 'dissimilitudo,' irreconcilable enmities. Obviously he cannot leave it at that, and even Folly serving as arbiter must finally come down on the side of the spiritual, but as being at one with the madness of Christian selflessness. Despite this attempted restoration, the real greatness of *The Praise of Folly* emerges in those pages where Erasmus presents conflict, clashes of visions, and the recognition of the liabilities of the life he has made his own, and eventually of the division within his own life between the practical man he was and the holiness toward which he aspired, but from which he knew he fell short.

In her classic work, *The Fool: His Social and Literary History* Enid Welsford draws upon the two discrepant elements for her understanding of *Praise of Folly* (236–42). On the one hand, by means of Folly Erasmus 'defends the creative vital instincts of humanity against the encroachments of the analytical reason …' Folly is really the sane normal world according to Nature.' She fosters the pleasing illusions, the counterfeits that make life possible, 'Without Counterfeit there were no living.' Under the watchful eye of the stern Stoic, who could accept without anxieties the pleasing measures offered by Nature? While noting that Folly expends a good deal of time on satiric portraits of the professions, Welsford turns to Folly's higher purpose, which is the appropriateness of another kind of folly for the true Christian. This higher folly disregards 'with a wild recklessness' the goods of this world, but in regard to the next world experiences an ecstasy which renders the soul 'beside herself,' swallowed up in the love of the divine (241) It should be noted that it is these two features – and not the satiric – that Huizinga invokes to account for the work's great appeal. The satire may dominate the middle parts of *The Praise of Folly*, 'but in the other parts it is something far deeper' (74). Here again he sides with posterity's judgment: '[*The Praise of Folly*'s] lasting value is in those passages where we grant that folly is wisdom and the reverse' (75).

By virtue of these divergent characteristics Folly finds her fullest literary incarnations in two of Shakespeare's greatest comedies, *As You Like It* and *Twelfth Night*, and even more imaginatively so, in *King Lear* (thus providing support for Craig Thompson's later notion of the influential roles of the Oxford Reformers in the flowering of Elizabethan literature). Walter Kaiser admirably supplements Welsford's repertoire by including as praisers of Folly, Erasmus's foremost French disciple, Rabelais, and Shakespeare's preeminent Lord of Misrule, Falstaff. Falstaff is dislocated: a figure from the happy world of comedy, he is misplaced in the iron world of history, from whence he must suffer his own tragic discharge. All the ironies of Erasmus's *Praise of Folly* and tensions of Shakespeare's *Henriad* are well observed by Kaiser.[2]

In *As You Like It*, the first contention indicated above occurs between Touchstone and melancholy Jaques, the wearied world traveller, who 'has sold his own lands to see other men's.' The clown is the real touchstone of the play, and Jaques is revealed to be a mere 'poseur.' The fool finds his natural home in the comic freedom of the world of Arden, from which 'the over-clever victim of ennui excludes himself' (Welsford 249–50). One could well picture Erasmus's own delight at this portrayal so consonant with some of the more piercing arguments of *Praise of Folly*. He would perhaps have had some moral scruples at the undoing of Malvolio in *Twelfth Night*, where Touchstone finds his true brother in comic arms in Feste the clown. A mutual dislike and more separates the worlds of Feste and Malvolio. The clown finds his congenial pace in the festival spirit of Saturnalian comedy. Malvolio, however, cannot even be denounced as a Puritan, but rather as a self-serving careerist, who in his eagerness to please his superiors abuses his powers by squelching the riotous behaviour of the free-spirited. He is rebutted by Sir Toby's immortal response to the up-tight: 'Dost thou think because thou art virtuous there shall be no more cakes and ale?' While this is supposedly a temporary seasonal licence (which most certainly Toby is guilty of abusing) it nevertheless serves its purpose in expressing a more exuberant attachment to living and in exposing the authoritarianism of the censorious. In Shakespeare's festive comedy clowns and fools speak for a spirited vitality while the worldly wise are cast out. Such comparisons are never perfect fits, and trite summaries are hardly helpful, but Jaques and Malvolio can certainly be enrolled in Erasmus's gallery of life-deniers who are undermined and exposed in their foolish wisdom by wise fools.

It is in *King Lear* that Shakespeare addresses the same dialectic as does Erasmus in the final, fitting climax to *The Praise of Folly*. In some brief sixteen pages that are among the best ever written on Shakespeare's greatest tragedy Welsford demonstrates how Erasmus's twofold argument is completed and enhanced, as kings and clowns are brought together, change roles, and achieve in their downfalls a universal wisdom. In the face of a classical decorum that would prohibit such cohabitation, Shakespeare insists on the dramatic effectiveness of bringing together these grandly representative types, in building on and altering the historical structures and traditions of their roles. The fool rises to the level of moral sanctity while the king in his madness expresses philosophical and human truths that represent the highest consciousness of the play.

King Lear is a morality play without that genre's predictable outcomes. The good characters are obviously good and the evil characters identifiable as evil. But in their differences they are mutually uncomprehending, just as Erasmus indicated they should be. There are no hands across the barriers. In many of their coolly rational arguments Goneril, Regan, and Edmund are obviously correct; only in their consequences are their reasonings catastrophic. The equally obvious good characters are innocently trusting and easily duped. That is, the one type, the malevolently rational, considers the other to be imbecilic, and the other cannot comprehend their deviousness or hardness of heart. Indeed, two worlds, with two different mental and emotional instruments, are in conflict. But in Shakespeare's tragedy, as in *The Praise of Folly*, such equivalency and irreconcilable warfare does not produce a stalemate. Each of the viewpoints 'is not equally valid, not equally true.' When pushed to the play's apocalyptic extremes, they all reveal their genuine natures. One great turnabout occurs in the nature of the fool. In the end, fidelity and loyalty are his true provinces:

> But I will tarry, the fool will stay
> And let the wise man fly;
> The knave turns fool that runs away:
> The fool no knave perdee.

Welsford makes a direct connection between this practice of foolish loyalty – a trait that finally distinguishes the 'good' characters – and the conclusion of *Praise of Folly*. 'That Shakespeare's ethics were the ethics of the New Testament, that in this play the mightiest poetry is dedicated to a reiteration of the wildest paradoxes of the Gospels and of St. Paul that seems to me quite certain' (268). But the presence of that doctrine as reassurance is not so clear, as the good suffer from what the evil have wrought and the evil devour themselves.

Voltaire had no need of a Shakespeare to bring his thoughts dramatically alive: he had a Voltaire. Yet, this was a Voltaire whose sense of artful decorum could not tolerate kings and clowns pitched together, or a prince and a grave-digger bandying wits. In Shakespeare's great imagination, however, they do represent universal types and conditions of humankind. Still, despite his unwillingness to step out of the decorum of his age into a more creatural universality, Voltaire did achieve greatness by virtue of the freedoms he allowed himself in the once demoted genre of *Candide*.

It is strangely wanting to seek in Voltaire that which he has in 'common' with us, as does Roland Barthes (94), when we should be seeking the exceptional, that which carries us beyond our normal worlds of perception. There are three main clasps that open up the books of *Voltairien* appeal. The first is found in *Zadig*, where Voltaire shows his rare faith in the possibility that good faith and rectitude will eventually be vindicated. Intellectual justice will pierce through the dense fog of slander, resentment, and ill-will. One can think back to the time when he turned the disaster after the Rohan affair into the opportunity of England, or the humiliation at Frankfurt into the rehabilitation at Ferney, but perhaps, looking ahead, his greatest vindication occurred when he returned to Paris, the site of his earliest triumphs, the native city he had known so well but which he had not seen in twenty-eight years, come back to be crowned with laurels and carried by the crowd to the old Comédie Française, the house that Voltaire built, with the splendid statue by Houdon fronting it all.[3]

The second clasp is of a different order. It reveals in *L'Ingenu* Voltaire's refusal to be comforted, to accept consolation. Not all the grave injustices that have been committed can be washed away. The complacent sexual banter and bartering of *Cosi-Sancta* falls short when compared with the death of Mlle Saint-Yves. The culture of mundanity does not suffice when there are some losses that are beyond repair, that do not lead to reconciliation, and like raw wounds have only to be touched to be reopened. Voltaire insists upon his God-given right to hold to such outraged conviction, not to absolve the sins of the world by the consolations of theodicy, which is only a type of fatalism that does away with the reality of things. Oddly enough, Voltaire needs a God as a warrant of his right to accuse the world as it is presented to him.[4]

The third clasp opens the world of *Candide* at those places where Voltaire argues with himself. It is present in the last of his *contes, Histoire de Jenni ou le Sage et l'Athée* (1775) in the debate between Freind and Birton. It may well be that Voltaire is showing the fatal consequences of the materialistic theories of Diderot and d'Holbach, but the greatness of the debate between Freind and Birton derives from the fact that Voltaire is arguing with himself (Deloffre's *'notice'* and notations are excellent, RC 1215–27, 1233–65). This clasp opens up the dramatic world where Voltaire is not arguing a settled case of Spirit, or Intelligence, against Stupidity and Fanaticism, engaging in too easy combat, where there is really no contest. There is another Voltaire, who arrives at his true stature when he is able in some ways to outface himself, to set in contention his own firmly held beliefs. While the outcome might still be a foregone conclusion, the presentations of Birton (who advances the arguments of the atheist, although he is not one) are too powerful to be simply trod upon or stepped over. Birton is ready to acknowledge that there is a Supreme Intelligence, but how or when this being enters into human affairs is open to question. As in the stupendous lengthy series of notes to the *Poème sur le désastre de Lisbonne*, Birton demolishes the assumptions of the great Chain of Being. He asks what possible relation there can be between the Infinite Being and us other 'worms of the earth.' This Being did not create the world as evidence of his glory, because that would be an act of vanity. And if this Being created the earth so that human beings could live happily, 'Je vous laisse a penser s'il est venu à bout de ce dessein…' (I leave it to your judgment as to whether he ever completed his design) (RC 647). He than affirms the question that Voltaire in other writings found unacceptable. We may call God that intelligent and powerful principal that animates all of nature, but did he deign to make himself known to us?

Freind in his more *Voltairien* counterarguments has recourse to the evidence of our senses, an appreciation of the magnificent order of nature, and the gift of life itself. Voltaire has him echo Rousseau's arguments so fully expounded in *Émile* about the ever-present power of conscience and even finally the mendacious wager of Pascal, hardly suitable for a true religious experience. At length, despite the pragmatic victory of Freind, there remains the comment of Voltaire's editor, Frédéric Deloffre, who concludes that Birton does not represent the adversary of Voltaire but rather 'that part of himself that rebels against his very fideism' (RC 1262). These are parts of himself exposed in a true dialectic, each taking animation from Voltaire's own firmest convictions, convictions that he cannot totally eliminate or crown in triumph (van den Heuvel 327).

Criticism can no longer treat *Candide* in superior isolation. While this means its primacy of place is open to some challenge (particularly from *L'Ingenu*, which Voltaire himself considered superior because of its greater *vraisemblance*, or truth to being), it also means we can gain a better understanding of this masterpiece. Burlesque in style, and lacking in affective power, *Candide* has a different field of interest. Yet, we are strangely moved by this young man's need to search out the truths of existence, *une raison d'exister*, to test the philosophies that encircle him. The candour of his name represents his openness to what experience brings his way. This is why Rousseau was intuitively correct in asserting that Voltaire did indeed respond to his *Letter on Providence* of 1756, Rousseau's impassioned answer to the pessimism of the *Poème sur le désastre de Lisbonne*. In it, Rousseau implicitly asks, if what you (Voltaire) say is true, that evil stalks the earth, then how are we to lead our lives? *Candide* is Voltaire's delayed answer.

While finally with *Candide* we open the third clasp, where Voltaire argues against himself, the first half of this *récit* teeters perilously on the brink of failure. Voltaire has little interest in arguing against Pangloss's philosophy, the Leibnizian quality of which he long before discarded, or embraced in only lukewarm fashion, riddled by the famous aborted questioning '*Mais…*' Pangloss is merely a figure of straw and the *roman* does not turn until the Eldorado episode, chapters XVII and XVIII. Eldorado is not Utopian, but rather *Voltairien*, where the author's most valued goals for human society are introduced. By its very inaccessibility, Eldorado might as well be 'nowhere'; nevertheless its practical ways are for Voltaire quite feasible. Borrowing from the comfort-seeking Voltaire of the *Mondain* poems, all the carriages are good and the cuisine is superb. For the exponent of natural religion and rational theology, there is only one God (it is beyond comprehension that anyone would think to worship more). There are no monks, and showing Voltaire's further leanings toward Protestantism, everyone is a priest and the only prayers are those of universal thanksgiving. For the progressive Voltaire, who learned well the lessons of his stay in England, Eldorado is a centre of technology, with its own palace of science and industry. The elements of Eldorado might be out of sight, but they are not out of reach.

After Eldorado the orbit of *Candide* changes. The murder and mayhem that existed in the first half – so reminiscent of the comic violence typical of Bugs Bunny or the Roadrunner cartoons, where the victims manage to escape uninjured or recover sufficiently – is notably lacking. So is the need to controvert the theological questions of Pangloss; his own words undo him. At the end, while averring that he had suffered terribly, he continues to sustain his thesis that 'tout allait à merveille,' to which Voltaire, in one of his typical ironic locutions, adds, 'et ne croyait rien' (and didn't believe a word of it; RC 230). Later, trying to resurrect his customary prying into the final causes of things, Pangloss gets the door slammed in their faces.

Now questions of Providence rarely intrude as Candide has acquired a new interlocutor in the person of Martin, and their discourse takes place on the plain turf of purely earthly understanding. As in *Jenni*, Martin represents Voltaire's worst fears, stated as matters of fact, meeting his best wishes. Rather than a satire of the emptiness of Pangloss's vapid thinking, there emerges a real encounter, an unbridgeable one (as in Erasmus's *Praise of Folly*) between benevolent hopes and the brute facts of evil. In this new ethos of significant exchange and encounter, it is quite striking that no statement in the second half of the *roman* is allowed to pass unqualified or uncontradicted.

The second half of *Candide* is an amazing venture in self-presentation, of the self in conflict. Voltaire's encounter with his own values is reproduced in two portraits, that of the savant and that of Pococuranté, where Voltaire is indeed showing portions of himself while not exempting these proto-Voltaires from serious criticism. The savant gives a splendid synopsis of Voltaire's own poetics of tragedy: to be new without being bizarre, to be sublime

yet always natural, to be a great poet while none of the characters appear as such, to know the human heart and to let it speak
simply and in a pure and harmonious language, and never to let
the rhyme control the meaning (RC 204–5). Like Shakespeare's
having Hamlet give advice to the players, Voltaire stands behind
the voice of his character. But not for long, as the hostess mar-
quise (whose gaming house is quite crooked) soon lets Candide
know that the savant's own literary success is quite meagre: his
one play was hooted off the stage and his book was left unsold.
Candide replies that this savant is another Pangloss. Pursuing this
advantage, and showing how diminished his former mentor has
become, he then asks the savant if everything is 'au mieux '(for
the better) in this world. But unlike Pangloss the savant embraces
the philosophy of the new interlocutor, Martin. Not at all, is his
answer; in fact 'chez nous' everything goes cross-wise (tout va de
travers). Eternal warfare is the rule and enmity of opposing forces
the composition of the times.

Pococuranté, that languid Venetian nobleman, also displays
much of the *Voltairien* critical manner (as Voltaire himself admits,
RC 882n1, 214). Like Montaigne, he reads for his own pleasure
and the exercise of critical judgment. Fools admire everything
from an esteemed writer (they are exegetes), whereas he only
reads for himself and for what he can take from a work ('Je ne lis
que pour mois; je n'aime que ce qui est à mon usage'). All things
must be brought before the bar of critical judgment, and in Voltaire's time, the canons of good taste. Accordingly, the seemingly
unending battle scenes of the *Iliad* are deplored; the *Aeneid* can
only be accepted in Books 2, 4, and 6, and Milton is beyond repair
(216–18). But more than critical judgment, one senses in Pococuranté the fatiguing weight of books. He has read all the books
and his flesh is weakened thereby. Candide is taken in by this example of independent critical thinking. But where Candide reads
full self-possession (a man who exists above all that he possesses),
Martin detects in Pococuranté a more disfiguring disgust at all
that he possesses. And when Candide questions whether there
is not great pleasure in this ability to criticize everything, Martin
answers, 'C'est-à-dire, qu'il y du plaisir à n'avoir pas de plaisir'
(219)? As if there can be pleasure in not taking pleasure. And the
delight that Voltaire always took in genuine works of art, even
where he was alert to their shortcomings, finds its voice to repeal
the part of himself that was abused in Pococuranté.

The real opposition in *Candide* exists between the jaded yet usually accurate views of Martin and the character of Candide. To this dichotomy there appears to be no resolution. But there is a reason for this: each represents permanent parts of the 'complex vocation' of Voltaire himself. On the one side, his is an 'esprit sans illusions' but on the other, this same esprit without illusions is capable of great enthusiasms, expressing a 'volonté prête à toutes les aventures' (Naves, 19). Thus Voltaire presents in his two main characters the opposing aspects of his own personality.

Yet like a cropped photo the conclusion of *Candide* is much diminished, as this gathering of war-torn refugees is confined to working a sparse farm under a limited motto – and perhaps this reduced picture of desolation is the true basis of its modern appeal. However, the problem with isolating *Candide* is that one tends to view Voltaire through the critical lens of these narrow passages. Able writers have felt the pressure to enlarge the dimensions of each, to gather up a philosophy more in keeping with Voltaire's larger aspirations and accomplishments. For some, the conclusion of *Candide* is already 'dépassée' (Pomeau, *De la Cour au jardin* 355). Van den Heuvel and Pomeau (along with others) are most instructive here, using extraliterary and literary methods to arrive at a fuller assessment of *Candide*. Each cites appropriately the great difference between the cold comforts offered by the *metairie* and the magnificent work of rehabilitation Voltaire brought both to the adjoining village of Ferney and its people (Pomeau, 353–6, van den Heuvel, 276–81). From a few barren and poorly cultivated farms (the region was badly hurt by the loss of the Protestant workers after the revocation of the Edict of Nantes), Voltaire at great expense and with much concern and diligence managed to restore it to a level of some 1200 households.

Both Pomeau and van den Heuvel also use the same kind of language when placing *Candide* in Voltaire's development. The oft-repeated phrase 'mais il faut cultiver notre jardin,' becomes both a conquest and a point of departure. It represents a conquest over the need to cut a figure with the great and also a contentedness with one's own more restricted possibilities. *Candide* thus contains 'the stirrings of a new humanism.' In itself, 'not very exalting,' the ending of *Candide* represents a new beginning, a certain 'ouverture' (RC 830). In van den Heuvel's more benign reading, the new, remodelled humanism, while more limited, also represents the possibilities of bringing into realization 'le rêve de l'Eldorado.' Pomeau for his part, as does van den Heuvel, situates *Candide* in the larger enterprises of Voltaire at this time. But he also calls it a masterpiece; *Candide* was 'une lecture roborbative pour les temps d'épreuve' (*De la Cour au jardin* 374). But the germination of *Candide* does not end there; it has its role as a point of departure: '*Candide* donne le coup d'envoi à la campagne contre l'Infâme' (Candide is the starting shot for the campaign against the *infâme*; 347–75, 374).

Quite clearly the critical tradition encasing *Candide* needs to be supplemented. The book needs to be seen in its relation with Voltaire's other works; it needs to be judged in balance with the larger aspirations and successes of Voltaire in reclaiming the farmlands near the chateau of Ferney, and it needs to be regarded as a new manifesto, an 'opening,' from which, with a more solid base, his public campaigning starts out on a solid footing. *Candide* is remarkable because within it Voltaire finds the insight and the courage to give full expression to his antiself, or to the portraiture of himself through others, to bring crashing down the outmoded philosophy ('of which he did not believe a word'), and to set in motion the challenges represented by the clash and conflict of new ways of looking at the world. *Candide* may not stand alone, but it does stand tall; witness its astonishing immediate success when an estimated 20,000 volumes were sold in 1759. Although Voltaire persistently denied authorship, he took great pains to have it printed in various outposts so as to elude the watchful authorities. The genre of the *conte philosophique*, to which he took reluctantly, became the capstone of his continuing fame, overshadowing other works which, by some criteria, should be better known. In this of course it is like *The Praise of Folly*. But in being so overbearing such classics have also the reverse effect of attracting some vagrant attention to the lives of their authors, and thus serendipitously to their other works as well.

PART THREE

DUALISMS

SIX

Never a Peace:
'Thus always Cain or Abel'

羚

By their enemies you shall know them.

The materials presented thus far provide ample means for bringing together Erasmus and Voltaire and measuring the far-reaching and pertinent nature of their thought. These are clearly not
men of a day, or only of their day. In their historical alignments
and personal involvements their characters, beliefs, and methods
stand clear to view. Expatriated either by choice or necessity, each
found refuge and glory in that international republic of letters,
of which they were the prime defenders and leaders in their day.
And what better phrase to describe the condition of literature today than that of an 'international republic of letters,'

Being part of a spreading, new intellectual movement brought
added spirit and confidence to their efforts. While steering by
such favourable winds of history, each directed acute critical intelligence against the legends of history, the heavy encumbrances
of superstition, false piety, fanaticism, and national pride. Each
was a historian by métier and by predilection, and while their resources and methods were of course different their goals were
similar – to reshape the culture of their day. Erasmus's *Adages*
were more than a collection of aphorisms, or even a means of sty-
listic enrichment; they offered a rich reservoir of classical wisdom,
granaries of practical employment. Similarly, Voltaire's copious
Essai sur les moeurs et l'esprit des nations is not a mere chronology
(as Mme du Châtelet objected), but rather 'l'histoire de l'esprit
humain' from which one was free to derive an 'édifice' of one's
choosing (*Essai sur les moeurs* 2:883). Representing different phases in the development of humanism, the one by collecting, collat-

ing, editing, but more importantly, by putting philology to critical use, the other by uprooting and debunking, each honoured presences from the past as positive supports and indeed as models for emulation. Erasmus venerated the gospels and the early church fathers (in fact, the pagan classics as well), while Voltaire honoured those periods of high attainment where culture and politics came together. Such great appropriations showed the way to their larger aspirations, their highly ambitious projects, and their roles as public intellectuals.

Each was divided by contradictions and subject to contrary pressures. Not willing to go all the way, or to let themselves go – for their own reasons of character and experience – they stopped at the water's edge and applied a brake on thought and action; they were reformers and not revolutionaries. Each showed an extraordinary concern with establishing limits. It was this practice of holding back, of playing a double game, that tarnished and diminished their reputations among later generations. Yet, despite their divisions they continued to speak out, showing that tenacity for which Erasmus was praised by Schoeck and Augustijn and Voltaire by Naves. They were indefatigable workers in their attempts to temper the more extravagant and paradoxical ideas of their days. They were able to do so because their divided and multiple natures were not just a matter of duplicitous behaviour but rather sprang from aspects of character and insight where they were very much aware of life's obscurities, of its contradictions and its contrasts. Moreover they each made judgments based upon a scale of proportionate values, which means in Voltaire's homely language, one does not beat one's nanny. Rather than adopting lateral oppositions, exclusionary practices based upon either/or distinctions, one subordinates, prioritizes. Matters of subaltern value are for that reason not to be rejected but rather incorporated into a fuller body of understanding. To be sure, in the pitch of battle both Erasmus and Voltaire violated these precepts, but they remained as constant points of reference for calmer and more judicious moments.

Even these observations, which may suffice for consolidating the works and purposes of Erasmus and Voltaire, do not adequately assess the revelations of character, the personal and public significance uncovered by the major event of their lives. As stated previously, in their times they each entered into an epochal encounter – Erasmus with Luther and Voltaire with Rousseau – that proved to be the defining debate of the age and helped to secure even more tightly the interests they held in common. Erasmus was given to retrenchments, if not retractions, of previously held positions: these included the Christian liberty that first brought Luther and Erasmus together as allies, the willingness to spread the Gospel's word among the people, and the strength of conviction provided by the inspiration of the Holy Spirit. On all three positions he backtracked. Where Erasmus was beset by his own misgivings, Voltaire took up the cudgels and became more aggressive, indeed to emotional excess, begging for explanation. Such reactions were not new-born but rather revelations of aspects of character that had been long present in the allegiances of each, in their rhetorics of inclusion and their scales of proportionate value. Luther and Rousseau did not create new personalities in Erasmus and Voltaire but did bring out qualities that were always present, now given greater focus. It was such reactive withholdings, emergent aspects of character, that placed a large dent in the later reputations of Erasmus and Voltaire.

More than any other, this engaging cross-rivalry on the parts of Erasmus and Voltaire revealed and determined crucial aspects of their beings. Avoiding mere repetition of elements already present in *Dualisms*, I confine my remarks here to the ways that Erasmus and Voltaire joined battle with Luther and Rousseau and thus even further revealed their own qualities in common. This show belongs to Erasmus and Voltaire. The epigraph of this chapter means more than what it says. Not only shall you be known by the enemy you choose, but the enmity induces responses that are themselves identifying marks (or scars). One is defined in contrast. But in taking the measure of their opponents what is remarkable is that each separately, Voltaire would say, *insensiblement*, arrived at the same indictments and in so doing managed to strengthen the intellectual comradeship that they shared across the centuries.

Their participation in a grand dualism prompts three additional areas of concern, only alluded to in the introduction and left untouched by my previous volume, *Dualisms*. (1) In the conflict each found in himself similar ways of approaching time and history, which stand in remarkable contrast with those of Luther and Rousseau. (2) Many valid reasons have been offered as to why Erasmus chose to come out against Luther, but the dualism of Voltaire and Rousseau has been mainly addressed from the side

of Rousseau, 'le cas' Rousseau. To be sure there were provocations, but do they explain the relentlessness with which Voltaire,
who so often came to the aid of victims, pounded in work after
work the exiled, proscribed, and helpless Rousseau? The issue
needs to be studied from the side of Voltaire, notably by taking
into account his involvement in a grand dualism, a dualism that
exerts its own demands. (3) Finally, Erasmus and Voltaire were
able to respond effectively to their more radical opponents, mark-
ing their special defects, and surprisingly their objections were
exactly the same. Erasmus found the same deficiencies in Luther
that Voltaire found in Rousseau, and these insights by rebound
can be used to define themselves in their truly joined natures.

TEMPORALITIES

> I do believe you think what now you speak;
> But what we do determine oft we break.
> Purpose is but the slave to memory,
> Of violent birth, but poor validity...
> What to ourselves in passion we propose,
> The passion ending, doth the purpose lose
>
> *Hamlet*

Moving from their similar career episodes and the comparisons
of their works to inspections of their more personal metabolisms,
we find that what looms large is Erasmus's and Voltaire's shared
attitude toward time. Each is in war with time, but this is a sense
of time that grows naturally from their own philosophies and motives for being. Time is a topic riddled by obscurity and obscured
by riddles. Augustine summarizes the paradox: when he doesn't
have to explain time he believes he understands it quite well, but
when he tries to explain it he is baffled. This is because time is like
the wind: we only see it when the trees bend. Or it is understood
by absence, by time lapsed, or experienced in the bones, 'You
have put old age into my days.' When discussing time in Erasmus
and Voltaire I am not looking at any abstract accounting of its
nature, but rather how time enters into their mental landscapes,
their personal metabolisms, in regard to change and their philosophies of history. Rather than time I would like to borrow the
phrase 'temporalities,' advanced by Heidegger and adopted by
Sartre, but put to very different use and meaning here (see below

page 187). This requires some rearrangement of furniture, as temporality for Heidegger and Sartre is not an approach to Being or even action but rather the very format of being. Being encounters its finitude in temporality, the waters in which we swim. To be outside of temporality is to be like a fish out of water. Rather than turn to Augustine and his self-professed ignorance, or to Sartre and Heidegger (whose language but not whose gist of argument Erasmus and Voltaire might have experienced some difficulties in comprehending), it is perhaps better that we turn to Woody Allen, when he declared, 'comedy is tragedy plus time.'

A more useful understanding of what Erasmus and Voltaire have in common is gained by contrasting their 'temporalities' with those of their compeers and rivals, Luther and Rousseau. There is a different tempo to their separate temporalities. In the tumultuousness of their personalities, Luther and Rousseau are given to ardent conversions. Their sense of time is dramatic, drastic, and urgent. The moment emerges as paramount, not contingent; it holds eternity in its sway, as if all of life were being determined in that decisive moment. There is no place for postponement or delay, or the thought that tomorrow will qualify what today has wrought, that in the long drawn-out drain of contingency, what Dante has called 'la pioggia continua,' things will not matter all that much. There is to be no faltering, no liquidation of conviction by temporal dispersions, by 'l'effritement progressif du temps,' the frittering away of our days. In Luther's and Erasmus's different senses of time, their keenest dramas of interaction are being played out, leading to their final rupture and the great debate over the freedom of the will. For Erasmus, as the moment passes, the ironies of a complex consciousness enter, undoing what was thought to be most certain, exposing to doubt the moment of the greatest enthusiasms. Again we can reflect on the pertinence of Hamlet. Erasmus's own gradualism in ethical improvement, the dominating movement of his *Enchiridion*, is dependent upon this non-imposing more contingent sense of time. Nothing is ever final, sufficient to the day ... There is always time to recover, to regroup, and to undo what has been done. Uniformity in the sequence of objects induces an equanimity in the subject. No moment stands out; there is no grandeur nor climactic defeat. Such sequence carries its own fallibilities, inducing not only a sameness but also a tendency to undo itself, to wither away. Such temporal dispersion makes Erasmus vulnerable to a faltering grip, to a lofty despair. It is this sense of time, produced by their very qualities, against which both Erasmus and Voltaire must muster their courage and determine their own reasons for existence. One is constantly at war with time, pitting its offer of recuperation against its inevitable deterioration and decay. There is no external intervention that redeems time, but only constant effort. Consequently both Erasmus and Voltaire are ethicists by vocation.

Luther wrote from the urgency of the moment. His very first words in his *Address to the Christian Nobility* are, 'The time for silence is over, and the time for speech has come,' and near the end he repeats, 'I cannot but speak.' While the first reference is indebted to Ecclesiastes, the entire drama derives from the Acts of the Apostles. The time for miracles, for the laying on of hands, for the gift of tongues might be over, but not the time of the Holy Spirit and bold speech. The living presence of Christ the person is dead, but resurrected by the power of God. The Holy Spirit thus becomes his surrogate, encouraging the apostles to bear witness to the resurrected Christ, to the remission of sins and to life everlasting and to do so by bold speech. One can see why Luther preferred the role of the Holy Spirit in Acts and Letters rather than in the Gospels, where, as in Luke, the Holy Spirit comes to make an announcement, an annunciation whether to Mary or to Elizabeth and Zacariah, and their roles are those of silent acceptance. But in Acts Peter astounds the elders when he, an unlearned man, can speak so powerfully (4:13). 'For we cannot but speak the things that we have seen and heard' (4:20). Like Luther Peter defies the prohibition of speech: 'We ought to obey God rather than men' (5:29). And Saul – Paul after his conversion, through his conversion, provides lessons for Luther in the importance of preaching, for which reason Protestant churches were constructed to facilitate communication of the word. The marvellous dramatic narrative of Acts thus provides Luther with the example and inspiration not to falter; in fact, the schema of his own career might well be contained within the drama of Acts. He then lists twenty-seven points of remediation, directly, without equivocation, demanding instant cancellation or demolition. As he tells us in his *De servo arbitrio* (*On the Enslaved Will*), the Christian by right indulges in assertion. If Christian faith, inspired by the presence of the Holy Spirit, particularly as related in Acts, is the determining issue, then the contrast between Erasmus and Luther is overwhelming. Erasmus simply pales in comparison. When submitted to the test of Acts, it is clear that Luther writes from the fullness of religious experience and Erasmus wrote for another age, another time.[1]

The oppositions that Erasmus and Luther present are extreme; that they are antitypes holds true along a line of measurements. Erasmus in *On the Freedom of the Will* was committed to writing a pacific *diatribe*, or *collatio*, that is, a gathering of various opinions. To the sword that Christ brings at the end of *The Praise of Folly*, Erasmus clearly attributes spiritual meaning: *gladium spiritus*, the sword of the spirit, 'that penetrates into the innermost depths of the bosom and cuts out every passion with a single stroke' (CWE 27:146), nothing remaining 'praeter pietatem' (AS 188). Luther's sword suffers no spiritualizing interpretation; instead it is a real sword, producing tumult, a sure indication that God's truth is being upheld. Not only does Erasmus's hermeneutics spiritualize, it also prioritizes. But here too Luther faces him down across the field of history. Erasmus's vertical schema is replaced by a lateral conflict borne out by the biblical accounts of the rival brothers. Conflict is endemic to human affairs, 'at all times we are either Esauites or Jacobites.' Unlike Erasmus, who can anticipate future resolutions of conflict, who in fact depends upon such resolutions however slow-paced, Luther is convinced that should even the papists and the Turks be defeated, from within their own triumphant midst, new and rival sects would emerge, 'thus always Cain or Abel, Esau or Jacob.'[2] In every way, along the field of temporalities, in the short or the long run, Erasmus and Luther stand opposed.

As they never were in life, in death Voltaire and Rousseau were for good and ill conjoined.[3] They march together down the Champs Élysées, they are both celebrated as heralds if not progenitors of the Revolution, they are together pantheonized, as they were each polemicized and red-flagged by partisans of the Left and the Right in the sharply contentious French intellectual life of the nineteenth century. Aesthetically and temperamentally there was soon discerned a sharp divergence between the two, already present in Mme de Stael's description of Rousseau issuing his blasts from the depths of some forest (Trousson, *Visages* 110). Stendhal found Voltaire to be 'pueril,' although he admired his great clarity. While Voltaire was eclipsed by the very issues he championed, and thus remained a man of his time, of historical importance, Rousseau continued to resonate, to enter into the lives and thoughts of his followers, and persisted in Romanticism and its aftermath. Like Luther's his very 'temporalities' were calls to attention.

Rousseau introduces his *Émile* with a characteristic rhetorical power. 'If I sometimes adopt an assertive tone it is not for the sake of making an impression upon the reader but for the sake of speaking to him as I think. Why should I propose as doubtful what, as far as I am concerned, I do not doubt at all? I say exactly what goes on in my mind.' Consequently he is not concerned with halfway measures, with what is merely feasible. His proposals are radical. Like Luther he must 'mean it' (see *Dualisms* 167–8). The state of doubt is a state too violent for his soul, he pronounces later. And although it only got him into trouble, he proudly appends his name as a citizen of Geneva to his works, while Voltaire, who experienced the hard knocks of some nine exiles, and two internments in the Bastille, adopted the ruses of anonymity or pseudonymity.

Like Erasmus Voltaire resorted to the rhetoric of qualification and modulation. His *contes* have their varied formats and reserves, and, as indicated above, their false endings, their lip-services and accommodations. He, of course, makes note of the conventional understandings of time, as when Zadig solves the first riddle as part of his testing to win Astarte's love. At the beneficent ending of *L'Ingenu* (which is not an indicator of the true temper of the *conte*, of Voltaire's refusal to be comforted), the motto is introduced 'le temps adoucit tout.' In *Les deux consolés* (RC 143–4) Citophile who, as his name indicates, brings consolation by enumerating the historical figures from the past who have endured similar hardships, is devastated himself by the death of his only son. When the lady whom his own attempts at consolation by citation had failed to comfort presents him with a list of all the kings who had lost their sons, he read it over but did not lament less. Finally after some months the two find they are able to rejoice again and they erect a statue of Time, with the inscription, 'A Celui Qui Console.' But this can be only the bitterest of ironies, suggesting how quickly time can bring forgetting. On the other hand, the more outgoing Voltaire, addressing the ills of society, looks forward to improvements, and changes do come, 'mais il faut du temps.' While personally irascible and energetic, given to action, Voltaire has a much more elastic view of the future fortunes of society. Having surveyed in all of his historical texts the misfortunes and evils that seem to reign throughout human history, he still knows that beneficial change can occur but in this he is only a soft ameliorist. Out of the horrors of war and assassination (the decades following 1600) some areas have shown improvements and enlightenment; but he is not a believer in any law of progress, as regressions can always occur (see above in chapter 4).

It is thus absurd to accuse Voltaire of ignoring history, of replacing time with space and its 'immobilisme.' In his oft-noted *The Philosophy of the Enlightenment* Ernst Cassirer opens a chapter entitled, 'The Conquest of History,' with the straightforward declaration, 'The common ('landläufige') assumption that the eighteenth century was an 'unhistorical' century is not and cannot be historically justified' (197). Thus, Barthes' charge of 'immobilisme' against Voltaire's sense of history, that it is more spatial than temporal, is not only a blunder; it is worse, culpable of repeating a commonplace years after it had already been rebutted. History is Voltaire's *métier*, it is his storehouse, his school-house, his staging ground, his field of inquiry, his plane of regard. But this is history critically scrutinized, stalked, and culled for principles favourable to conduct. Raymond Naves succinctly summarizes Voltaire's historical humanism: the same historical figures whom as a modernist Voltaire can disdain, as a moralist he can make the object of his study, drawing from their actions the principles that enter into his great compilations of the 'manners and the spirit' of peoples. Naves adds that Voltaire's meditations always end in the values and understanding of the present (158). Voltaire scrutinizes history not as a detached scholar but as an engaged man of the world

Nevertheless, as has already been suggested by the different codes of the three clasps, there is a dominant complexity to Voltaire's view of the world. He understands its changefulness, its resistance to generalities and to rules. This is most notably apparent in his entry 'Contradiction' and those that immediately follow in the *Philosophical Dictionary*, where he shows by the piling up of succinct instances that the inclination toward irony and paradox, the capacity to abide within contradiction and contrast, are hallmarks of his genius. In his republic of moral reflection, contradiction and inconsistency are the unwritten rules of the land. 'The more we see of the world, the more we see it abounding in contradiction and inconsistency' (1:331). To wish for regularity would be like wishing for rivers to run straight, for the mountains and the valleys to become as one. Only in games are lined rules observed; 'in the meantime irregularity is part of our nature.

Our social world is like the natural world, rude and unshapely'
(1:333). This is true of peoples, of princes, of institutions, and men
of letters. Montesquieu, who disparaged the Académie Française
for the vapid panegyrics of its members, was nevertheless in-
ducted into that august body and praised for his skill in 'drawing
likenesses' (1:333). Voltaire goes on, 'men are everywhere incon-
sistent alike. They have made laws by piecemeal, as breaches are
repaired in walls' (1:333). We are back in the late 1730s, the worlds
of *Babouc* or *Memnon*: just as it would be folly to wish that nature
functioned in a straight manner, it would be still greater folly to
expect from man the 'perfection of wisdom.' Nevertheless, there
is a 'principle of preservation,' a muddling through that works
(1:333–4).

But there are other more formidable principles. One is the
desire for order and regularity in relationships. This might be
termed the law of contracts. The other is his belief that separated
from the customs of tribes and cults, there is a 'raison universelle,'
which all societies and people observe (*Essai sur les moeurs* 1:27).

In judging human affairs Voltaire substitutes the principle of
contrast for that of contradiction (1:284–6). This opens the way to
the exercise of critical judgment, the capacity to appreciate contrasts within the individual and even to extend this critical judgment to revered works of art. These are some of the qualities that
made Voltaire the premier critic of his day, indeed called the first
great French literary critic by Naves (102). The excellent critic does
not contradict himself when he praises or blames the same author,
be it Dante, Shakespeare, Pascal, or Corneille. It is the author who
contradicts himself by not writing all of a piece. Sometimes even
the great nod, thus requiring the application of attentive critical
judgment. Indeed, the stupid statements of great men could form
a volume in itself.

Voltaire had a great respect for industry and commerce. Under
the topic, 'Liberty of Conscience' (which he alleges to be a direct
translation from a German source) he values the manufacturing
resources of an Anabaptist, and the commerce of the English exchange where men of all religious persuasions can come together
peacefully to carry on business (1:240–1). It is thus that throughout his work Voltaire shows great curiosity in and respect for the
moral fortitude and the simplicity of the ways of the Quakers.
The first four of the *Lettres philosophiques* are devoted to them as
is a lengthy section of the *Dictionnaire*, from which I have been

quoting. So intrigued is he that many of their ways and beliefs – forming another 'golden age' – found themselves reproduced in Eldorado. In the *Lettres,* however, he is quite naturally suspicious of their 'inspiration,' as he was also of Socrates' *daimon.* He argues that one does not reason with an 'enthusiast.'

Nevertheless, Voltaire was also extremely taken with the quiet simplicity of Quaker practice and their return to the ways of early Christianity. Seeking refuge from the religious and civil wars that wasted Great Britain (an instinct similar to what accounted for the origins of Eldorado), William Penn established 'the primitive church' in America. Voltaire's admiration for what Penn was able to accomplish shines through in every paragraph. Primary among the achievements were complete civil liberty and religious freedom. Such grounding is responsible, Voltaire believes, for the enormous flourishing of Pennsylvania from a community of 500 at the time of Penn to the then current population of over 300,000. While one half of the population remains Quaker, twenty different religions comprise the other half. Philadelphia is a model for a flourishing modern city, prosperous in its industry, based upon civic and religious freedom. Voltaire transcends himself when he compares the Anglo-Saxon North to the Hispanic South of the Americas; by their general imitation of Pennsylvania, in the colonies at large 'no one is molested in his creed.' It is this which has rendered the English power in America equal to that of Spain: 'If any method could be devised to enervate the English colonies it would be to establish in them the Inquisition' (1:297). His doctrine of universal change governing all things leads to another startling conclusion of some prescience: 'Perhaps the Americans will in some future period cross the seas to instruct Europeans in the arts' (1:311).

Erasmus is similarly aware of the ironies of history. He of course had his period of buoyant optimism in the years immediately preceding the Lutheran intervention, after which his view of human society became pessimistic and his own sense of himself defeatist. In subsequent years Erasmus continued his fight with integrity. One could, of course, credit his rational intelligence or his opposition to Luther, but his later thought was not an anomaly, but rather something found in the grain of Erasmus's character. Erika Rummel argues rightly for a strong current of Christian scepticism in Erasmus. Thus he was sharply aware of the irregularities in the run of life, irregularities that resist order, obscurities that elude clarification. From this particular perch Erasmus was an acute observer of his times and like Voltaire had some powers of prescience. In a letter from Basel in 1527 Erasmus now regrets his earlier advocacy of Christian liberty: 'I am deeply grieved at having preached freedom of the spirit in earlier writing' (*Erasmus and His Age*, 204) But what is important is not the recantation (Luther had already anticipated this recantation in his response to *On the Freedom of the Will*) but rather the reasons for it. From experience itself Erasmus's arguments acquire a new density and texture. Where before, he had argued, it was permissible under certain conditions to forego compliance with man-made ordinances, now in the full fury of the protestant onslaught, such refusals have become obligatory. He goes on, 'Now what kind of freedom is this: not to be able to say prayers, or to offer sacrifice, or to fast, or to abstain from meat?' (204).The argument of freedom has yielded its own despotism. (Dostoevsky's Shigalyovism is not far off.) One arrives at a new kind of obligation, where one is required not to do certain things, and this can represent an equally great hindrance to Christian liberty. A new kind of requirement has intervened, the requirement of adversarial denial.

In January 1525, Erasmus develops a thought that had been gaining ground with him and that many perceive to be a fatal flaw in the 'protestant' consciousness, one responsible for its splintering effects, and that is a certain relentlessness in change. Where good will is absent, or the spirit of benevolence, all restrictions, even the smallest are bound to be thought oppressive.

> Human affairs will never be in such a happy condition that one will not have to overlook many things, no matter what changes are made. At present some people are displeased by everything – clerical garb, sacred chant, bells, images, the tonsure, anointings, regulations, ceremonies even the sacramental rites and laws. (*Erasmus and His Age*, 184)

He then goes on to the crucial sentence: 'And there is no end to this; there is always something to replace the old complaint.' I have already discussed these memorable pages in *Dualism* (95–6). A culture of complaint believes that history is symmetrical, that all complaints are equally justified because validation is enshrined in the spirit of protest itself. Erasmus argues that this culture never arrives at equilibrium, with a capacity to distinguish true grievances from petty ones.

Lewis Spitz had ample reasons to regret the 'tragic denouement' of Erasmus's last years, particularly 'for a man who had once been the literary and intellectual arbiter of his age' (106). Yet all was not lost or Erasmus committed to silence, as the preceding comments show. In one of his last and fullest works, *On Mending [Restoring] the Peace of the Church* (*Liber de Sarcienda Ecclesiae Concordia*; 1533), he does seek out an equilibrium. It is to the last pages of this commentary on Psalm 83 that we turn to find Erasmus at his best. Not being contested, it bears no handicap of psychological defensiveness. That is, it is not about Erasmus himself, but is rather the product of thirty years of involvement in the events and controversies of his day as counsellor to an emperor and as adviser to kings and dukes. It represents a survey of the issues that have divided Christians and that have shredded the seamless garment of Christ. It breathes the spirit of conciliation and brings to the front Erasmus's benevolent imagination. His separation from party or faction has paid off and he can speak with the maturity and wisdom that he has earned. While he remains, as he has always been, a son of the church, he is able now with the best of credentials to address the errors of each: 'One side is unwilling to accept changes, while the other wishes nothing of the old to remain' (Dolan 377).

His usual historical gradualism comes into greater play, 'Most evils creep in little by little and on different occasions. They ought to be eliminated in the same way, provided this does not cause a disturbance' (Dolan 377).The church must endeavour to eliminate the superstitions that have alienated the adult layperson. In Erasmus's defence of the church two principles emerge, one that has run like a thread throughout his debates and another that is relatively recent. The first requires that whatever reforms are undertaken, care must be exercised 'not to do away rashly with those things that have been handed down with the authority of the past and that long usage and general agreement have confirmed' (378) (temere desciscere ab iis quae maiorum autoritate tradita sunt, quaeque longo seculorum usu consensuque confirmata; ASD V-3, 304). Erasmus, like many of the humanists who will follow him, bows before the authority of the ages. The mass, 'accepted for so many centuries' (383) (missam tot seculis receptam; ASD V-3 308) should not be stamped out as if it were some pestilence. Or, 'is not that baptism that was good enough for over fourteen hundred years for the Church satisfactory to them' (386) (Non sufficit illis baptismus, qui mille quadringentis annis suffecit ecclesiae catholicae; ASD V-3 312)? Ever the humanist, Erasmus finds comfort and more, 'authority,' in the continuities and consensus of the ages. The second also comes from: those who advocate change; they should show greater respect for the needs of the simple, the uneducated, who need the 'silent poetry' of the icons and the paintings and the murals. They require 'externals.' Whereas formerly Erasmus had condemned such flocking to a materialized religion, here he defends not only their usefulness for the common people but also their being essential to religion itself. Superstition is prevalent in the prayers to saints, but such prayers of simple folk will be heard by Christ, because he always loved the simple of heart (380). And if he does not grant us what we seek through ('per') the saints, he will do so on behalf of ('pro') the saints (ASD V-3 305).

Thus it is that now, as earlier, Erasmus is able to give a quali-fied acceptance to matters that do not have scriptural sanction but have become so much a part of the fabric of life that their extirpa-tion would prove more harmful than their retention. Like Voltaire Erasmus is unwilling to break through the larger matrices and conditions of existence. To be sure he prioritizes, but such a prac-tice enables preservation. True confession is delivered to God in the privacy of one's soul; but confession to a priest can help (not running to the various confessors). As to whether Christ founded confession in its present form, there should be allowed a diver-sity of opinions to prevail until a council can render a definite judgment (382). Many of the abuses of the mass must be elimi-nated, particularly the various masses that have sprung from the growth of sodalities. Erasmus outlines the contents of the mass (382), simple and pious with a definite form. The mass is a sac-rifice in which grace is renewed by participation in a symbolic rite, the remembrance of the death of Christ and his resurrection. Feast days ought especially to be reduced in number, particularly those pertaining to the Virgin Mother (385). Fasting should be left to the judgment of the individual. In all these cases, Erasmus supports what might be called a qualified acceptance of current practices, provided proper emphases are understood and are in place. Diversity should be tolerated until a council can settle the especially thorny matters. Above all, force and charges of here-sy are to be avoided. But to return to the previous section, 'it is mere contumacy to reject useful practices just because they are or-dained by the Church' (385) (quase rogo contumacia est, velut in odium ecclesiae hoc reiicere, quod tantam adfert utilitatem; ASD

V-3 311). While breathing a spirit of equanimity and calm, these profoundly moving reflections (and they in their spirit of justice are more that than recommendations) had little effect on either camp (despite being translated into German by Melancthon). The die had already been cast by Erasmus's debate with Luther.

Beyond his truly religious sentiment, what is *Voltairien* emerges in the remedy: with Erasmus as well as Voltaire this can only occur through the use of reason and the passage of time. Reason will eventually be heard when the passions have subsided; then the proponents of opposing arguments will be more willing to relax the stubbornness of their positions. It takes time 'We have put up for too long a time with strife; perhaps mere exhaustion will enable us to find peace' (387). Clearly here the sanity of both Erasmus and Voltaire emerges: their arena is not only history but also historical time, through which slowly after the conflict and the explosions a kind of compromise or consolidation may emerge. It is a conditional world view, a diminished world view and one that has seen its triumphs from time to time, but which also does little to stem or even to comprehend the on-rushing historical cataclysms of revolution.

THE 'CASE' OF VOLTAIRE

Voltaire's break with Frederick II he himself likened to a 'lovers' quarrel' (Besterman 668). There were too many enduring strands of affinity and affection to produce an enmity. Although hampered by the inequality of condition, they shared an appreciation of wit, a philosophical turn of mind, and an expressed concern for tolerance, for openness to foreign intelligences, and an opposition to fanaticism. It was not surprising that in their friendship after estrangement reconciliation should have occurred.

With Maupertius, the situation was different. First, they had a 'history.' Each had been at Cirey with Mme du Châtelet, where Maupertius had also been one of her lovers, and each had been early expounders of Newtonian science. At the court of Frederick, their positions had changed. Voltaire was present as literary adviser and editor of the king's works (the rumoured remark by Voltaire that his task was to clean up Frederick's dirty linen was reported back to the king by Maupertius). Maupertius had acquired a position of some power and favour with Frederick. As 'president' of the Academy of Science he had authority to appoint academicians and to award subventions (or 'pensions') on his judgment of the merits. Here a third party intervened. Samuel Kônig had taken public issue with many of Maupertius's pet theories, and one in particular he claimed to have been derived from a letter by Leibniz. Unfortunately he was unable to produce the letter and thus was chastised by Maupertius. Maupertius, however, did not attempt to refute the substance of Kônig's arguments, but instead exerted his 'despotic' powers as president and succeeded in having Kônig discharged from the Academy. Here Voltaire intervened, taking Kônig's side, abhorring Maupertius's actions as hostile to the freedom of thought and the debate essential to the republic of letters. The various exchanges of letters (in their details too far off our course to be presented here; see Mervaud in Pomeau (*De la Cour au jardin* chapter 6) soon took on a European dimension. Voltaire's biting satire, *Histoire du docteur Akakia*, drew down the displeasure of Frederick, who burned a copy of it. This confirmed Voltaire in his conviction that the time had come to depart from the court of Frederick.

Despite the wide interest this dispute provoked, and the substantial intellectual nature of the arguments (even if treated satirically by Voltaire), it has not entered as vividly into the cultural imagination. One must ask the question why it slips into virtual disregard when compared with the quarrel between Voltaire and Rousseau. That is, it does not have the same psychological dimensions, the same off-setting powers of attraction as the great dualism between Voltaire and Rousseau had.

But here some remediation is in order. What I did not see in my previous work is another problem which awareness of dualisms can help resolve. Reductive pathologists are excessively eager to diagnose the 'case' of Rousseau but rarely if ever, except for expressions of disgust or chastisement, do they explore the 'case' of Voltaire. While frequently criticized for his merciless pursuit of Rousseau, Voltaire's conduct has not undergone the same degree of analysis. Perhaps the very bluff confidence and the seductive humour of satire signal equanimity. But Voltaire was just as much bothered by Rousseau as Rousseau was by Voltaire and just as unsettled emotionally by his rival as Erasmus was by his – although their reactions took opposite turns. In the time of Rousseau's greatest troubles, when he went from being a celebrated author, even a cult figure, to having his books confiscated, burned, and he himself placed under bodily decree,

Voltaire attacked him with increasing verve in work after work. At first he had no eyes for Rousseau. Then he considered him a 'fou de famille'; he may have been a crazy but he was 'our' crazy. But the aspiration toward greatness that once moved Philoctète succumbs to the grand enmity that dualisms provoke. The 'fou de famille' then became a 'frère-ennemi,' an object of constant attack. Of course there were provocations to explain the change in attitude. Rousseau wrote the *Lettre à M. d'Alembert*, which succeeded in damaging Voltaire where he lived and worked, among the play-going patrician class of Geneva, eagerly attracted to the productions that Voltaire staged. Rousseau wrote the infamous letter of 1760, where he managed to get off his chest that he 'hated' Voltaire. Then, finally, in *Lettres écrites de la montagne.* Rousseau 'outs' Voltaire as the author of *Sermon des cinquante*, the authorship of which Voltaire had worked to conceal and which if formally conceded would have meant a third more prolonged sojourn in the Bastille, or worse. Rousseau had thus become a traitor, an informer.

But Voltaire had withstood worse experiences of insult and humiliation. Even after his detention and arrest in Frankfurt, attempting to flee the court of Frederick, he continued to be a sympathetic admirer. And Voltaire and Frederick were codependents in a mutual admiration society (see Frederick's letter of 1776 above, cognizant of Voltaire's approaching end).There was something else afoot in the relentlessness of Voltaire's attacks on the vulnerable Rousseau. There is a pathology in piling on, when leave-alone, or silence would have sufficed. Such relentlessness in punishment that is so exorbitant and out-of-scale tempts one to reach for Coleridge's ascription to Iago of a 'motiveless malignity.' Reasons, provocations offered do not satisfy the cause; they are not reason enough. One searches for other explanations. Voltaire was not an evil man. The extraordinary 'case' of Voltaire requires the larger screen and manifestations of a dualism if we are to understand the unrelenting and steady stream of abuse that he was so intent in inflicting on the hapless Rousseau. Within a dualism there is a life-long animosity, not even deterred by death. Moreover, within a dualism difference is both rigorously intellectual and temperamental. There is little room for twinning the twain. Another sure gauge of a dualism is the constant attentiveness, despite denials, that each pays to the other. In the later *Lettre au docteur Pansophe* (see below, page 172) it is clear that

Voltaire had read almost everything that Rousseau had written. Such constancy of surveillance reveals a genuine and passionate involvement. Although Voltaire had many 'combats,' this was the strangest. Of all the people at the ball, this was the one his eyes were fixed on. Knowingly or unknowingly, Voltaire had finally come to treat Rousseau as a true antagonist in a great dualism. According to Roland Barthes, Rousseau was Voltaire's only genuine contestant, his only comparable adversary, an 'anti-Voltaire,' rising to the generality of his true antitype (100). Vituperation is a response to a threat, and Rousseau, despite his helplessness, still seemed threatening, painful to the sight like an ulcer in the eye. Voltaire was in the grips of a greater passion, one that others before him (Luther and Erasmus) and after him (Sartre and Camus) would also endure. He encountered a genuine antitype, the quarrel with whom became inevitable because together in their radically opposed values and characters they represented the perennial tensions of Western culture.

DUALISMS AT LAST

Like other great historians of an epoch such as Huizinga, Cassirer, and Pirenne, W.K. Ferguson was given to synthesis, to searching out the unifying aspects of the Renaissance. He did this in contrast to narrow specialization, or in opposition to the disaggregative methods of some historians who, because of the various additions made to a house, believe there is no design at all. Ferguson valued periodization when amply supported by a combination of facts and thought. But such valid quests for the unifying elements of a culture should not blind us to the fact that a period may be equally defined by its divisions. Thus dualisms may correspond to the divergent needs of a culture.

Erasmus and Voltaire are joined when they confront their antagonists in the cross-rivalries. They may have been diminished, but neither was blinded or silenced by the more radical, even more tumultuous qualities of their opponents. Each held tenaciously to his own position, and challenged Luther and Rousseau at the most fundamental levels of their thought and beliefs. Interestingly enough each focused on the same faults, the same insistencies in Luther and Rousseau, and in opposing and denouncing these qualities they revealed the more essential values that they themselves held in common.

In their great debate of 1524–5 over the freedom of the will, which Heinrich Bornkamm ranks 'among the greatest documents of intellectual history' (418), Erasmus and Luther gave their utmost, with the result that their differences were as much over method as over meaning. After many diplomatic efforts at peacemaking both by detailed exchanges of correspondence between Luther and Erasmus as well as through well-intentioned intermediaries, Erasmus finally decided to come out against Luther (although with his typical disingenuousness, he refused to admit that his work was directed against Luther). Thus appeared the *De libero arbitrio* (*On the Freedom of the Will*), followed after a lengthy delay by Luther's responsively entitled, *De servo arbitrio*. Shocked by the vituperation of Luther's response, in quick order Erasmus answered with two installments of the *Hyperaspistes*, each much longer than the original effort. The two responses are marred by a tiresome self-defensiveness (Erasmus was never one to let a disagreement go unanswered). The three works combined show Erasmus's retrenchments on previously held principles, principles that he shared with Luther in earlier days. Ever the *Voltairien* 'citophile,' Erasmus professes not to be a judge or advocate but rather, with some superior detachment, simply to be presenting the various opinions of learned authorities. But so perplexing are the issues, so conflicting the opinions, that one reaches an impasse – Erasmus's epistemological scepticism – and is forced to suspend judgment and rely on the accumulated opinion of the church, its doctors and theologians, and the enduring beliefs of custom (see Huizinga 162, 165, on this reversion). Against these and similar retrenchments on Erasmus's part Luther is appalled. The absence in his argument of any passionate belief astounds and repulses him. Erasmus has tripped over his own courtesy, over his tactic of sticking to the high road. For Luther this is the road that leads nowhere, or if anywhere, back to a confirmation of the currently prevailing conditions.

Such redress was not new to Erasmus. In a much earlier letter to Justus Jonas, Erasmus expresses his frequently stated regret at the turn the movement of reform has taken: 'Had I known that a generation such as this would appear, I should neither have written at all some things that I have written or should have written them differently' (CWE 8:209). But in the *Freedom of the Will* and the *Hyperaspistes* his revocations are even more specific. Luther himself points out that Erasmus in effect denies the Christian liberty that had been the keystone of their earlier presumed alliance. Erasmus believes that he has adopted a middling position, leaving only the smallest of windows open for free will. Somewhere between God's initiating grace and his 'shaping ends' there is an area where the person is free to accept or deny God's grace, to show gratitude or to believe that all that comes their way is by their own doing. Luther comes crashing down on such attempts at mediation. In his spiritual economy there is no middling way. All this apparently modest concession does is open the door for all the works and ceremonials, the human ordinances against which they had each separately warred. Erasmus is thus guilty of revoking on the critical notion of Christian liberty, for, as Luther declares, 'Human statutes cannot be observed together with the word of God, because they bind consciences while the word sets them free' (LE 127–33).

In abundant page after page in *Hyperaspistes I* Erasmus makes some acute observations, entering the first of the two arguments that both he and Voltaire adopt. Erasmus rebukes Luther for his need to be 'singular.' Who is Luther to go against the accumulated wisdom of one thousand years, the consensus of the church and its doctors, the weight of the universities and their theologians, and the sheer endurance of custom through the ages? In the balance of probabilities it is more likely that Luther and his confederates are wrong (CWE 76:224–5, 230–1). If, as Luther maintains, 'the Church is hidden, the saints are unknown' (LE 158), why should not the same cloud of unknowing hang over Luther's assertions as well? Should not the same scepticism calling for a suspension of judgment prevail? The voices of the past, invoked as authorities, and the gag of scepticism are being used to quell the voice of this upstart man of the present. According to Carducci, Petrarch, Erasmus, and even Voltaire felt a personal shortcoming in contrast with their rivals. When earlier Erasmus had defended culture and civilization in his quarrel with Dorp he was in the vanguard, and those values were confidently on display; but here in contest with Luther the same evocations of culture and the values of civilization become a protective bunting by which one wards off the more astonishing character. Erasmus blanches before the existential reality of Luther's religious experience. Luther's 'singularity' is not based upon a need to stand out but rather by the willingness to stand alone. Everyone stands alone in the conquest of faith, which must not be sought after (because 'hope would be hope for the wrong thing'),[4] but rather arrived at, and that mysteriously, inadvertently, understood as an action of grace. This is not individualism but aloneness. Thus in Luther's *The Babylonian Captivity*, the mass is not a sacrament, a 'work' whose benefits can be transferred to others. 'The mass is a divine promise which can benefit no one, which can intercede for no one, be communicated to no one, except only to the believer himself by the sole virtue of his faith' (Dillenberger 283). Everyone must endure the challenge of faith alone in their innermost being, outside history, outside tradition, outside models and exemplars. We see here how wide the divergence is between Erasmus and Luther. Erasmus was an educator and an ethicist; he recoils against the 'enslaved will' because that would obviate the educational models provided by the community of the saints. But for Luther such a model theory must be scrapped. The exemplary lives of the saints, whether Bernard, Francis, or Dominic, come under a cloud of uncertainty. For us, 'the number of saints are unknown'; only God knows who the saints are. If Erasmus has an epistemological scepticism which nevertheless falls back on the accumulated wisdom and consensus of tradition, Luther's struggle toward belief affords no such alleviation, for they are the very standards that he calls into question.

We come here to the core of radical Protestantism and the line of sharpest demarcation between Erasmus and Luther, a line that grows deeper, clearer, and more unbridgeable in the great debate. Despite his complex intellectual formulations, such as his epistemological scepticism, Erasmus is still beset by a need to belong. Having endured one bereavement, one orphanhood in time, he was psychologically incapable of enduring the same spiritual aloneness that Luther felt was necessary for the access of faith. Erasmus needed the ministrations of the church, the panoply of the saints, the sense of communication with the continuities of history, the accumulated wisdom, and the traditions of the centuries. These are the arguments, the emotional needs that his contest with Luther brought out in him. Erasmus understood very well the challenge Luther represented both to himself and all that he believed in from the *Enchiridion* on, and above all he felt the terror that was represented by the responsibilities of spiritual aloneness.

There were other revocations. For instance, where he had once thought, in his period of buoyant optimism, that the Gospels and Psalms should be spread among the people, so that they might even be sung by the ploughman at his labours, now he believes that there are certain abstruse and ambiguous questions which should not be bandied in the streets but rather reserved for think-tank seminar sessions. Even there they should be considered with moderation (CWE 76:164–78). Erasmus correctly notes that these are two separate issues. But the question remains, if the common person is to have the Gospels available and to hand, why would not the same questions occur as were thought only suitable for responsible thinkers and seminar sessions?

The greatest revocation occurs in regard to the Holy Spirit and here, as in the attack against 'singularity,' Erasmus and Voltaire share a common position. But it is something of a sore point with Erasmus. Erasmus went to war against Luther out of pique. He understood Luther to be saying that Erasmus is old hat, that he is standing in the way, that like Moses he has led them part of the way but now must be buried in the desert, but most important that Erasmus was lacking when it came to matters of the spirit. In the same letter (CWE 10:109–10), he adds, 'This means war.' The decision to come out against Luther was thus determined. And in the *Hyperaspistes* Erasmus does mount quite acute and telling arguments about the role of the Holy Spirit and the various individuals who pretend to possess it (CWE 76:235–61). Given the diversity of the claimants and the variety of their views how are we to know who is in possession and who is possessed? Are there not places in scripture that are obscure and over which it is better to suspend judgment? Is the Holy Spirit clear in all matters, and not spotty, here clear and there unwieldy? Rather than good fruit has not Luther's call to the Holy Spirit turned gentle souls (he is speaking of Justus Jonas) into 'violent and supercilious' imitators? Are you Luther, he asks, with your Holy Spirit, the only arbiter of truth and is everyone else mistaken? The summary (261), putting in Luther's voice Erasmus's objections, has Luther maintain 'though all are blind, I am not blind; for I am conscious that I have the Spirit of Christ.' Once again Acts opens up the issue and not in Erasmus's favour. The same question was put to Moses, 'Who made thee a ruler and a judge?' Thus he was refused and rejected before the intervention of the angel and the burning bush (CWE 7:35). The question itself is narrow-minded and niggardly.

The movement from the fervour of the Paraclete to the more questioning role attributed to the Holy Spirit did not occur overnight. Already in the apologia addressed to Latomus Erasmus was beginning to reframe his position. This quixotic work shows

Erasmus at his best and at his worst. He puts himself in the curious position of answering charges ('suspicions and rumours') that he claims were not directed against him (and yet as Rummel has shown, entire swatches may be derived from his works – 'his disclaimers strain credulity' *Catholic Critics* 86–9). It revives the lingering dispute over the *Collegium Trilingue*, academic turf wars, and the need for Latin, Greek, and Hebrew, if one is to in some ways offer credible interpretations of obscure texts. Yet his rhetoric is even more inclusive. Very early in the text he reminds the reader of his long-term goal, which was 'to link linguistic skills, elegant expression, and a knowledge of ancient authors with the traditional methods of study.' He then adds, 'But I have always stopped short of despising any subject' (CWE 71:38). In this work emerge most clearly the two facets of Erasmus's thought that will enrage Luther. Oddly enough, on the day in 1519 when Erasmus finished the apologia he received his first adulatory letter from Luther. But this was all to change over the inherent scepticism of his conjectural method and even more so over Erasmus's divided mind on the role of the Holy Spirit. Against the predominance of such Spirit, Erasmus raises the flag of true knowledge, of the necessary application of available resources in order to comprehend sacred texts adequately. He accepts the description of 'grace' as that 'which gives us some share of the divine nature,' but adds that in the pursuit of human knowledge we should embrace whatever forms of assistance are helpful. 'For the truth of the Gospels is not so closely linked to grace that it can turn away the disciplines that prepare the mind to receive it' (71:65). He then mounts in rapid succession criticisms that he will make later. It is one thing to have sufficient knowledge of the essentials of Christianity – that is adequate for the faith of the common person – but for the person who wishes to become an authority in the interpretation of sacred texts, much learning is required, and that involves abundant philological tools. How are we to distinguish if everyone claims the movement of grace for himself? Even here he reverts, invoking his favourite rhetorical trope, the yes/ but, the so/ yet: this, the reliance of grace, is a rule he would prefer not to criticize. Yet how can we safely rely on this personal conviction of 'grace' when such figures as Ambrose and Augustine wander from the Gospel truth (71:65)? On these two points, the advocacy of conjecture sliding into mere talking issues and the sufficiency of grace to insure the accuracy of biblical interpretation, the letter

'Apologia' shows the way to the dispute with Luther. Erasmus's 'unclearness' does not arise from any obscurity in thought or language but rather from his balancing act in satisfying various internal and external pressures.

Erasmus in the debate is on even less sure footing, because he is aware that he himself is lacking in the Holy Spirit left by Christ. He loves Christ, he exhorts the people to follow the model of Christ, he feels ardour and love can impel the eloquence of one's writing, but the true spirit of Christ to whom one must abandon himself has not possessed his life. His practical-minded critical intelligence seems unable to open itself to a life lived according to the vision of the spirit, lived at the level of intense whole-heartedness and self-sacrifice. Thus his well-reasoned objections to Luther's appropriation of the spirit must be read against his own misgivings. This is not hypocrisy but rather honest self-analysis, if not expiation.

The dualistic confrontation with Luther had exercised a perverse effect. In fact the closer Erasmus gets to Luther the more he falters over the Holy Spirit. The presence of Luther's conviction confronted him with a personal lack. And this lack is most poignantly expressed in his long letter to Marcus Laurinus of early 1523. It is a passage that shows Erasmus's full eloquence, an eloquence that propels one forward (therefore I quote it again in full):

> Anyone who cannot love Erasmus as a Christian, though a feeble one, must adopt towards him what attitude he pleases; I for my part cannot be different from what I really am. If Christ has given anyone a grander measure of the gifts of the Spirit, and he has the self-confidence, let him use them for Christ's glory. I feel happier meanwhile in following a humbler but a safer course. I cannot fail to abominate discord. I cannot fail to love peace and concord. I see the great obscurity there is even in the affairs of men; I see how much easier it is to rouse uproar than to pacify it, and I have learned how many are the tricks Satan can play. I would not dare trust my own spirit in everything; far less would I be able to give a reliable opinion on the spirit of other men. I could wish to see all men make a concerted effort to secure the victory of Christ and the establishment among all men of concord in the gospel, so that disorder might be ruled out in favour of sound reasoning, and measures might be taken to promote on the one side the authority of the priesthood and on the other the freedom of the people, whom

the Lord Jesus wished to be free. Anyone embarked on this course can rely on me to the utmost of my power. But those who prefer to cause universal confusion will not have me, at any rate, as a leader or a colleague. They put forward as their excuse the working of the Spirit. Let them dance then among the prophets – and good luck to them – if they have been inspired by the Spirit of the Lord. That spirit of theirs has not yet seized on me; and when it does, they may well say, 'Is Saul also himself among the prophets?' (CWE 9:400–1)

This long paragraph conveys the essence of Erasmus in all its varied strands and all its varied complexity – its moving in and out, to and fro, from a recognition of his own character, determinism, to his quest for peace and disavowal of any approach of Spirit, to his appreciation of the darkened meanings in human affairs, let alone the divine, to his suspicion of his own claims on truth and the consequence for the claims of others, to his envy of those who claim the Spirit, and to his own not quite vanquished thought that his revilers might still yet see him like Saul become proverbial among the prophets. The 'non dum' (the 'not yet' reservation) reveals that he has not quite given up on himself. Rarely is there a passage of such full self-revelation and modest self-defence, such truth-telling, as Augustijn says about the similar passage, where Erasmus, still filled with self doubt, fears that he will resort to Peter's denial.

Erasmus was the voice of a Christian scepticism that, after all the intellectual transformations and qualifications, still came out in support of the *status quo ante*. Luther detected this, denying any effectual practice, at least those that he could agree with, as emanating from Erasmus's thoughts. He pounces on one offending passage, in which Erasmus may have been saying more than he intended.

And I take so little pleasure in assertion that I would gladly seek refuge in scepticism whenever this is allowed by the inviolable authority of Holy Scripture and the Church's decrees; to these decrees I willingly submit my judgment in all things, whether I fully understand what the Church commands or not. (CWE 76:7)

Luther can barely contain his outrage, calling Erasmus by his favourite epithet, 'Proteus,' as one who writes of the inviolable authority of scripture and the hallowed decrees of the church, while at the same time maintaining that if left to his own devices, he would be a sceptic. Several paragraphs later, Luther intones, 'The Holy Spirit is no Sceptic' (LE 109). One does not know where to pin Erasmus down, and his words are neither here nor there, as Luther judges in his vilification of Erasmus throughout *Table Talk* and in an open letter of 1534. But one thing Luther does know, such words undermine the belief in Christian liberty, the concept that had formerly forged their putative alliance. 'What new religion, what new humility is this that you would deprive us by your own example of the powers of judging the decrees of men, and subject us in uncritical fashion to men? Where does the Scripture of God impose this on us' (LE 108)?

Luther then summarizes Erasmus's thought in a way that reaches far into the future. For Erasmus, Christian truth is, according to Luther, 'no better than philosophical and human opinions, about which it is stupid to wrangle and contend since nothing comes of it but strife and the disturbance of outward peace. Things that are above us, you say, are no concern of ours. So with a view to ending our conflicts you come forward as a mediator, calling a halt to both sides, and trying to persuade us that we are flourishing our swords about things that are stupid and useless' (LE 109). Luther is in effect calling Erasmus a sceptic, which in the lexicon of early sixteenth-century theology is equivalent to calling him an atheist. The next paragraph ominously seems to imply as much (with the special insight that one party to the dualism has into the other, and with the cryptophasia that typifies the communication of twins): 'That is what your words seem to mean, and I think you understand, my dear Erasmus, what I am driving at' (LE 109). What is Luther driving at but the undeclared assertion that Erasmus so values the human over the divine that his allegiance to the divine is suspect, that he is not a true believer.

Erasmus was no *Voltairien*, but that does not mean that aspects of Erasmus's thought would not find their welcomed place and allotted home in the thought of the Enlightenment. We can almost hear Voltaire, with Gibbon and later others, exclaim: Surely a second reformation is at hand. We readily accept – almost to the point of triteness – that all historical adaptations require transformations, that reading in the grand sense of taking over is a two-way street, and that in a take-over much has been jettisoned: companies are sold. Prototypically, the cultural *traduttore* is a *traditore*, and all intellectual migrations undergo their own refractions. All of this rings true until we contemplate Luther's insight into the ramifications of Erasmus's thought. There is hardly a better description of the full theological and practical underpinnings of the Enlightenment. Luther, with the gifted insight of a coconspirator in a grand dualism, would not have been surprised at the characterization of Erasmus introduced by the upholders of a second Reformation. He would have asserted that it was there all the while, simply awaiting detection. He did not need the subterranean streams by which Erasmus resurfaced, nor the hindsight of Dilthey or Huizinga or many others who saw in Erasmus the predecessor of the Enlightenment. Not that Luther foresaw or predicted the Enlightenment; but from his own time and station, from his own estimate of Erasmus's character, he understood the way Erasmus would travel, because he understood the man, his citophilia, his moderating positions, his reliance on reason as the head of the virtues in his hierarchy of values, his need for consensus, his commitment to peace and unity, and above all his scepticism. Erasmus would have had no true role in the Acts of the Apostles. With unerring accuracy, which tells us something about the abnormal powers of a true dualism, Luther had found out his man, had detected him before his time. The advocates of a second Reformation did not have to remove Erasmus's *philosophia Christi*, because, as Luther sensed, that was already diluted, lacking in emotive power. Luther did not doubt the sincerity of Erasmus's belief, rather the depth of his religious conviction. Erasmus did not show the willingness to abandon all. And to Erasmus's great credit he acknowledged and regretted the same want in himself.

Some of Voltaire's later *contes* and *romans* have been relegated to the inferior status of pamphleteering, but from *La Princesse de Babylone* and in the *Histoire des voyages de Jenni* valuable arguments have been rescued. Similarly in the discounted pamphlets, important accounts are rendered. The virtues of Voltaire shine in these passages with all their foresight and historical judgment, but when it comes to his obsession with Rousseau these virtues are somewhat tarnished. In the *Lettres sur la Nouvelle Heloïse*, in the *Lettre au Docteur Pansophe*, and in his *Sentiment des Citoyens*, Voltaire would not let up in his unrelenting attacks, denying authorship but rarely succeeding in concealing his hand. They at times show him at his satirical best and his personal worst and in

Sentiment des Citoyens, they have the unintended consequence of provoking Rousseau one last time into the inspired composition of his masterpiece, *The Confessions*.

The *Lettres sur la Nouvelle Héloïse*, allegedly written by the Marquis de Ximenes, were so obviously written by Voltaire himself that even Ximenes, a willing ally and faithful accomplice, later admitted to only having had his hand in a small portion of the first letter. Because of their nit-picking over small points of language, their evident class prejudice and xenophobia, the letters backfired, even drawing the disapproval of Voltaire's friends, d'Alembert among them.

The *Lettre au Docteur Pansophe* (who is directly addressed throughout as Jean-Jacques; *Mélanges* 831) is a much different matter and should be much better known. It is a masterpiece of polemical satire, and makes clear that despite his public disclaimers, Voltaire seems to have read every word of Rousseau – the major works, the prefaces, the letters, thus fulfilling the attentiveness required of a true dualism. In fact, even his marginal commentaries are themselves scholarly troves. The *Lettre* is a survey of Rousseau's works to date, and Voltaire's criticisms remain as they were from the beginning, but are given a new point and sharpness. Better than any other document it helps us to understand the principles that Rousseau seems to have violated and the reasons for Voltaire's persistent acerbity toward his one-time subservient ally. For one, Voltaire is out of patience with Rousseau's defence of ignorance, the strain he sees permeating his works from the first *Discours* onward. Voltaire regards Rousseau as a traitor to all that a modernizing, enlightened Europe has come to represent, all the combined accomplishments since the Renaissance (which was the starting point for Rousseau's sense of the moral decline that accompanies the advancement of the arts). If Rousseau wishes to return to the eleventh century he would be signing his own death warrant. Voltaire stands out as a clear defender of the development of modern culture: 'Nous ne sommes plus esclaves de ces tyrans spirituels et temporels qui désolaient toute l'Europe; la vie est plus douce, les coeurs plus humaines et les États plus tranquilles' (We are no longer slaves of the spiritual and earthly tyrants who used to desolate all of Europe; life is sweeter, sentiments are more humane and the [countries] more tranquil; (*Pansophe* 833). It would take a man of Voltaire's certitude, of his confidence in his own critical judgment, of indeed confidence of where and when he is standing to make so forthright a defence of the values of the culture of his day.

Rousseau in attacking the *philosophes* is biting the hand that feeds him: 'C'est à la philosophie que vous devez votre salut et vous l'assassinez' (You owe your whole well-being to philosophy and yet you assassinate it; (*Pansophe* 833). But there is more than this in Voltaire's exasperation with Rousseau. Behind this betrayal of the intellectual brotherhood, of the common enterprise of the 'république littéraire,' there are two other more fundamental complaints that in their expression unite Voltaire and Erasmus. The first is the charge of singularity. Just as Luther had to withstand the question, Who are you to go against the combined wisdom of the ages? so Rousseau had to endure the charge of being out of step, of breaking ranks, and of flying in the face of the proprieties of dress and behaviour and thought. Thus Voltaire instructs Rousseau that were he a better person, '[Il] pourrait cependant apprendre que le vrai mérite ne consiste pas à être singulier, mais à être raisonnable' ([He] would know that true merit consists not in being singular, but in being reasonable; 836). The charge also measures the distance travelled from the time of Erasmus to that of Voltaire: Erasmus was defending the wisdom of the ages embodied in the structures and teachings of the church; for Voltaire, Rousseau's need for singularity is a violation of the social code of reasonableness, the trademark of the *honnête homme*.

But Rousseau is listening to a different music. His singularity is the consequence of heeding the promptings of the Spirit, of the *'sentiment intérieur,' 'la voix intérieure.'* If Luther's 'singularity' represents spiritual aloneness, Rousseau's singularity is based upon solitude, removal from the importunities of friends and seclusion from city life. This internal dictation does not come unawares but is rather the end product of long thought and deliberation. It represents no dark night of the soul, but rather in the midst of doubt a resurgence of positive sentiment that helps to open the way to beliefs and practices. In the midst of rational debate it seems to settle the score. Despite its role in rational deliberations, it still represents a spiritual divide that separates the two, separating the character of good sense and practical wisdom, who comprehends the complexities of his historical conditioning, from the person who follows some inner compulsion, some voice of mysterious yet palpable design. Where Erasmus could only feel misgivings that he was 'not yet' endowed with the light of the Spirit and did not find possible martyrdom for Luther's cause to be truly suitable to his nature, Voltaire with his typical pointed satire undoes the pretensions of such 'illumination.' Voltaire allies Rousseau with the English Quakers and evangelists, who are equally obedient servants 'à cette voix divine, qui parle si haut dans les coeurs des illuminés, et que personne n'entend' (to this divine voice which speaks so loudly in the hearts of the illuminated and that no one else seems to hear; 837). In an age of Faith the more tender-hearted Erasmus falters in the absence of the Spirit; in an age of Thought, Voltaire can securely lampoon this divine voice as inaudible to most sensible people. When Rousseau makes his famous distinctions between Christ and Socrates, defending the divinity of the former, referring to Jesus in his life and death as a god, but to Socrates as a mere wise man, Voltaire in one of his furious marginalia can inscribe, 'What do you know of the life and death of gods?' (Gouhier 188, modified). Remarkably enough, both Erasmus and Voltaire define themselves by this same opposition to 'singularity of belief' and their varied inabilities to share in the promptings of the Holy Spirit.

But there is one other persistent claim that separates the radical Protestantism of Luther and Rousseau from the more ameliorative continuities and sense of belonging that Erasmus and Voltaire share. Just as Luther can claim that in their existential reality everyone is responsible for his own faith and salvation, outside of history, outside the lessons of the saints, and that the moment of recovery occurs to the individual in the separateness of his spiritual functioning, so Rousseau adheres to what Cassirer has called the central principle of protestantism: 'nul n'est exempt du premier devoir de l'homme, nul n'a droit de se fier au jugement d'autrui' (no one is exempt from the first duty of man; no one has the right to rely on the judgment of others; OC IV.623; Bloom 306). Erasmus had a need to belong; Voltaire had an ineradicable sense of belonging; each was a prominent member of the 'literary republic' and while critical still felt history and its continuities and its attainments were their domain. Both Luther and Rousseau found such dependencies to be inadequate. They each introduced a Spirit, in Luther's case a terrible and demanding spirit, into the conditions of life. But why should they be cast as the rival powers to Voltaire and Erasmus, who after all were not slugs, lie-abeds, average hedonistic pursuers of physical delight, but rather hard working, critically minded and innovative intellectuals? But that is precisely it. They were not dullards but exponents of civilization at its highest level of attainment, and ones with profoundly different spiritual motives from their cross rivals. Only at the heights of a culture do such contests take place, the best against the best, because each with his opposing claims on the nature of humanity and the shape of the future, offers the most compelling and competitive alternatives. And this is why these two earlier dualisms persist until our own day. Oddly enough, the logic and the even linguistic tenor of the debate undergo little change. What we can know is that the quarrel with the philosophy or mentality of the Enlightenment both preceded the Enlightenment and continued long after it. The heirs of Erasmus and Voltaire continued to be heard eloquently (and with greater supporting arguments from the heavy costs of war and history) throughout the twentieth century. This is evidence enough that in establishing these rival pairs we have hit upon a fundamental tension, if not chasm in the modern Western psyche. All that is required is that we make use of the powers of recognition.

Epilogue: Recurrence and Recognition[1]

ꙮ

Little did I realize when I set out to restore the dimmed reputations of Erasmus and Voltaire that by its own natural pressures such a necessary act of remediation would become the second complementary volume of a continuing discourse. In the epilogue to *Dualisms,* aware that dualistic presentations had been receiving considerable intellectual attention, with new volumes on the subject appearing virtually on a monthly basis and continuing to do so, I did not wish to preclude such further discussion. In fact, by following the tangled fates and fortunes, even the historical functions of Erasmus and Voltaire, I have added to it in unanticipated ways. With all their differences intact and observed, they still remain kindred spirits when their career episodes are studied, and when the complexities of their works are examined. Even their participation in the major dualism of their day is given sharper points of contrast.

Thus where I closed one chapter, here I open another, bringing Erasmus and Voltaire down through the centuries and entering them into the perilous confines of European thought in the third and fourth decades of the twentieth century (and even beyond). The kernel of this book, the core that the convergences of Erasmus and Voltaire expose is that this is not a story of two stations, but rather of three. Given the historical connections of Erasmus and Voltaire it can be argued, as Martin Luther so insightfully intuited, that there was an 'enlightenment' before The Enlightenment. The similarities between the two personages and between the strivings of the epochs, mutatis mutandis, are clear. But so do the enmities and the accusations persist. And both hold true – the similarities within one alignment and their differences from the other line – even down to the third station, that of the twentieth century. Where one could expect the phrasing and issues to be different, in some cases they differ not at all. Tony Judt has aptly remarked on the tendency to regard the Western liberal democracies as 'shallow' (89);' that and similarly belittling epithets Erasmus and Voltaire had to endure both from contemporaries and in their reputations alike. James Joyce, employing the same method of recurrence and recognition, borrowed from Giambattista Vico's *Nuova Scienza,* called it the 'sehm asnuh.' The same as new, the same as now, the same to you – such manifold meanings accumulate in *Finnegans Wake,* that multilayered book of cultural globalization. But one central theme may be verified and that is Joyce's own preoccupation with dualities: 'Two bredder as doffered as nors in soun … No peace at all' (620). Two brothers as different as north and south, but also as norsemen in the sun – such readings only begin to address the proliferating meanings of Joyce's last unsurpassed work of genius. But what is clear from this ultramodernist text is that a revitalized Erasmus and Voltaire may acquire a new pertinence in the dire cultural wars of the twentieth century, particularly when their renewed arguments land us smack in the middle of the crisis of German intellectual thought – ('la tragédie de l'intelligence'; Camus, quoted in *Dualisms* 346). This is underscored when the values they represent, the conflicts in which they were engaged, recur and may be recognized in yet another dualism, that of Ernst Cassirer and Martin Heidegger in their debates at Davos in 1929.

Ernst Cassirer deserves to loom large in the argument of this book. In his *The Question of Jean-Jacques Rousseau,* he brings into sharply drawn contention the ameliorist eudaemonism of the *philosophes* and the daemonic quality of Rousseau, the former relying on an ethic of accommodation and an inclusive rhetoric,the latter holding to an either/or ethical imperative and a habit of challenging accusation (*Dualisms* 6–9). Moreover, this present volume shares many purposes with Cassirer's *The Philosophy of the Enlightenment* (the German original published – and the timing is crucial – in 1932).[2] In my introduction I declared one of my intents was to rescue Erasmus and Voltaire from the time-worn epithets suggesting lack of depth (10). Similarly, Cassirer, in his large, synoptic study, worked to preserve the Enlightenment from the accusation of 'shallowness.' 'A major objective of this study would be achieved if it succeeded in silencing that slogan [Rede]' (xi). Cassirer credits the reliance upon Thought among the thinkers of the Enlightenment, but he does not leave it as Thought for its own sake but rather as being committed to 'the task of shaping life itself' (viii). By purposeful action the aims of the advocates of Enlightenment were to bring culture to the aid of civilization. He thus confirms in advance that notable comparison made by Sartre of the joint interventions in public life of the reformers of the sixteenth century and the *philosophes* (see above, page 6). Thus Erasmus and Voltaire can join hands across the centuries as working to achieve a second Reformation. In this new alliance with humanism, Protestantism has now become in the minds of many the religion of freedom. The classic confrontation of Erasmus and Luther was played out again, but this time Erasmus was victorious (160).

Defending the Enlightenment (and by inclusion our two thinkers as well) from charges of 'shallowness' also means validating some basic tenets of the Enlightenment. Cassirer writes, 'The age which venerated reason and knowledge ("Wissenschaft") as "man's highest faculty" cannot and must not be lost even [also] for us' (xi). The quoted phrase within the quotation derives from Goethe and is an indication that the challenge that Goethe already faced is 'auch' ('also,' not 'even') a recurrent challenge for Cassirer. Given the darkening nature of German thought in the interwar years this was a call of renewed relevancy – the dispute might be called the Quarrel over the Enlightenment, its resources, and its implications. Such arguments take us back to the very first questions that prompted this study, why Erasmus and Voltaire, and why now? In actuality they are not two but the same question: to answer the one is to answer the other. Their importance emerges from their being parties of interest in the third station of the post-Enlightenment development. The causes that Cassirer invokes and the modes of thought that in their combined fullness Erasmus and Voltaire represent were under attack in the twentieth century and among their major defenders is Cassirer himself. Not only did he retrieve the revalued goals of the Enlightenment, he himself entered into the great debate of the time as to their merits. His very methodology, searching out the structures of thought and their unifying principles, makes him a great defender of culture and of civilization. As he saw the recurrence of the Luther-

Erasmus dispute in the eighteenth century, so we can witness the recurrence of that debate in the twentieth century and today. Erasmus and Voltaire continue to live, continue to matter, because the representative fullness of their modes of thought is involved in the major intellectual struggles of our time. They espoused the same causes as did Cassirer: Erasmus knew and feared that the attacks against Luther were subversively directed against him and his defences of the humanities and *bonae literae*, and among Voltaire's many objections to Rousseau one persists: the fear that as a renegade he is undermining the work of the *philosophes*, biting the very hand that fed his fame in the commonwealth of letters. For all three, joining Cassirer with the continuing presence of Erasmus and Voltaire, the essential argument is that culture and civilization must not be estranged. Thus, despite the centuries of separation, the convergent powers of Erasmus and Voltaire show an eminent adaptability in the midst of recurrence. We have seen and heard of these wars before. As Cassirer's presence in the debate and as the fuller import of his many works clearly indicate, his vindications of the values of the Enlightenment were acts of self-defence and self-restoration. It was himself that he was defending in the midst of the crisis of his time.

The remarkable exchange between Cassirer and Martin Heidegger was the culminating event of three weeks of philosophical conferences extending from 17 March to 6 April 1929.[3] Much anticipated it was both monumental and mesmerizing. It may be likened to the exchanges between Turgenev and Dostoevsky at the Pushkin festivities in 1880 – while there were other speakers, all eyes were centred on the two, Turgenev and Dostoevsky, who represented such opposing poles of thought and modes of being (*Dualisms* 291–3). In the same way Cassirer and Heidegger, these two antitypes in thought and personality, show the recurrence of the arguments that *Dualisms* presented. They further summarize so much of what divided Erasmus and Luther and Voltaire and Rousseau. The baggage of philosophical language may have shifted but the carousel of argument remains the same. Their exchange may have constituted a 'strange' dialogue but it was a superb dualism, the opposing qualities of each admirably described by Pierre Aubenque: 'il y a de l'irenisme chez l'un, une fureur de néophyte et de l'iconoclaste chez l'autre. D'un coté, un personage qu'un témoin décrit comme "olympien," héritier d'une culture cosmopolite qu'il doit à ses origines citadines et bourgeoises, habitué au commerce des hommes…; de l'autre, le provincial jeune encore mais déjà célèbre, mais timide, entêté et tendu…' (in the one, an irenic quality, in the other the fury of the neophyte and iconoclast. On the one side, a person whom a witness described as 'Olympian,' the heir of a cosmopolitan culture which is owing to his bourgeois origins, and thus accustomed to the interchanges with people … on the other, the proviincial, young yet already celebrated, but still shy, stubborn and tense …). The one harkens back to the philosophy of the Enlightenment ('se réclame de la tradition européenne de la philosophie des lumières'); the other, the herald of a new beginning in philosophy, does not hesitate to proclaim the 'destruction de ce qui a été jusqu'ici les fondements de la métaphysique occidentale (l'Esprit, le Logos, la Raison)' (the destruction of what had up to then been regarded as the basis of Western metaphysics – Spirit Logic, Reason). On the one side, the representative of culture, organized around the central principle of the subject; on the other, an extreme radicalism which only sees 'laziness' in the consumption of the objects of culture and which dares to throw humankind back into the hardness of its 'fate.' Writing in 1972 Aubenque is able to indicate the future violence anticipated in Heidegger's language and position, violence that was cultural, hermeneutical, and unfortunately political.[4] More than a forerunner, he was a founder, while Cassirer was one of the greatest, but unfortunately the last of the representatives of bourgeois humanism, of culture and form itself (Aubenque 14–16).

   While the debate was restrained by politeness of exchange, the differences in their two positions stand out none the less. In fact, as frequently occurs, they are even more pronounced, given greater distilled clarity by virtue of the pressures of public debate. Their debate has extensive reach, stretching backward and moving forward into the future. Rüdiger Safranski in his exemplary philosophical biography of Heidegger reminds the reader of the shadowy but close presence of Thomas Mann's synoptic novel, *The Magic Mountain* (it appeared in 1924) standing behind the debate between Cassirer and Heidegger. On a more personal level, in 1981 I attended a debate in Florence between Eugenio Garin, one of our premier students of Italian humanism, and a young philosophy professor. Garin spoke of the importance of history and of cultural continuity, while the younger man referred to empty spaces in Nature and of ruptures in history, After the event I had occasion to mention to Garin that I had attended that debate before – in the pages of *The Magic Mountain*, where Settembrini, the voice of Italian and Renaissance humanism, of the Enlightenment, and of the progressive tendencies of Western civilization. engages the radical reactionary Naphta. Dualisms possess such powers of transfer.

In their different philosophies, Cassirer and Heidegger face in opposite directions, yet eye to eye, point to point. 'Cassirer was regarded as a great representative of a humanist tradition and a universally attuned cultural idealism ... This grand seigneur of political humanism had been invited ... to be the opponent of Martin Heidegger, who stood for what was new and revolutionary' (Safranski 184). While what was 'new and revolutionary' is a statement that needs to be parsed, nevertheless the opposition of two such antitypes in thought and personality and mannerisms is manifest. If like his prototypes, Erasmus and Voltaire, Cassirer was a lowlander, Heidegger was a mountaineer both figuratively and literally. He courted the precarious. He sought out true being, better found in the isolation of the mountains than in the domesticated thought of the quotidian flatlands. Even in their respective literary afterlives, the pattern of dualisms holds true: like his own predecessors, Cassirer's cultural presence is now met unfortunately by the unaccommodating question, 'Who reads Cassirer?' while Heidegger has appealed to a multitude of interpreters, disciples, and followers.

Their argument extending outward and backward was larger then themselves. At the time of their debate the shaky Weimar Republic was nearing its end, besieged by the Left and the Right (the elections of 1930 gave Hitler's National party a total of 107 seats – a dramatic surge). The intellectual class, with notable exceptions like Karl Jaspers, lent little support to the venture in democratic politics that, while enjoying some good moments, may have been unfairly disabled and doomed from the start. Paraphrasing Dante, it had come before Germany was ready (*Paradiso* XXX, 133–8). While hardrock economic troubles and political ambitions certainly predominated, the intellectual climate did not help. The very conditions of the times marked a rupture between culture and civilization, those two formations that while separable are better enjoyed together. Civilization has been regarded as representing an advancement in social culture; it depends upon amenities, accessibility, and convenience; it relies upon the civil converse of peoples and attention to those things that constitute the well-being of a community and that contribute to the right ordering of a polity. But German intellectual life in the late 1920s manifested a divorce between culture and civilization, in essence, a clash between consciousness and civics, between the strenuously intricate and abstruse efforts of the intellect in its solitude and private life and an opposing need for active public participation in the equivalent of town meetings. These latter involvements were regarded as democratic banalities in contrast with the attainments of culture. Webster's International Dictionary inserts a coy postscriptum in regard to culture: 'The term is occasionally abused by a somewhat arrogant and exclusive restriction of its meaning.' The debate between Cassirer and Heidegger, while drawn along these lines, engaged an even narrower focus. It is culture itself that is on the spit. Each exponent has his ancestors and progeny. Like Luther and Rousseau before him and Sartre after him, Heidegger can find no salvation in culture but only in the attentive aloneness of the individual mind. For Luther the benefits of the mass cannot be passed on to another; Cassirer correctly saw into the principles of Rousseau's essential Protestantism. Sartre himself in *Les mots* finally reaches the conclusion that culture saves nothing: 'La culture ne sauve rien, ni personne; elle ne justifie pas' (*Dualisms* 399). The family resemblances, the similar imprints of voice are unmistakable, and include Heidegger's quest for authenticity in relation to temporality and death: no one can exist for you and no one can face up to the inner 'ownness' of your own death except yourself. *Solus ipse.*

Two Latin phrases may be used to summarize the directions of the debate: the terminus a quo, or the beginning from which, and the terminus ad quem, or the end toward which. They are used more provocatively by Heidegger and Cassirer, meaning in Heidegger's phrasing, the prior starting point to which thinking must return – that before which, and in Cassirer's thought, the goal of cultural attainment toward which finitude strives, and that is symbolic form. In belief and person Cassirer represented the smiling benignities of culture and cultivation. His entire intellectual life was spent in defence of culture in its unifying aspect, and in the advancement of which symbolic understanding is its highest attainment. His intervention in the debate summarizes not only the fundamental *Philosophy of Symbolic Forms* and the smaller works that went into its making, it also brings together the volumes of historical understanding at which he truly excels, *The Individual and the Cosmos in Renaissance Philosophy* (1927) and *The Philosophy of the Enlightenment* (1932). His arguments also anticipate their condensed formulations in *An Essay on Man*, whose subtitle situates us better: *An Introduction to the Philosophy of Human Culture*. His quest as always was the philosophical unity of culture, and thus made of him a natural antitype to Heidegger.

Cassirer argues in the debate that the objective nature of culture is to be found in its form. By this he means the advancement of thought beyond the material and relational toward the symbolic, from numbers to geometry, from political realism to imagined Utopias, from the stasis of myth and ritual in primitive religions to freedom, and in art toward the awareness of the unifying coherence in its very informing premises, its 'design.' There is that in the development of human culture which tends toward a perceptible unification of all disciplines; the goal of philosophy is to make this unity clear. Language, Cassirer's earliest interest, is the natural starting point, as well as the defining point of his difference with Heidegger. It represents the basic test of providing for a unity in the multitude of phenomena. Despite this diffusion of tongues, both generically and individually, 'we understand ourselves through the medium of language. Hence there is something like *the* language. And hence there is something like a unity which is higher than the infinitude of the various ways of speaking. Therein lies what is for me the decisive point. And it is for that reason that I start from the objectivity of the symbolic form, because here the inconceivable has been done. Language is the clearest example. We assert here that we tread on common ground ... This is what I would like to call the world of the objective spirit. From Dasein [consciousness of individual being] is spun the thread, which through the medium of such an objective spirit, again ties us together with another Dasein. And I believe there is no other way from Dasein to Dasein than through this world of forms' (*Kant*, Appendix 4, 205). Knowledge itself is an example of this paradigm, namely 'that an objective statement can be formulated about a matter and that it has the character of necessity which no longer takes notice of the subjectivity of the individual' (ibid). Despite the differences of time and language one can well imagine both Erasmus and Voltaire aligned by means of yet another convergence with this sophisticated defence of culture, one that provides a common ground for mutual comprehension.

The argument is made even more explicit in *An Essay on Man* : 'If the term "humanity" means anything at all, it means that in spite of all the various differences and oppositions existing among its various forms, these are, nevertheless, all working toward a common end' (96). Modern humanistic culture combined with philosophy finds one of its greatest paladins in the work and person of Ernst Cassirer, but this also means that he had to undergo the same diminishment and neglect, particularly when contrasted with the more pressing and challenging personal philosophy of Heidegger. Where the 'Olympian' Cassirer would seek to rescue humanism from the merely subjective, the multitude of variants coming together in the human capacity to evolve objective forms, Heidegger's so-called 'antihumanism' would seek to submerge the objective in the deepest workings of the self.

Heidegger holds to the terminus a quo, that behind which and from which. He argues that behind the allure of humanism and spirit lie the basic encounters of humankind with anxiety (*Angst*), with thrownness (*Geworfenheit*), with care (*Sorge*), with nothingness, with temporality, and with death. All these issues emerge in the debate with Cassirer. It is not my purpose to enter into the full complexities of Heideggerian thought, but rather to condense and to centralize and to indicate its electric charge (the reason why the best bookstore on the Westside of Los Angeles, has on its shelves some fifteen separate titles by and about Heidegger and not one concerning or by Cassirer). Such thought abominates the sublimations and the ideal pretensions of art and culture.

Being and Time is revolutionary because it in part invents a language for the new dispositions of philosophy. It holds to this language with a technical and systematic consistency in order to explain matters that had long been ignored by philosophy. For this reason but not this solely, it catches on and it stays on. There is urgency and challenge in Heidegger's prose, confronting his reader with the need to avoid the tranquillizing effect of the everyday. The important matter is that he himself writes with a confidence of saying something new in a way that was new. He reminds us – in *Kant*, Appendix 3 (192) – that his philosophy, the brink of which Kant approached before turning away, means, as Heidegger thought, the destruction of the former foundation of Western metaphysics. His work demands a 'radical, renewed unveiling of the grounds for the possibility of metaphysics as a natural disposition of human behavior ... which must pose the question concerning the essence of human beings in a way which is prior to all philosophical anthropology and cultural philosophy' (ibid.) He renders meaningless the traditional divisions between realism and idealism, between scepticism and truth, subject and object. Yet he had a profound knowledge of the dimensions of the circle he was voiding (*Kant*, Appendix 6). One can see why in the debate with Cassirer Heidegger barely conceals his impatience. 'Every page in this book [*Being and Time*] was written solely with a view to the fact that since antiquity the problem of Being was interpreted on the basis of time in a wholly incomprehensible sense' (198). The same with death (199), anxiety, nothing. If we ignore the presence of these matters as existing prior to the formation of culture (*a quo* not *ad quem*) 'then it is an absolute impossibility to say something about what is under discussion here. All these questions are inadequate with respect to my central problem' (199–200). The final one of three questions he poses to Cassirer formulates not only the different directions of their thoughts but also their different standpoints and origins.' To what extent does philosophy have as its task to be allowed to become free from anxiety? Or does it have as its task to surrender man, even radically, to anxiety' (200)? Not only in concept but in impulse Heidegger's argument in debate resumes the dimensions of his book *Being and Time*. One must enter into the abyss; there is a difference between knowing and being. And with this statement we are removed historically back to another debate, that of Luther with Erasmus, and the recognitions that recurrences nourish.

Anxiety (*Angst*) before existence has several sources and roots. Anxiety arises before humankind's fundamental position of thrownness, of being accidental, of being nothing and nowhere. Thus it searches for solace in the 'they' (in German, 'Man' or the generalized 'one'), the easy accommodations of public existence which have a tranquillizing effect. But even in this resort anxiety occurs because the Dasein is always 'ahead of itself' in thinking of other possibilities, in breaking out of the frame it has itself established. Thus the comfort is not comforting, because the Dasein suspects that it has made an inauthentic choice. But even when not prey to the public consolations, the Dasein feels Angst, because that is natural to its position, of not being there, of feeling that its thoughts are wanting, insufficient, as being a hollow echo. We utter statements whose veracity or sincerity of belief in almost the same breath we doubt or abjure. Heidegger disclaims any consistency of 'self,' yet there is an 'I,' or subject, who experiences this nullification and who is thus thrust into the position of being a truth-seeker. Angst is thus an attribute of the *solus ipse*, the individualized thing itself, but without a selfhood. We cannot help but think what we are thinking. Angst is an indication of Dasein's own responsibility of stewardship for its own being. And it alone. Angst is a basic, a priori, constituent of existence itself. Its presence is part of the constitution of Dasein. Thus it must be encountered if the original questions of metaphysics are even to be posed.

Just as there is an individualizing 'ownness' in Angst, so death enters Dasein as its 'ownmost non-relational possibility of being not-to-be-bypassed' (*Being and Time* 235). Everydayness tries to disguise death by making it an objective event that one reads about, not as something belonging to Dasein itself. It cannot be covered over. 'The they does not permit the courage to have anxiety about death' (ibid.). As with Angst, so death falls prey to tranquillization and estrangement (funeral eulogies 'celebrate' life). Rather than an 'eminent imminence' death is evaded. But even such attempts of flight into inauthenticity reveal death as a not-to-be-bypassed presence, as the end of time. The upshot of the presence of death is to introduce a new resoluteness into Dasein, a sense of caring that tempers existence. Make no mistake, for Heidegger, and perhaps accounting for his appeal, humankind is subject to a special spiritual calling.

These involvements require a new attitude toward time, not the time of the philosophers which has been spatialized and dissected into separate segments, but rather time as temporality. We exist in time, time is finite. But only through time, or temporality, through Dasein's being toward while being in the present, can any wholeness, or authenticity of being be attained. 'Temporality reveals itself as the meaning of authentic care' (300), or 'the primordial unity of the structure of care lies in temporality' (301). This time is especially our own to encounter. This means that the past is not past as long as the Dasein exists, but instead persists as the 'having been'; the Dasein is the 'I-*am*-as-having-been.' Temporality is a horizontal structure of modes of being, an arena, or more likely the very atmosphere of being, containing the I as having been, the future as being toward, and the present as a thrownness looking toward the future. But if care is a being-toward-death, and death is the not-to-be-bypassed, this future fate is daunting in that it shuts down any potentiality-for-being – there is no open future – and reveals the nullity of Dasein. A time will come when there is no being-there (Dasein) to be there. But this makes possible 'the resolute existentiell understanding of nullity,' which is an understanding of oneself in the finite conditions of temporality. 'Primordial and authentic coming-toward-oneself is the meaning of living in one's ownmost nullity' (303). Resolute care emerges from these absences, or movings out of and movings toward that is human existence. At last, then, at least then, something. One is left with an attitude, that of care, whose one imperative seems to be not to insult, bring hurt to, or destroy the struggling Daseins of other humans.

Karl Jaspers was a confederate and ally of Heidegger from 1920 on. But after 1933, when Heidegger joined the Nazi Party, they no longer met, and after 1936 they no longer corresponded. This estrangement was followed by a reconciliation of sorts – at least in resumed correspondence, but their relationship remained a love *affaire manqué*. Jaspers, perhaps better than any one else, distrusted the implications of Heidegger's renewed post-war tone and style. His same oracular, 'poeticizing' language, apocalyptic, seems to anticipate nothing so much as the advent of another totalitarianism. The one, the more charismatic, believed that thought was being, while the other, Jaspers, believed that thought must have some existential relevancy both to the inner and to practical life (Safranski 386–7). Both he and Hannah Arendt were arrested by the 'unrelatedness' of Heidegger's thought. It is not the object that is estranged but rather the vision of the beholder that fails to involve itself, that literally cannot see itself in a shared humanity with the person seen.[5] One cannot see one's own eye-balls. And concerning language, for Jaspers and Arendt, there should be a concomitant closer rapprochement between philosophizing and ordinary conversation. As Erasmus and Voltaire would agree, language must not make a virtue of the needlessly obscure. Yet Jaspers, like Heidegger, and like many others of this 'lost' generation, was a mountaineer rather than a lowlander. And when from the mountainous heights he looked around for company he found only one person there, his 'polite enemy.' However, the powers they served were incompatible (Safranski 388–9). And if it seems a chance had been missed, yet Jasper's admiration persisted for the darkened and perverse yet searching genius of Martin Heidegger. His powerful presence was confirmed by the fact that Jaspers, as well as Arendt, were always interested in what Heidegger was thinking; he never reciprocated with interest in their thought.

Virtuoso of philosophical discourse, Heidegger was a born master of the technical philosophical trade, and yet in his most important piece after *Being and Time*, his *Letter on Humanism*, we see Heidegger reversing the current of philosophy, sending back the waters as with a magical wand to that from which they came and which existed before logic and metaphysics, before philosophy, back to an ultimate simplicity. Oddly enough Sartre, against whose essay 'Existentialism is a Humanism' this work is directed, underwent a similar turnabout as described in *Les Mots* (*Dualisms* 386–90). It appears that in modern phenomenology there is a need for reversion, some ulterior purpose driving the king to become a commoner, and that the philosophy of existence is pervaded by a nostalgia for what is. 'Let Being: be.' The playing-out of such a determination, the Holy Grail being found in what is ordinary, is movingly transcribed in Heidegger's *Letter on Humanism*, which Hannah Arendt rightly called a *Prachtstück*, an exemplary, a gorgeous piece. Heidegger's scorn for current thinking, for practical technology, for the division of university disciplines, induces a need to go back, to uncover the simplicity of words. Thinking's only reward is thinking, not to be found in praxis or in objectified values. Thus, while joined at the start, he and Sartre travelled in opposite directions. A newly won contentedness in Being must supply for Heidegger the natural centre of existence. But thinking has become fussing about minor verities and semi-truths rather than standing a post of guardianship at the sacred grove of Being, which is only to be found in truth to being. Such a call to truth, which is far from the marketplace of slogans, is Heidegger's dearest dream. Somewhere is a place called Truth, and it is a place, an abode (*Letter on Humanism* 256). It is a place we pine after, yet hovering beyond us it can never be possessed. But we know it is there and to it, for it, and by it, we make our dismissive judgments of lesser things that are objects of willing, adjuncts of praxis, things that do not matter as much as truth. To nihilate such negation – that difficult Nietzschean chore – is to make some progress toward approaching being. Truth cannot be so coerced or cornered; it visits us and tells us in obscure moments that thinking true is the only way to thinking the truth. We are its shepherds; we maintain it by negation even when it sustains us. To say what it is always falls short of being what it is. And yet being is always preferable to knowing. It is its own business, unrelated. Arendt has called Heidegger the last of the Romantics (she adds, 'let us hope'; *Essays* 187n2). And others have subjected him to well-deserved criticism, particularly when in 1933 he defected from his own dream of truth, and succumbed to the allure of power. Entering the cage he provided for the raging beast, but he himself became the provender, the greatest thoroughbred philosopher of his time. This is not a modern novel but rather a medieval romance, or fit for one, with its high mountain peaks and bevy of knights, of solitary adventure, triumph, and separation after desolate betrayal. It is not a quest story but rather one of vigil, whose better and more enduring offering was summarized by Robert Frost, when he wrote in 'Neither Out Far Nor in Deep:'

> The land may vary more;
> But wherever the truth may be –
> The water comes ashore,
> And the people look at the sea.
>
> They cannot look out far.
> They cannot look in deep.
> But when was that ever a bar
> To any watch they keep?

Recognition of the importance of the exchanges at Davos was belated and slow-coming. In part this was because the participants adhered to a strict philosophic discourse. The site itself was secluded, 'far from the madding crowd,' but also far from the enclosed tightness of the metropolitan city, where news travels fast and competition within the narrow intellectual space is closely followed.[6] Nor did it reach out and grasp the popular imagination, in the good sense of encapsulating the basic divisions of a society. All of this was to come later. Thus there are no suggestive monographs but rather publications in which the actual exchange is incorporated as an appendix or as one among other parts of a debate that extended from 1928 to 1931.[7]

There was no sensed immediacy of consequence to the exchange, which means that, while in importance the debate between Cassirer and Heidegger might rival, it can never replace any of the four pairs that constitute the substance of the book, *Dualisms*. For one, it lacked an itinerary of encounter, a longer run of development, the besetting entanglements of thought and belief and personality. This meant, of course, that between Cassirer and Heidegger there were no prior affinities, no joined beliefs that when transgressed by collisions of temperament and events resulted in nuclear explosions. Opposites they were and opposites they remained, and only briefly did their paths cross and then, under pressure of external politics, diverge sharply. Then it became more than a contest of two philosophies, but rather of two modes of reading culture and civilization, two ways of being. Heidegger joined the National Socialist Party and assumed the deeply compromised rectorship of Freiburg University. More foresightful Cassirer made his way to Sweden and from there to the United States of America and to a readily offered and much appreciated home at Yale University, where his last two works, *An Essay on Man* and *The Myth of the State* were written in English. Showing that at times the last may be the best, *The Myth of the State* is Cassirer's masterpiece. Written under the shadow of death, and in the language of his adopted home, it summarizes all of his work with driving succinctness and powerful clarity of formulation. In this work, written he tells us, twelve years after the onset of National Socialism, he confronts Heidegger one last time, and does so in the name of culture and civilization: 'A theory that sees in the *Geworfenheit* of man one of his principal characteristics [has] given up all hopes of an active share in the construction and reconstruction of man's cultural life. Such philosophy renounces its own fundamental theoretical and ethical ideals. It can be used then as a pliable instrument in the hands of its political leaders' (293). Certainly an injustice would be committed if this brilliant thinker were shunted to the side-tracks of our intellectual life.[8]

BETTER PURPOSES

This modern German revival of dualistic typologies possesses the strange power of bringing with it the living presences and arguments of Erasmus and Voltaire. A lineage of convergences may be determined. More an attribute than a coincidence, like Erasmus and Voltaire, and like the other 'writers of consciousness,' whose fuller natures and activities I described in *Dualisms,* Cassirer was an Anglo-(Americano)phile. Like Voltaire he became expert in the language of his adopted home. But more important, throughout his life he promoted the noble tradition upheld by defenders of culture and of civilization. There was however one revealing difference: unlike Erasmus and Voltaire Cassirer never felt the need to recant, nor did circumstances oblige him to. This intriguing difference to one side, despite the changes in language, the shared content of thought was amenable, isotropic. Indeed, Erasmus, given to the saving grace of allegorical interpretation, would have had no difficulty in seeing the value of Cassirer's symbolic forms. And Voltaire would have valued a shared intellectual brotherhood that eschews singularity and that finds in reasonableness the restraints and modulations necessary to civilization. In the new debate with Heidegger the old flames were revived and Erasmus and Voltaire were reactivated and restored. Their story of reclamation carries us to such farther vistas.

In this larger sense, dualisms constitute one of the pillars of knowledge in Western culture, another way of knowing. They may not represent the whole story but they certainly touch on many of its parts. They may be put to work in broadening our approaches to the humanities, in reevaluating venerable and enduring frameworks of historical understanding and philosophical theories, and even in exploring the complex and historically changeful nature of humanism itself. For instance, dualisms show that the humanities must not be limited to subject matter (however valuable the Greek and Latin, or other later classics are) but must be conditioned by attitude and approach. I have already discussed this in my epilogue (*Dualisms* 396–9), but it bears repeating here. The humanities require the living presence of the past, the *presence totale* of the participants with a more affective appropriation of what is studied and taught, and find their ways by the necessary collision of ideas in the contest of the agonists. Stoic disengagement or distancing, as both Erasmus and Voltaire have shown, is not part of their repertoire. What I did not emphasize sufficiently in the previous work was that these new determinations go a long way toward opening up the field of humanistic study to other cultures and other disciplines.

Despite its denial of permanent resolutions or any higher synthesis, such as might be found in a Hegelian dialectic, that is, and despite its prospectus of unending enmity, recurrence should provide no cause for pessimism. Quite the contrary; the related notions of recurrence and its recognitions should be acknowledged as being among the higher forms of our knowing and one of the substantial bases of humanistic learning. To find discord deriving from early affinities, to recognize compatibilities throughout the differences of time and station requires audacious acts of imagination. This is another way of saying that in their eminent transferability dualisms are sources of creativity, engaging such witnesses as Coleridge, with his bold alignments of diverse figures, or Cassirer, who imagines the dispute between Luther and Erasmus as being reborn in the eighteenth century. Such carrying-over is the fruit of profound recognitions, the finding of remarkable similarities even in the midst of real differences. Cross-rivalries themselves, moving from affinities to difference to epochal clash provide clarification and illumination. Their endurance must have some connection with essential divisions within the nature of Nature and human society. At least we know real contact has been made.

It is more remarkable than disappointing that out of our human-animal world, out of the historical world, those worlds of which they are a part but from which they stand apart, there should rise up such commanding and competing proponents of spiritual belief and conduct. Moreover, in their historical alignments, their persevering modes of thought, they represent formidable if opposing modes of apprehending experience. In fact, it is their very recurrence, their transferability, that provides signs of their creative and humanizing potential.

Rather than humanist versus antihumanist what is represented in dualisms are two dimensions of spiritual life. On the one side, those values that Cassirer sought to defend in the culture of the Enlightenment and that the convergent Erasmus and Voltaire fully represent, are composed of the valuable interchanges of community, the notable effects of a faith in historical continuity that is gradual, ameliorist, the crucial role of education in forming human conduct and personality, and the importance of having theoretical language bear some resemblance to the language of daily conversation. That might at least avoid the necessity for derisive satire and even eliminate the prevalence of cloudy thought. From the other side, the so-called daemonic, what cannot be ignored are their roots in a religious calling, an ultimate dissatisfaction that is in need of justification and in search of wholeness of being, even a restoration of what has been lost. Life itself is a beggary that requires transcendence of some sort and even restitution. These are two equally valid understandings of existence. Neither can be regarded as more 'humanistic' than the other; each has its vulnerabilities. Moreover, as dualisms they receive their confirmation, their arguments are elevated, when willy-nilly they tap into the profound schism of the Western psyche whose types they have come to represent. They are much greater than they know: in their dualistic alignment they are taken over by forces which they believe they grasp but which in fact grip and lead them.

To identify truly baleful conflict, we can see that war is the total opposite of dualisms. In dualisms the original affinities are divided into differences that yet produce clarification and illumination. War, on the contrary, begins with differences that yield sameness. In the accelerating reciprocal violence each side comes to resemble the other. There is a deadly mirrored likeness. Clash does not reveal difference, nor the clarifications brought by polemics, but rather the search for justification that relives the back-and-forth past histories of mutually incriminating complaint and offence. Recurrences and transferability bring the past into the future not as a basis for exoneration but rather as a source of recognition and illumination.

Notes

❦

1 Despite the many observations comparing the two, only E.N. Ten-haeff, in his inaugural address, *Erasmus en Voltaire als Exponenten von hun Tijd* (Groningen: Wolters, 1939) and Peter Gay's *jeu d'esprit The Bridge of Criticism*, 1970, give Erasmus and Voltaire special extended treatment. Gay's trialogue deserves some fuller attention. Following the advice laid down by Edward Gibbon (reprinted as an epigraph) *The Bridge of Criticism* brings together Lucian, Erasmus, and Voltaire. As could be expected there are notable clashes of ideas. Lucian at times speaks as a Christian, Erasmus is always conventionally so, except at times when he faults Voltaire's lack of imagination when compared with Michelangelo, Raphael, and others, or with the Romantics (each of whom Erasmus either did or would have ignored), and Voltaire always speaks as a liberal of the twentieth century. But the ideal behind the volume is laudable: 'I wrote these dialogues to serve two distinct but related purposes: to show the continuing vitality of the Enlightenment and to rescue it from persistent misreading' (155).

2 In his still reverberating essay, 'Religion, the Reformation and Social Change,' Trevor-Roper makes the same point. Three hundred years of European history, 1500–1800, begins with the Renaissance and ends with the Enlightenment, 'and these two processes are in many ways continuous' (1) in his volume of the same name. Ferguson establishes the same principles of continuity between the Renaissance and the Enlightenment ('The Interpretation of the Renaissance' 129).

INTRODUCTION

1 The European Union did see fit to name its travelling student fellow-

ships after Erasmus rather than Voltaire. Rotterdam has the Erasmus Universiteit and Basel its Erasmus gymnasium. There is a lycée Voltaire in Paris, Orleans, and Wingles, and even one founded in 2007 in Qatar. There are numerous exchange programs named after Voltaire.

2 Naves 53.

3 'September 1, 1939' in *The Collected Poetry of W.H. Auden* 59.

4 Born in periods of religious controversy, the term(s) continue to arouse dispute. Erasmus was the first to experience discomfort at his designation. It was not in his nature to be so singled out. He consistently declined or deplored the term, perhaps fearing to be involved in an exchange of epithets with Lutheranism (Collected Works of Erasmus, henceforth CWE, 9:398–9). Most recently, in an excellent anthology of essays, *Erasmianism: Idea and Reality*, ed. Mout et al., Cornelius Augustijn in the lead essay advises against the phrase, declaring that he uses it not at all, and he encourages scholars to limit discussion to Erasmus's influence. Mout, one of the editors of the volume, says it is so ambiguous it should be put on ice (199, 208). As Augustijn tells us, even in England Erasmus served more as a corrective than an alternative (199), and he insists: 'There was never an Erasmian renaissance' (200). This may have been the case but as James McConica and Craig Thompson make clear (see below chapter 2) the Erasmian influence in England was tremendous, particularly in two phases: his *Colloquies* provided some of the rationale for the confiscation of monastic wealth and his *Paraphrases* much later were widely used, even required reading. But under Mary this expansion of Erasmianism was quickly curtailed, not even recovering under the reign of Elizabeth. But as Enid Welsford and Walter Kaiser have shown, *The Praise of Folly* (other works could be included) found tremendous resonance in the comedies and tragedies of Shakespeare (see chapter 5). Except for England and briefly in Spain, Erasmus and Erasmianism had some honour in being condemned by both sides, with Reformer and Catholic frequently employing the same language. His books were among the first to be included by Paul IV's commission in an Index of prohibited books, although followers of Ignatius Loyola unknowingly read expurgated versions of Erasmus's works – with the title page removed. After that the pace of dispute slackened; it was only by indirect, subterranean forces that he reemerged in the Socinianism and Arminianism of the seventeenth century (Trevor-Roper, 'Desiderius Erasmus,' in *Historical Essays* 53). And under such new provisions this new Erasmianism after Erasmus found favour with Voltaire. The term seems to have had persistence as well as resiliency. Of course, adoption always implies transformation, and the Erasmus that appealed to the Enlightenment and to the liberal wing of Protestants was the Erasmus of rational theology, with a critical turn of mind, and with some capacity for a moderating scepticism.

It should be noted that this conception of a cooperative historical functioning as part of some larger design is an historic afterthought and does nothing to dislodge the bitter dualism in which Erasmus and Luther had engaged, nor does it remove, based on specifics, the recantations that under the pressure of the Lutheran onslaught Erasmus felt obliged to render. Also stressing the second reformation of a later age, Preserved Smith in his *Erasmus: A Study of His Life, Ideals and Place in History* provides a preamble to Mansfield's larger compendium. In this still readable study, Smith writes: 'Its publication [that of *The Praise of Folly*] marked the real beginning of that immense international reputation that placed its author on a pinnacle in the world of letters hardly surpassed or even approached by anyone later save Voltaire' (125). Making one of the arguments advanced in *Dualisms* and repeated here, Smith sees the basis of the quarrel between Erasmus and Luther as originating in their very propinquity: 'The two fought together because they were so near together; because both cultivated and both sought to dominate one sphere of human interest, the spiritual-mental…the *geistig*' (322).

There should be no confusion between the 'second Reformation' of a later date and the thesis of 'la trosième Église,' advanced by Augustin Renaudet in his *Érasme et l'Italie*. Erasmus remained a son of the church, and while he sought and wished for many improvements and reforms, he did not seek in any essential way another church (Augustijn, *Erasmus* 182). We can gauge with a due amount of diffidence Erasmus's attitudes toward the changes brought about in his own time, but how about the future? P.S. Allen alerts us to one quite plausible conclusion: 'Neither [Erasmus] nor his opponents [Luther?] saw where he was tending; if he could have foreseen, he would have been shocked, no doubt, but not deterred. For God to him was *Via, vita, veritas*; and Truth shirks no questions, however startling' (*Erasmus: Lectures and Wayfaring Sketches* 73). Erasmus is thus a happy warrior, a portrait more befitting the earlier Erasmus than the one beset by so many compunctions about not telling truths in all seasons and all places. Still it is a bracing conjecture, one that welcomes Erasmus into the second Reformation.

5 Voltaire's literary afterlife, indeed, his life, was different (see Trousson). Unlike Erasmus, Voltaire did not fall between the press of opposing camps but became the standard-bearer for the Left and tarred by the Right (with the revolutionary Assemblies such denominations came into vogue). That is, down through the Dreyfus affair, Voltaire became a figure not on his own but as a subject of polemical dispute. But the extent of his hold was even increased by the Frankfurter *Rundschau* when, upon the death of Sartre, it wrote *finis*: the era of the French public intellectual begun with Voltaire had ended. But long before, contention against *Voltairiens* had lost its force. One

would have to say that it lasted more than a hundred years and entered in many ways into the lives of the greatest figures of the nineteenth century, in France as elsewhere. But with this endurance what it meant to be *Voltairien* also changed. Little by little was eroded the Voltaire of high aspiration, the successor to Corneille and Racine on the stage, the epic French Virgil. Gradually, but also quite early, the Voltaire who survived was the Voltaire of the Regency, the heady Voltaire, who lacking genius possessed only 'esprit,' or wit. This writer was not a 'great poet'; lacking in lyricism, 'il ne se laisse aller' (Naves 114). Voltaire thus lost any appeal for the Romantics who found him dry, lacking in sublimity. As was said of the English neoclassical poets of the eighteenth century, he was the greatest prose writer of his time. Still his was a name and a personality to contend with. For the religious right – which had a remarkable persistency from de Maistre down to Maurras and the Action Française – he himself became the 'infâme,' and was frequently associated with – Luther. By having his deistic faith discounted, Voltaire became the symbol of the drift of irreligion, moving from his attacks on superstition, to anticlericalism, to irreverence, and finally to disbelief. This represents travesty. But powerful literary evidence attests to Voltaire's presence in the households undergoing dechristianization in the course of the nineteenth century. Sartre in *Les mots* writes that his family was 'touched by the slow movement of dechristianization which came to birth within the voltairien upper bougeoisie and which took a century to spread through all levels of society' (82). Even in Russia the education of both Turgenev and Tolstoy was similarly secularized.

Many of the major figures of French Romanticism (the generation of Balzac) very early imbibed a taste for Voltaire. He was part of a familial legacy which, however, led to a later disenchantment. His subject matter, his poetics, his diction, his versification, his philosophy itself all lost their interest for the post-Revolutionary generations. Thrown into the pit he was only able to emerge in the just fullness and rightness of his interests and stature when the polemics became less intense. Most recently Roland Barthes (in *Essais critiques*) would indicate other 'isms' that blocked Voltaire's access to modernity. While the universal 'we' on whose behalf Barthes writes seems to be lacking in specifics, still his essay invokes other intellectual trends that swept Voltaire aside. In his alignment with intelligence against systematic intellectualism, Voltaire would have, Barthes argues, hated the major nineteenth-century movements in science, history, and the philosophy of existence: 'marxistes, progressistes, existentialistes, intellectuels de gauche Voltaire les aurait hais, couvert de lazzis incessant ...' (99–100). And just as he would have hypothetically underserved them, so they undermined him and his works. Barthes's arguments will be encountered again throughout this book, both favourably and unfavourably, but what is sure is that he makes a substantial contribution to our understanding of the slackened and changed presence of Voltaire, to which could be added that of Erasmus as well. Still one can imagine with some hilarity the treatment some of these movements would have received at the hands of Voltaire. And his 'jeering' would not have been universal, but reserved for those which threatened human liberty.

6 Quoted from Conrad Busken Huet, in Mansfield, *Man on His Own* 306. See Busken Huet, *Het Land van Rembrand* 173. In the twentieth century Rudolph Borchardt prophesied that the name of Benedetto Croce would fulfil the same eponymous function for his time that Petrarch, Erasmus, and Voltaire did for theirs, to which notation René Wellek adds, 'a prophecy which has not been fulfilled' (58).

7 McConica, *Erasmus* 99. Augustijn will argue for Erasmus's 'uniqueness' (7). But it is hard to understand how the term is being used, except in the sense that every individual is unique, particularly when he associates Erasmus with the broad-sweeping movement of biblical humanism, and later Augustijn correctly attributes the final outbreak of the dualism between Erasmus and Luther to their being too much alike: 'The two men were closer to each other than they were willing or able to admit' (132).

8 *Voltaire* 603.

9 *Situations II* 154. But long before either epoch, Dante defined himself as the lay intellectual who took the manna from the tables of the philosophers and applied his learning to the issues of the day. Jacob Burckhardt makes special note of this: 'In his letters [Dante] appears as one of the earliest publicists and is perhaps the first layman to publish political tracts in this form' (1:97).

10 Charles Homer Haskins would include Petrarch to this dubious distinction: 'Already in the fourteenth century Petrarch is remembered for his Italian sonnets and not for the Latin epic *Africa* on which he expected his lasting fame to rest' (153). Perhaps even more relevant is Giovanni Boccaccio, whose learning is almost equal to that of Petrarch, who delivered the first university lectures on Dante's great *Comedia*, whose poems were 'adapted' by Chaucer, but who is solely remembered for his *Decamerone*.

11 Opinion did not change in the course of the twentieth century, despite the fact the Erasmian scholarship continued but in latter days somewhat thinned out. Mansfield builds his last volume of the history of Erasmus's reception around the three centenary celebrations devoted to Erasmus, which were frequently accompanied in Europe, and particularly in Holland, by extended public festivities. To his

credit Mansfield confronts honestly this 'paradox' of the continuing celebrations along with the lapses in scholarly attention: 'The bonding of Erasmus more closely than ever to the humanist tradition, one of the achievements of twentieth-century scholarship, has located him in an enclave to which diminishing numbers, even among the educated, have access.' And when it comes to the new critical theories, Erasmus will acquire (or has acquired) a garb 'even more specialized and esoteric than the humanist' (228–9). In the general decline of Latinity (see Chomarat) and in the general decline of literacy what happened to the fortunes of Erasmus is not unique. What is unique is the particular form that it took, and the shared fate that *Praise of Folly* enjoys with *Candide*.

12 See Naves 143, to which might be added Cousin's 'Voltaire, c'est le bon sens superficiel' (quoted in Naves). A fuller register of such tendencies to quips may be gained from Trousson's *Visages de Voltaire*. Augustijn, *Erasmus*, quotes Joseph Lortz as to Erasmus's 'vollendete Undeutlichkeit' (187). But one of the points this book will emphasize – the real issue – is how inadequately these amusing quips render the fuller natures of Erasmus and Voltaire, and how readily each of them transcends the aphoristic mug-shots.

13 It is equally erroneous to seek a reconciliation of the two, to twin the twain, which is most likely an exercise in wishful thinking, a desire to bring into some ideal union the characteristics that are so opposed. Thus Huldrych Zwingli in 1521, admiring the separate qualities of Erasmus and Luther, could only imagine the superiority of the person who combined both (quoted in Rummel, *Erasmus* 91). But Zwingli's mistake is a common one: it is the confusion of philosophical dualities with dualisms. Dualities, whether as philosophical principles (mind versus matter), or given more localized designations (Matthew Arnold's Hebraism and Hellenism, Schiller's realist and idealist, Turgenev's Hamlet and Quixote), are separated only as ideal abstractions, outposts that serve to identify the intervening terrain. In practical reality their qualities merge and reemerge, interpenetrate, so no one or no one thing can fully fit one of the terms. Dualisms, however, square off in unflinching opposition, unreconciled and unreconcilable up to the end and even beyond, as is evidenced by the recurrence of the divisions they commanded.

Here once again, Zweig is on the mark. Calling it 'foolishness' to wish for the forces of Erasmus and Luther to come together in a common cause, he asserts: 'The twain were organically different, and there existed no meeting-ground for their mutual collaboration' (138). Nor, as is true of any dualism, is there any hope for their eventual reconciliation. Late in life Erasmus rejected an olive branch offered by Luther, just as Voltaire refused to allow Rousseau to contribute to the subscription drive organized to commission a statue in the patriarch's honour.

14 Mme de Stael advanced this oft-repeated thought. See Trousson, *Visages* 110–11.

15 With Voltaire, according to Naves, we have no fear of coming up against a pose of embellishments or sublimations. Voltaire's task was to reduce all the 'narcissismes et toutes les transcendances' (78). Obviously this statement needs to be qualified in regard to Erasmus, as it will be when discussion is directed toward 'temporalities' in chapter 6. When Erasmus's Christianity is fused with Platonism, as at the end of *The Praise of Folly*, his rhetoric takes wing. But there is a difference between knowing the way of the saint and following it, as T.S. Eliot makes clear at the end of *East Coker*, where he distinguishes between the saint's lifetime of surrender in selfless love, which 'for most of us … is the aim / Never here to be realized' (*Complete Poems* 136).

16 'Not everyone has the strength needed for martyrdom. I fear that, if strife were to break out, I shall behave like Peter' (CWE 8:259), quoted by Augustijn, citing this not as an indication of cowardice but rather as an 'example of an unusually honest self-analysis' (125). Naves ascribes remarkably similar qualities (virtues included) to Voltaire: 'Le courage de Voltaire n'est pas spectaculaire. Il ne brandit pas l'épée. Il ne cherche pas le martyre' (71). But like that of Erasmus his virtue was in his tenacity, his refusal to remain silent.

CHAPTER 1. NAMES FOR BASTARDS

1 Gerhard Ladner, '*Homo Viator*: Medieval Ideas on Alienation and Order,' *Speculum* 42 (1967): 233.

2 Evidently Shakespeare may also have shared the belief that Brutus was the bastard son of Caesar; hence the very touching recourse to the familiar Latin, 'Et tu Brute?' While not present in Plutarch such a possibility was advanced by Suetonius, but Shakespeare in any event would not have been able to read him. Nor did he need to, since the Latin phrasing was well heard on the English stage from 1592 on. See Nuttall 191. But also see the incisive review of the Nuttall argument by David Wootton which was itself well corrected by Brian Vickers's letter.

3 See *Actes du congrès Érasme, Rotterdam, 27—29 Octobre 1969* (1971), 14–28.

CHAPTER 2. ENGLAND, ALWAYS ENGLAND

1 CWE 1:198–9.

2 For an interesting sociological survey of England at this time see Derek Wilson, *England in the Age of Thomas More* (London and New York: Hart-Davis McGibbon, 1978).

3 See separate entries in *Contemporaries of Erasmus: A Biographical Register* (CEBR).

4 See also Rousseau, *L'Angleterre et Voltaire*, preface to vol. 145 and the substantial chapter, 'Voltaire Dramaturge,' vol. 2, where Rousseau discusses the numerous translations, imitations, and adaptations of Voltaire's plays throughout eighteenth-century England.

5 For an excellent account of the largely political lessons gained by Voltaire during his stay in England, see Peter Gay, 'England a Nation of Philosophers,' *Voltaire's Politics*, 13–65.

6 'Shakespeare and the Drama: 1726–1776' in *Voltaire*. For a more up-to-date bibliographical account, see Robert and Isabelle Tombs, 'The French and Shakespeare: The Age of Voltaire,' *That Sweet Enemy* (New York: Random House 2008), 104–7. The following books are pertinent to this discussion: OC 3B, ed. David Williams, *Essai sur la poésie épique* 410–23; Williams, 'Voltaire's War with England'; and OC 53, ed. David Williams, Introduction; Williams, 'Voltaire and the Problem of Shakespeare,' in *Studies on Voltaire and the Eighteenth Century*, ed. Theodore Besterman, 314–41; OC 5, ed. John Renwick, 'Discours sur la tragédie à milord Bolingbroke,' 156–83; OC 24, *Appel à toutes les nations de l'Europe*, 191–221; OC 30, 'Lettre de M. de Voltaire à l'Académie française,' 349–70; Le Tourneur, *Préface du Shakespeare*; and Genuist, *Le Théâtre de Shakespeare*.

In his *Shakespeare in France* (1899) J.J. Jusserand was ideally positioned to grasp the full range of Shakespeare's presence in France. The 1820s were decisive: 'from that moment Shakespeare was admitted into the Pantheon of the literary gods' (450–9). Shakespeare became the court of appeal for new standards in taste, in diction (by neoclassical decorum the word 'pistol' was inadmissible on the stage), and the broader sweep of human experience (453–64). But Jusserand adds that the victories of Shakespeare as shield-bearer for advancing French romanticism is only a half-told tale. Shakespeare helped bring about a national literary transformation, but 'to believe that he had become acclimatized in France, that his genius had penetrated and transformed the French mind is an error' (466). Utilizing the racialistic theories so prevalent at the time, Jusserand argues that the French 'national genius' – built upon a 'Latin substratum' – could not totally relinquish its adherence to regularity of form, action, and speech, and that while playgoers will admire individual lines, speeches, and episodes in Shakespeare, they will be swept away by Racine's *Iphigénie*. Indicating how history trumps such 'racializing theories,' it is doubtful whether such a statement could be confirmed after 1945.

In the light of the epilogue to this book, it is noteworthy that in
Germany the situation was entirely different. As Roger Paulin explains in a brilliant work of detailed scholarly exposition, *The Critical Reception of Shakespeare in Germany 1682–1914*, the Germans, not
having a Golden Age of their own (except for the inexpungeable Luther), used Shakespeare to create their own national literature. Paulin uses his subtitle as a leitmotif throughout: 'Native Literature and
Foreign Genius,' that is, the ways by which the Germans, unlike the
French, annexed and appropriated Shakespeare making him 'ganz
unser.' Emphasizing feeling rather than form, personal empathy
rather than regularity of taste and rules, German criticism from Less-
ing to Herder to Goethe and Schiller and to the Schlegels established
some of the bases of modern Shakespearean criticism. Eventually
this strain could lead to the sense of a 'deep reading' that ignores the
literal, the positivistic, to arrive at the privileged understanding be-
stowed by the kinship of spirit.

7 Jusserand, in a notable paragraph, indicates why this might be so.
'Some men have the gift, of whatever they say, of being listened to;
whatever they write, of being read ... When others spoke no one
paid any attention; now that they open their lips, everyone is all
ears.Their voice is clearer; it seems as though their ink were blacker.
This precious gift was at all times Voltaire's; he possessed it from his
youth and retained it till his death' (180).

8 While a 'revolutionist' to the core when it came to theatre, Voltaire,
according to Jusserand, 'upsets nothing; he is prudent; he is seized
with fear. He has to deal with an art so holy in his eyes that his hand
hesitates. The audacious reformer becomes circumspect; he cannot
turn away from the high road without trembling. He will go and
attack God on his altars without fear of hell ... but the idea that it
might be possible to renounce alexandrines makes him shudder
...' (245–6). A tragedy in prose is a sin against the Holy Ghost, for
which there would be no remission. Among the many other virtues
of Jusserand's still highly readable and valuable work, there is both
philosophical and psychological acuity.

9 In a judicious work of thorough scholarship and, I might add, in
more sophisticated terms, René Wellek arrives at the conclusion 'that
romanticism centers on a concern for the reconciliation of subject
and object, man and nature, consciousness and unconsciousness'
('Romanticism and Literature,' *Dictionary of the History of Ideas*,
http://etext.lib.virginia.edu, 22).

CHAPTER 3. ERASMUS'S LETTER TO VAN DORP AND VOLTAIRE'S LETTER TO ROUSSEAU

1 See Rummel, *Erasmus and His Catholic Critics* 2:152.

2 See Klawiter ¶33, quoted in Quinones, *Dualisms* 28.
3 *Erasmus and His Catholic Critics* 1: 67–93.
4 Augustijn, *Erasmus: Der Humanist* 125.
5 It should be noted that when the CWE translators employ contemporary sounding terms like 'stalking horse,' 'renaissance,' and 'humanities,' some liberties have been taken with the text. Erasmus actually wrote, 'si renascantur bonae litterae' (CWE 3:122; Allen 2:99).
6 See Preface, note 1, above.

CHAPTER 4. WORKS FINDING THEIR WAYS

1 See in particular pages 191–3, 201–2, 207, 226, 252.
2 *Ten Colloquies of Erasmus.*
3 Paul Hazard, 'Le problème du mal dans la conscience européene du dix-huitième siècle,' *The Romanic Revue* 31 (1941): 167.
4 See the full account of Voltaire's experience with Frederick in Pomeau and Mervaud, *De la Cour au jardin* esp. 21–177.
5 Such an argument inevitably involves the so-called Weberian thesis, developed by Max Weber in *The Protestant Ethic and the Spirit of Capitalism*. Fernandez-Armesto and Derek Wilson in their efforts of disaggregation represent the most up-to-date rebuttals of some of the implications of Weber's ideas (see *Reformations* 277–85). But their arguments were anticipated by Landes in *The Wealth and Poverty of Nations* 173–81, which offers substantial support to Weber's main arguments.

H.R. Trevor-Roper does much to turn the arguments around. In the aforementioned key essay, 'Religion, the Reformation and Social Change'(see pages xv, 195 note 2), arguing that capitalism existed before Protestantism and that the great financial entrepreneurs were all émigrés, he cites two causes for the association of new financial possibilities with mainly the northern states. One was positive, the survival of Erasmianism, and the other negative, the regression of the Counter-Reformation countries under the banner of Spain and the union of church and state into a forbidding theocracy. The shiver of absolutism in religion and politics sent the most industrious and ambitious to other circles where they could reap their fortunes in relative freedom. Clearly this fear of the union of church and state and the emphasis on industry and finance complies very closely with the description of the northern states in *La Princesse de Babylone*. While Trevor-Roper may have made too sharp a distinction between Erasmianism and Protestantism, clearly the mediating humanism that Erasmus represented was squeezed out by the hardliners of the Roman church and the radical Protestants. It later knew its own revenges, coming back in the seventeenth and eighteenth centuries, and quite obviously joining hands with what Voltaire had to offer.

For the general importance of geography in the work of Voltaire, see Scherer, 'L'univers en raccourci.'

6 See Menchi, *Erasmo in Italia* 352.

7 See note 5 above. Among the elusive 'firsts' Machiavelli must be included. Certainly by virtue of their unification into nation states the north could be contrasted with the division of Italy into smaller and weaker principalities and republics. But Machiavelli does not stop there. In his *Discorsi* he makes a distinction between *morale* and *virtù*, or what he calls *bontà*, or goodness, without which no republic can flourish. Italy suffers from *corruzione*, as do France and Spain but in these countries the blight is in part offset by a powerful monarchy that establishes good order ('l'ordine'). Otherwise the character of their people is no different. Machiavelli then establishes a notable difference with Germany, where *bontà* and *religione* among the people are still *grande*, with the result that people observe the laws (without fraud) and many republics there are free without fear of foreign domination (*Discorsi* I. LV). Machiavelli's ignorance of the actual conditions of the German states seems invincible. See also Cassirer, *The Myth of the State* 147–8.

While it is customary to oppose Machiavelli and Erasmus (as Cassirer has so significantly done), in some ways Erasmus joins his Italian compeer (whom he never mentions) in this alignment. However, this is done in a work, *Julius Exclusus*, whose single authorship by Erasmus is in dispute (see the full argument of this complex issue in the ntroduction by Michael J. Heath in CWE 27:156–63). Pope Julius II, whom Erasmus had seen enter into the conquered Bologna, resurgent in military glory, is defending his version of the papacy as against the spiritual foundations of Christianity provided by the examples of Christ and Peter and Paul. Trying in Erasmus's dialogue to take heaven by storm he is denied entrance by Peter. In his ironic defence he lauds Italy as against the French and Germans, who are attempting to keep to the message of Christ. To his mind, they are 'barbarians' and the Italianate papacy is trying to live according to the standards of the present day, and in so doing revel in the same 'corruzione' that Machiavelli deplores. They share this characteristic with the Spaniards. See, in particular, CWE 27:187 for a full listing of the points of difference. It should be added, however, that Julius is quite adept at the political cunning and manoeuvering that Machiavelli, at least in *The Prince*, admires. In any event, it is clear that the first glimmering of the north/south axis had its origins in the Reformation, and the migration of the intellectual centre of gravity to the north. See Ferguson, who says, 'The preoccupation of the papal curia with temporal politics during these crisis years made it peculiarly unfitted to combat the spiritual revolution that broke out in Germany and that, within two generations, separated half of northern Europe permanently from the Church of Rome' ('The Church in a Changing World' 166). See also Landes 174, 177, 178, 179, 180, 181. Whatever the causes, something clearly and decisively had happened. Perhaps Landes is on the better trail, combining a mixture of Trevor-Roper's negative argument of the adverse effect of the Counter-Reformation and Weber's thesis of the development under Protestantism of a 'new man – rational, ordered, diligent, productive'(177). Even Fernández-Armesto and Wilson must admit to a three-hundred-year-long deep divide between Protestant and Catholic.

CHAPTER 5. THE SURVIVORS:
PRAISE OF FOLLY AND CANDIDE

1 See the introduction to Clarence Miller's translation of *The Praise of Folly* ix. For the Latin original I have been obliged to resort to the *Erasmus von Rotterdam*, Ausgewählhlte Schriften (AS), vol. 2. Where the Latin original is given in the text, the page number after the slash refers to this edition.

2 See Kaiser, *Praisers of Folly*.

3 Jacques Gengoux has written an admirable suite of essays, '"*Zadig*" et les trois puissances de Voltaire,' *Les Lettres Romanes* 16 (1962), wherein he introduces the three powers that, brought together, form the *Voltairien* ideal. They are body (*corps*, including bravery and physical appeal); mind (*esprit*, including wit, intelligence, and philosophical bent); and heart (*coeur*, or the capacity for affection that underlies the others). Taken individually each of these powers is insufficient, but brought together into a developing whole, as in *Zadig* or *L'Ingenu* (note the absence of *Candide*), they represent the fullness of *Voltairien* virtue (in marked contrast to the same triadic elements employed by Pascal.) The three clasps I invoke are not individual forces or qualities but rather subjects of concern – one could call them personal myths or themes. Two of them refuse to enter into any ideal development or notions of reconciliation. They balk at any attempt to show the unity of Voltaire's thought and instead reveal its dire complexity.

4 Paul Hazard, in the aforementioned essay, 'Le Problème du mal dans la conscience européene du dix-huitième siècle,' traces the widespread appeal of the Leibnizian adage that this is the best of all possible worlds. He attributes its dissolution to the developing confidence in the powers of observation and common sense. In Voltaire, this may be confirmed by his long-standing allegiance to Locke, but it would appear that Hazard's thesis would have the consequence of locating Voltaire in that genius of mediocrity by overlooking his in-

sistence on the just expression of an outraged sense of humane sentiment.

CHAPTER 6. NEVER A PEACE: 'THUS ALWAYS CAIN OR ABEL'

1 While Erasmus may have felt himself deficient in 'possessing' the
   Spirit, there is no question but that he understands what was meant
   by the coming of the Holy Spirit, especially in Acts. To bestow faith
   in the minds of men after the Son was taken into heaven, 'from
   heaven the Holy Spirit was sent, renewing the minds and tongues
   of all' (*On Mending the Peace of the Church*, 335). We do well to place
   Erasmus and Luther at the crisis point of the Reformation. Their
   central differences hold but some modulations can occur. While
   firm in the centre Luther underwent some modification around
   the periphery. This was because, as Jaroslav Pelikan has pointed
   out in that indispensable small book *Spirit versus Structure*, he was
   obliged to provide some structures for evangelical Christianity. In
   educational practice he was of the humanist camp, insisting on instruction in languages. 'I know full well that while it is Spirit alone
   that accomplishes everything, I would surely have never flushed
   a covey if the languages had not helped me' (Pelikan 73). Luther's
   more mature opinions were thus defined from the midst of controversy, against the church's reliance on 'works' on one side, and the
   number of more radical opponents on the other: Andrew Karlstadt,
   John Oecolampadius, Ulrich Zwingli, and Martin Bucer over the real
   presence in the Eucharist; and the Anabaptists over infant baptism
   (113). Luther requires polemics to see his way clearly. Throughout
   these controversies, because of these controversies, Luther, ever the
   man of spirit, showed his capacity for balance, which resulted in
   his enormous success. In matters of church practice this was clearly
   the case, but also in some philosophical concerns as well. If he was
   able to say that one should close one's eyes to 'use, tradition, and
   great numbers'(Pelikan 39), thus emboldened by the word of God,
   in time he was able to see that some practices, such as ordination
   and matrimony, while not sacraments, helped foster the tranquility
   and order of the church. As with continuity itself, this has little to do
   with salvation, but much to do with the discipline required for good
   order. Like Erasmus he came to detect a knee-jerk adversarial consciousness in hostility to the papacy: it is as if 'whatever comes from
   the pope is wrong. If something goes on in the papacy in a particular
   way, we must do it some other way' (Pelikan 88). In contrasting
   Erasmus and Luther it must be borne in mind that after the critical
   debate each underwent subtle changes in his thought, but this was
   not in regard to core issues and did nothing to soften hostility.

2 Quoted in Fernandez-Armesto and Wilson, *Reformations* 30.
3 See *Dualisms* 422n1, 424n4.
4 T.S. Eliot, *East Coker*, 125

EPILOGUE: RECURRENCE AND RECOGNITION

1 See above, page 195 note 1.
2 Trans. Fritz A. Koelln and James P. Pettegrove (Boston: Beacon 1955); for modifications, see the original German Ernst Cassirer, *Die Philosophie der Aufklärung*, vol. 15. Additional references in the text are to Ernst Cassirer, *Philosophy of Symbolic Forms* 1953, *An Essay on Man* 1956, and *The Myth of the State*, 1946).
3 The substance and context of the debate are contained in two translations: Martin Heidegger, *Kant and the Problem of Metaphysics*, 175–217, and Aubenque, *Cassirer-Martin Heidegger, Débat sur le kantisme et la philosophie et autres textes de 1929–1931*.
4 The reference to violence has many applications, most particularly to hermeneutics. It was employed by Heidegger himself in his justification for making of Kant what suited him. One is not confined to the prison house of the letter, of what was expressly stated, but rather by any 'violence' that should break through or out of the text. In order to go beyond what the words say to what they mean ,to what is unexpressed, one has recourse to interpretive violence. Cassirer rejects outright this method of interpretation, calling Heidegger a 'usurper' rather than an interpreter, and warning that such reading can only be partial (being both incomplete and subjective), while true criticism or interpretation depends upon an understanding of the work as a whole. Max Kommerell (1902–44) made similar charges against Heidegger's method, calling it not an explication but an encounter, and perhaps even a misfortune (Wellek 31, 85–91). The basic derivation of future directions is obtained right here, as Heidegger in his willingness to commit violence to the text, to eschew explication, to go beyond what was literally expressed to what was subtended, laid the way open for Jacques Derrida and the vogue of deconstruction. The entire issue is a fertile one for critical inquiry. Several comments are called for. First, the method can be quite creative: witness the insightful essays by Dobrolubov and Pisarev on the novels of Turgenev in the nineteenth-century; their essays saw through the text into things the text did not say but meant. By virtue of their own experiences they understood what the text was meaning to say, and thus were able to construct its prehistory (*Dualisms*, 241–53). Creative texts themselves are ready subjects for mauling, exploitation, and even usurpation. It is an expression of their potency that they may be put to purposes other than those their author may have intended. This exploitability may be more pertinent in works of art

than in works of philosophical statement, although the borders between the two are certainly porous as Heidegger would maintain. In lesser hands this method can lead to mish-mash with no really gainful insights. But in creative hands it can produce new departures, new ways of seeing into both a work and society itself.

Such essays I would call essays of contestation. They do not exist alone but rather in a dialectical relationship with the opposing efforts they provoke. They are inseparable from the responses they inevitably elicit. Essay and response are like characters in a drama, participants in a duet, each with prescribed roles to play. The key element is that under the pressure of such essays of contestation the responses rise to a higher level of understanding and perception than their more conventional readings had at first allowed. They are pushed to more perceptive, more appealing understandings. Thus, Roland Barthes' essay 'Le dernier écrivain heureux,' prompted more searching inquiry into Voltaire's abiding thoughts, contained within the three clasps (see above, 136–42). Thus 'violence' done to a text does not call for simple complaint – one does not respond to insanity with banality, but rather with a better comprehension. I leave open the question as to whether Cassirer's accusation of partiality of a reading as against a comprehension of a work in its totality is adequate.

5 In 'What Is Existential Philosophy?' in *Essays in Understanding 1930–1954*, Hannah Arendt discusses in juxtaposed sections the contrasting philosophies of Heidegger and Jaspers. These are admirable and accurate précis of their thought. The key word for Jaspers is 'communication.' Arendt writes, 'Existence is, by its nature, never isolated. It exists only in communication and awareness of others' existence. Our fellowman is not (as in Heidegger) an element of existence that is structurally necessary but at the same time an impediment to Being as Self. Just the contrary: Existence can only develop in the shared life of human beings inhabiting a given world common to them all' (186). This is the point readily expressed in Voltaire's down-to-earth humour.

6 See Randall Collins, *The Sociology of Philosophies* (Cambridge: Harvard UP 1998), 26–45 but everywhere provocative and useful.

7 See in particular note 3 above.

8 Although Trevor-Roper's classic essay 'Religion, the Reformation and Social Change' does not explicitly point a moral or draw a lesson, its overall implications are clear enough. In the sixteenth and seventeenth centuries, autocratic states, those combining religion and state into a theocracy, chase away their best talents, who then bring their skills to the enrichment of other nations and places, where the allowances of political and religious liberties leave the ways open for the pursuit of personal riches. The comparative, trans-

historical approach shows much the same thing happened in the twentieth century. While Cassirer, in name and influence, could not be fully compared with Erasmus and Erasmianism, still as a symbolic figure he represents a similar phenomenon. Escaping the restrictive demands of state ideology, the new totalitarianism of terror, European intellectuals fled en masse to the more receptive freedoms of the United States and other countries of the Western hemisphere, bringing in most cases a bright enrichment to the lives of the countries that welcomed them.

Works Cited

꧀

Allen, P.S. *Opus epistolarum Des. Erasmi Roterodami*. Allen. Oxford: Clarendon, 1906–58. Especially volumes 1–4.

– *Erasmus: Lectures and Wayfaring Sketches*. Oxford: Oxford UP, 1934.

Arendt, Hannah. *Essays in Understanding: 1930–1950*. Ed. Jerome Kohn. New York: Schocken, 1994.

Aubenque, Pierre. *Cassirer – Martin Heidegger: Débat sur le kantisme et la philosophie et autres textes de 1929–1931*, Paris: Beauchesne, 1972.

Auden, W.H. 'September 1, 1939.' *The Collected Poetry of W.H. Auden*. New York: Random House, 1945.

Augustijn, Cornelius. *Erasmus: His Life, Work, and Influence*. Trans. J.C. Grayson. Toronto: U of Toronto P, 1991.

– *Erasmus: Der Humanist als Theologe und Kirchenreformer*. Leiden: Brill, 1996.

Bainton, Roland. *Erasmus of Christendom*. New York: Scribner, 1969.

Barthes, Roland. 'Le dernier écrivain heureux.' *Essais Critiques*. Paris: Gallimard, 1962.

Bataillon, Marcel. *Érasme et L'Espagne*. Paris: E. Droz, 1937.

– 'Actualité d'Érasme.' *Colloquia Erasmiana Turonensia*. Tours, 1969. 871–90.

Besterman, Theodore, gen. ed. *Studies on Voltaire and the Eighteenth Century*. Vols 145–7. Preface by André Michel Rousseau. Oxford: Voltaire Foundation, 1976.

– *Voltaire*. 3rd ed. Chicago: U of Chicago P, 1976.

Bierlaire, Franz. *Érasme et ses Colloques: Le livre d'une vie*. Travaux d'humanisme et Renaissance 159. Geneva: Droz, 1977.

– *Les Colloques d'Érasme: Réforme des études, réforme de moeurs, et réforme de l'Église au XVIe siècle*. Liège: UP de Liège, 1978.

Bietenholz, Peter G., and Thomas B. Deutscher, eds. *Contemporaries of Erasmus: A Biographical Register of the Renaissance and Reformation*. CEBR. Toronto: U of Toronto P, 1985–7.

Billaz, André. 'Zadig.' *Dictionnaire Voltaire.*

Bornkamm, Heinrich. '*Erasmus und Luther.*' *Das Jahrhundert der Reforma-tion.* 2nd ed. Göttingen: Vandenhoeck and Ruprecht, 1966.

Burckhardt, Jacob. *The Civilization of the Renaissance in Italy.* 2 vols. New York: Harper, 1958.

Busken Huet, Conrad. *Het Land van Rembrand.* 8th ed. Haarlem: Tjenk Willen and Zoon, 1946.

Carducci, Giosue. *Studi litterari.* 2nd ed. Bologna: Zanichelli, 1907.

Cassirer, Ernst. *The Myth of the State.* New Haven: Yale UP, 1946.

– *Philosophy of Symbolic Forms.* New Haven: Yale UP, 1953 (orig. 1924).

– *The Question of Jean-Jacques Rousseau.* Ed. Peter Gay. New York: Co-lumbia UP, 1954.

– *The Philosophy of the Enlightenment.* Trans. F.C.A. Koelln and J.P. Pet-tegrove. Boston: Basic Books, 1955 (orig. 1932).

– *An Essay on Man.* New York: Doubleday, 1956.

– *The Individual and the Cosmos in Renaissance Philosophy.* Trans. Mario Domandi. New York: Harper and Row, 1963.

– *Die Philosophie der Aufklärung, Gesammelte Werke.* Vol. 15. Hamburg: Felix Meiner Verlag, 2003.

Chomarat, Jacques. *Grammaire et rhetorique chez Érasme.* 2 vols. Paris: Société d'édition Les belles lettres, 1985.

Coleridge, Samuel Taylor. *The Collected Works of Samuel Taylor Coleridge.* Gen. ed. Carl Woodring. Bollingen 75. Princeton: Princeton UP, 1969.

– *The Friend.* 2 vols. Ed. Barbara E. Rooke. Vol. 4 of *Collected Works.* Ed. Kathleen Coburn. Princeton: Princeton UP, 1969.

– *Literary Remains.* Ed. H.N. Coleridge. 4 vols. London: Pickering, 1836–9.

Cronk, Nicholas, ed. *The Cambridge Companion to Voltaire.* Cambridge: Cambridge UP, 2009.

Devereux, E.J. *Renaissance English Translations of Erasmus: A Bibliography to 1700.* Toronto: U of Toronto P, 1983.

Dictionnaire Voltaire. Ed. Jacques Lemaire, Raymond Trousson, and Jeroom Vercruysee. Brussels: Hachette, 1994.

Dillenberger, John, ed. *Martin Luther: Selections from His Writings.* New York: Anchor Books, 1962.

Dolan, John. *The Essential Erasmus.* New York: Meridian, 1983.

Ehrard, Jean. *L'Idée de nature en France dans la première moitié du XVIIIe siècle.* 2 vols. Paris: S.E.V.P.E.N, 1963.

Eliot, T.S. *The Complete Poems and Plays: 1909–1950.* New York: Harcourt, Brace, 1957.

Elliott, J.H. 'The Decline in Spain.' *Crisis in Europe, 1560–1660.* Ed. Trevor Aston. New York: Doubleday 1967. 177–205.

Erasmus, Desiderius. *The Praise of Folly.* Trans. John Wilson. 1668. Repr. Ann Arbor: U of Michigan P, 1958.

– *The Colloquies of Erasmus*. Trans. Craig R. Thompson. Chicago: U of Chicago P, 1965.
– *Opera omnia Desiderii Erasmi Roterodami*. ASD. Amsterdam: North Holland, 1969–.
– *Erasmus and His Age: Selected Letters of Desiderius Erasmus*. Ed. Hans J. Hillerbrand. New York: Harper Torch, 1970.
– *Colloquia*. Ed. L.-E. Halkin, F. Bierlaire, R. Hoven. ASD. Vol. 1, part 3. Amsterdam: North Holland, 1972.
– The Collected Works of Erasmus. CWE. Toronto: U of Toronto P, 1974–
– *Institutio principis christiani*. Ed. O. Herding. ASD. Vol. 4, part 1. Amsterdam: North Holland, 1974.
– *The Correspondence of Erasmus*. Preface James K. McConica. Trans. R.A.B Mynors and D.F.S Thomson. CWE. Vol. 3, 1976.
– *Encomium Moriae Erasmus von Rotterdam*. Ausgewählte Schriften. AS. Vol. 2. Darmstadt: Wissenschaftliche Buchgesellschaft, 1976.
– *The Colloquies of Erasmus*. Trans. Craig R. Thompson. CWE. Vols. 39–40, 1977.
– *The Polemics of Erasmus of Rotterdam and Ulrich von Hutten*. Trans. Randolph J. Klawiter. Notre Dame: U of Notre Dame P, 1977.
– *Querela Pacis*. Ed. O. Herding. ASD .Vol. 4, part 2. Amsterdam: North Holland, 1977.
– *The Praise of Folly*. Trans. Clarence H. Miller. New Haven: Yale UP, 1979.
– *Adages*. CWE. Vol. 31 (1982), trans. Margaret Mann Phillips, ann. R.A.B. Mynors; vol. 35 (2005), trans. Denis L. Drysdall, ed. John N. Grant.
– *On Mending [Restoring] the Peace of the Church* (*De sarcienda ecclesiae concordia* 1533). Trans. John P. Dolan. *The Essential Erasmus*. New York: Meridian, 1983.
– *A Complaint of Peace*. Trans. Betty Radice. CWE. Vol. 27, 1986.
– *De sarcienda ecclesiae concordia*. Ed. R. Stupperich. ASD. Vol. 3. Amsterdam: North Holland, 1986.
– *The Education of a Christian Prince*. Trans. and ann. Neil M. Cheshire and Michael J. Heath. CWE. Vol. 27, 1986.
– *The Praise of Folly*. Trans. Betty Radice. CWE. Vol. 27, 1986.
– *Enchiridion*. Ed. and intro. John W. O'Malley. Trans. Charles Fantazzi. CWE. Vol. 66, 1988.
– *Hyperaspistes I and II*. Trans. and ed. Charles Trinkhaus. CWE. Vols. 76–7, 1999.
Ferguson, Wallace K. *Europe in Transition 1300–1520*. Boston: Houghton Mifflin, 1962.
– 'The Church in the Changing World: A Contribution to the Interpretation of the Renaissance.' *Renaissance Studies*. New York: Harper, 1963. 155–170.

- 'The Interpretation of the Renaissance: Suggestion for a Synthesis.' *Renaissance Studies*. New York: Harper, 1963. 125–35.
- 'Toward the Modern State.' *Renaissance Studies*. New York: Harper, 1963. 137–53.

Fernández-Armesto, Felipe, and Derek Wilson. *Reformations: A Radical Interpretation of Christianity and the World, 1500–2000*. New York: Scribner, 1996.

Gay, Peter. *Voltaire's Politics*. Princeton: Princeton UP, 1959.
- *The Bridge of Criticism*. New York: Harper and Row, 1970.

Genuist, André. *Le Théâtre de Shakespeare dans l'oeuvre de Pierre le Tourneur, 1776–1783*. Paris: Didier 1971.

Gibbon, Edward. *The Decline and Fall of the Roman Empire*. 2 vols. New York: The Modern Library, 1932.

Gouhier, Henri. *Rousseau et Voltaire: Portraits dans deux miroirs*. Paris: Vrin, 1983.

Groos, René. *Le siècle de Louis XIV*. 2 vols. Paris: Garnier, 1947.

Hadot, Jean. 'La critique textuelle dans l'édition du Nouveau Testament d'Érasme.' *Le Christianisme d'Érasme: Sources, modalities, controversies, influences*. Ed. Jean-Claude Margolin. Colloquia Erasmiana Turonensia. Tours: Stage international d'études humanistes, 1969; Paris: Vrin, 1972. 749–60.

Haile, H.G. *Luther*. Garden City, NY: Doubleday, 1980.

Haskins, Charles Homer. *The Renaissance of the Twelfth Century*. 1927; repr. New York: Meridian 1955.

Heidegger, Martin. *Being and Time*. Trans. Joan Stambaugh. New York: State University of New York, 1996.
- *Kant and the Problem of Metaphysics*. 5th ed., enlarged. Trans. Richard Taft. Bloomington: Indiana UP, 1997.
- *Letter on Humanism. Basic Writings*. Revised and expanded ed. San Francisco: Harper Collins, 1997.
- *Introduction to Metaphysics*. Trans. Gregory Fried and Richard Polt. New Haven: Yale UP, 2000. Heuvel, Jacques van den. *Voltaire dans ses contes*. Paris: Armand Colin, 1967.

Hobsbawm, E.J. 'The Crisis of the Seventeenth Century.' *Crisis in Europe, 1560–1660*. Ed. Trevor Aston. New York: Doubleday, 1965. 5–62.

Huizinga, Johan. *Erasmus and the Age of Reformation*. New York: Harper & Row, 1957.

Jacobs, Eva. 'Tragedy and Didacticism in the Case of Voltaire.' *Voltaire and His World: Studies Presented to W.H.Barber*. Ed. R.J. Howells. Oxford: Voltaire Foundation, 1985. 51–66.

James, William. *The Varieties of Religious Experience*. New York: Modern Library, 1936.
- 'The Present Dilemma in Philosophy.' *Pragmatism*. New York: Meridian Books, 1955. 17–37.

Joyce, James. *Finnegans Wake*. New York: Viking, 1955.

Judt, Tony. *Reappraisals*. New York: Penguin, 2008.

Jusserand, J.J. *Shakespeare in France*. New York: Putnam's, 1899.

Kaiser, Walter. *Praisers of Folly*. Cambridge, MA: Harvard UP, 1964.

Klawiter, Randolph J. *The Polemics of Erasmus and Ulrich von Hutten*. Notre Dame: U of Notre Dame P, 1977.

Kohls, E-W. 'Érasme et la réforme.' *Le Christianisme d'Érasme: Sources, modalités, controverses, influences*. Ed. Jean-Claude Margolin. Colloquia Erasmiana Turonensia. Tours: Stage Internationale d'études humanistes, 1969. Paris: Vrin, 1972. 837–47.

Landes, David. *The Wealth and Poverty of Nations*. New York: W.W. Norton, 1998.

Le Tourneur, Pierre. *Préface de Shakespeare traduit de l'Anglais*. Paris: Droz, 1990.

Luther, Martin. *Martin Luther: Selections from His Writings*. Ed. John Dillenberger. New York: Anchor Doubleday, 1962.

Machiavelli, Niccolò. *Discorsi: Tutte Le Opere*. Ed. Francesco Flora e di Carlo Cordie. Florence: Mondadori, 1968.

Mansfield, Bruce. *Phoenix of His Age: Interpretations of Erasmus c. 1550– 1750*. Toronto: U of Toronto P, 1979.

– *Man on His Own: Interpretations of Erasmus, c. 1750–1920*. Toronto: U of Toronto P, 1992.

– *Erasmus in the Twentieth Century: Interpretations c. 1920–2000*. Toronto: U of Toronto P, 2003.

Margolin, Jean-Claude. 'Érasme et la France.' *Erasmus und Europa*. Ed. August Buck. Wiesbaden: Otto Harrassowitz, 1988. 58–64.

– 'Érasme et l'Angleterre.' *Notulæ Erasmianæ II: Érasme et l'Angleterre*. Ed. Alexandre Vanautgaerden. Brussels: La Lettre vole à la Maison d'Érasme, 1998. 61–7.

McConica, James. *English Humanists and Reformation Politics*. Oxford: Clarendon, 1965.

– *Erasmus*. Oxford: Oxford UP, 1991.

McGann, Jerome. 'Byron and Wordsworth.' School of English Studies. Nottingham: U of Nottingham, 1987.

Menchi, Silvana Seidel. *Erasmo in Italia, 1520–1580*. Turin: Bollati Boringhieri Editore, 1987.

Mourreaux, José-Michel. *L'Œdipe de Voltaire*. Paris: Archives des Lettres Modernes, 1973.

Mout, M.E.H.N, H.H. Smolinsky, and J. Trapman. *Erasmianism: Idea and Reality*. Amsterdam: Elsevier Science, 1997.

Naves, Raymond. *Voltaire*. 8th ed. Paris: Hatier, 1972.

Nuttall. A.D. *Shakespeare the Thinker*. New Haven: Yale UP, 2007.

Oberman, Heiko O. *Luther: Man between God and the Devil*. Trans. Eileen Waliser-Schwartzbart. New York: Doubleday, 1992.

Ogg, David. *Europe in the 17th Century*. 6th ed. London: Adam and Charles Black, 1952.

O'Rourke Boyle, Marjorie. 'The Eponyms of Desiderius Erasmus.' *Renaissance Quarterly* 30.1 (spring, 1977): 12–23. Published by U of Chicago P on behalf of the Renaissance Society of America.

Paulin, Roger. *The Critical Reception of Shakespeare in Germany 1682–1914*. Hildesheim: Olms Verlag, 2003.

Pelikan, Jaroslav. *Spirit versus Structure*. New York: Harper and Row, 1968.

Phillips, Margaret Mann. *The 'Adages' of Erasmus: A Study with Translations*. Cambridge: Cambridge UP, 1964.

Pomeau, René. *La Religion de Voltaire*. Rev. ed. Paris: Nizet, 1969.

– *D'Arouet à Voltaire*. Oxford: Voltaire Foundation, 1985.

– *De la Cour au jardin* (with Christiane Mervaud). Oxford: Voltaire Foundation, 1991.

– *On a voulu l'enterrer*. Oxford: Voltaire Foundation, 1994.

Quinones, Ricardo. *Dualisms: The Agons of the Modern World*. Toronto: U of Toronto P, 2007.

Rabelais, François. *Gargantua. Oeuvres complètes*. Ed. Pierre Jourda. Paris: Garnier, 1962.

Renaudet, Augustin. *Erasme et l'Italie*. Geneva: Droz, 1954.

Rousseau, André-Michel. Preface to *L'Angleterre et Voltaire: Studies on Voltaire and the Eighteenth Century*. Gen. ed. Theodore Besterman. Vols 145–7. Oxford: Voltaire Foundation, 1976.

Rousseau, Jean-Jacques. *Lettre à M. d'Alembert sur le théâtre. Oeuvres complètes*. Vol. 5. Paris: Gallimard, 1998.

– *Emile. Oeuvres complètes*. Vol. 4. Paris: Gallimard, 1969.

Rummel, Erika. *Erasmus and His Catholic Critics*. 2 vols. Nieuwkoop: De Graaf, 1989.

– *Colloqui di Erasmo da Rotterdam*. Milan: JACA, 1998.

– *The Confessionalization of Humanism in Reformation Germany*. Oxford: Oxford UP, 2000.

– *Erasmus*. New York: Continuum, 2004.

Rupp, E. Gordon, and Philip S. Watson, eds. *Luther and Erasmus: Free Will and Salvation*. LE. Library of Christian Classics 17. London: SCM, 1969.

Safranski, Rüdiger. *Martin Heidegger: Between Good and Evil*. Trans. Ewald Osers. Cambridge, MA: Harvard UP, 2002. Trans. of *Ein Meister aus Deutschland*.

Sartre, Jean-Paul. *Situations II*. Paris: Gallimard, 1948.

– *Les mots*. Paris: Gallimard, 1964.

Schalk, F. 'Erasmus und die *Res Publica Literaria*.' Actes du congrès Érasme, Rotterdam, 27–29 octobre 1969. Amsterdam: North Holland, 1971. 14–28.

Scherer, Jacques. 'L'univers en raccourci': quelques ambitions du roman voltairien.' *Studies on Voltaire and the Eighteenth Century*, vol. 179. Geneva: Institut et Musée Voltaire, 1979. 117–42.

Schoeck, R.J. *Erasmus of Europe*. Edinburgh: Edinburgh UP, 1990–3.

Seebohm, Frederic. *The Oxford Reformers: John Colet, Erasmus and Thomas More*. London: Longmans, Green, 1869.

Smith, Preserved. *Erasmus: A Study of His Life, Ideals and Place in History*. New York: Harper and Row, 1923.

Spitz, Lewis. *The Protestant Reformation 1517–1559*. St Louis: Concordia; repr. with additions and corrections, 2001.

Strauss, William, and Neil Howe. *Generations*. New York: Morrow , 1991.

Thompson, Craig R. *Ten Colloquies of Erasmus*. New York: Liberal Arts P, 1957.

– 'Foreword.' *Desiderius Erasmus Concerning the Aim and Method of Education*. New York: Bureau of Publications, 1964. vii–xxvi.

– 'Erasmus and Tudor England.' *Actes du Congrès Érasme Rotterdam 1969*. Amsterdam: North Holland, 1971.

Tombs, Robert, and Isabelle Tombs. *That Sweet Enemy, Britain and France: The History of a Love-Hate Relationship*. New York: Vintage, 2006.

Trevor-Roper H.R. *Historical Essays*. London: Macmillan, 1957.

– *Religion, the Reformation and Social Change*. London: Macmillan, 1967.

Trousson, Raymond. *Visages de Voltaire*. Paris: Champion, 2001.

Tyndale, William. *New Testament*. Intro. David Daniell. New Haven: Yale UP, 1995.

Vickers, Brian. Letter. *TLS*. 25 January 2008, 6.

Voltaire. *Philosophical Dictionary*. 2 vols. London: W.W. Dugdale, 1843.

– *Oeuvres complètes*. OC. Paris: Garnier, 1877–85.

– *Appel à toutes les nations de l'Europe*. OC. Vol. 24. Paris: Garnier, 1879. 191–221.

– *Lettre de M. Voltaire à l'Académie Française*. OC. Vol. 30. Paris: Garnier, 1880. 349–70.

– *Correspondence*. Ed. Theodore Besterman. Paris: Gallimard, 1953–77.

– *Lettre au Docteur Pansophe*. *Mélanges*. Ed. Jacques van den Heuvel. Paris: Gallimard, 1961.

– *Lettres Philosophiques*. *Mélanges*. Ed. Jacques van den Heuvel. Paris: Gallimard, 1961.

– *Melanges*. Ed. Jacques van den Heuvel. Paris: Gallimard, 1961.

– *Candide*. Ed. René Pomeau. OC. Vol. 48. Oxford: Voltaire Foundation, 1968.

– *Voltaire to Jean-Jacques Rousseau*. OC. Vol. 100. Oxford: Voltaire Foundation, 1971. 259–62.

– *Romans et contes*. RC. Ed. Frédéric Deloffre and Jacques van den Heuvel. Paris: Gallimard, 1979.

– *Letters on England*. Trans. Leonard Tancock. London: Penguin, 1980.

– *Essai sur les moeurs et l'esprit des nations*. Ed. René Pomeau. Paris: Garnier, 1963.

– *Discours sur la tragédie à milord Bolingbroke*. Ed. John Renwick. OC.

Vol. 5. *The English Essays of 1727*. Oxford: Voltaire Foundation, 1996.

– *Essai sur la poésie épique*. OC. Vol. 3B. Oxford: Voltaire Foundation, 1996. 412–24.

– *Œdipe*. Ed. David Jory. OC. Vol. 1A. Oxford: Voltaire Foundation, 2001. 15–284.

– *Discours de M. de Voltaire à sa reception à l'Académie française*. Ed. Karlis Racevskis. OC. Vol. 30A. Oxford: Voltaire Foundation, 2003.

Weber, Max. *The Protestant Ethic and the Spirit of Capitalism*. Trans. Talcott Parsons. New York: Scribner's, 1908.

Wellek, René. *A History of Modern Criticism*. Vol. 7. New Haven: Yale UP, 1991.

Welsford, Enid. *The Fool: His Social and Literary History*. New York: Farrar and Rinehart, 1935.

Williams, David. Introduction. *Commentaires sur Corneille*. Vol. 1. OC. Vol. 53. Banbury: Voltaire Foundation, 1974.

– *Studies on Voltaire and the Eighteenth Century*, Vol. 48. Geneva: Institut et Musée Voltaire, 1966.

– 'Voltaire's War with England: The Appeal to Europe 1760–1764.' In *Studies on Voltaire and the Eighteenth Century*. Vol. 179. Geneva: Institut et Musée Voltaire, 1979. 79–100.

Weber, Max. *The Protestant Ethic and the Spirit of Capitalism*. Trans. Talcott Parsons. New York: Scribner's, 1908

Wilson, Derek. *England in the Age of Thomas More*. London and New York: Hart-Davis McGibbon, 1978

Woodward, William Harrison. *Desiderius Erasmus Concerning the Aim and Method of Education*. New York: Bureau of Publications, 1964.

Wootton, David. 'The Vibes of Marx.' *TLS*, 4 January 2008.

Zweig, Stefan. *Erasmus of Rotterdam*. Trans. Eden and Cedar Paul. New York: Viking, 1934.

Index

Allen, P.S., 24, 38, 40, 41, 42, 43, 51, 53, 59, 60, 63, 72, 74, 75, 111, 124, 138, 142, 149, 162, 165, 178, 179, 185, 197n4, 204n5

Arendt, Hannah, 78, 98, 188, 189, 209n5; on Heidegger 189–90; on Jaspers 209n5

Aubenque, Pierre, 180–8, 190

Auden, W.H., 5, 196n3

Augustijn, Cornelius, 74, 75, 86, 89, 101, 146, 169, 196n4, 197n4, 199n7, 200n12, 201n16, 204n4

Bataillon, Marcel, 8

Beard, Charles, 11

Besterman, Theodore, 33, 52, 53, 54, 58, 62, 77, 119, 120, 159, 202n6

Bierlaire, Franz, 85, 89, 91, 106

Billaz, André, 8, 105

Bolgar, R.R., 43

Bornkam, Heinrich, 163

Busken Huet, Conrad 76, 199n6

Capito, Wolfgang, 47, 92, 120

Carducci, Giosue, on Petrarch, 14, 76, 164

Cassirer, Ernst, xiii, xvi, 96, 116, 153, 162, 174, 177–86, 190, 191, 192, 193, 205n7, 208n2, 209n4, 210n8, 211, 212; Cassirer in America 191; Cassirer's arguments 183–5; debate with Heidegger 178, 180–91; on Erasmus and Machiavelli 96; final words on Heidegger 191; *The Myth of the State* 191; Reform and the Enlightenment 178–82

Chomarat, Jacques, 21, 28, 87, 133, 200n11; and Erasmus 21, 28, 87

Coleridge, Samuel Taylor, vii, viii, 21, 70, 132, 161, 193; discussion of Erasmus and Voltaire vii–viii; and dualisms 21; and recognition viii–ix

Colet, John, 22, 36, 37, 38, 39, 40, 41, 42, 44, 45; and Erasmus 38

comparative literature, ix; and Jean-Claude Margolin x; and Jean Ehrard xiii–xiv; and recognition ix

convergences (Erasmus and Voltaire), viii, ix, xi, xvi, 6, 12, 177, 191

Cousin, Victor, 200n12

Cromwell, Thomas, 44, 46, 47, 48;
  and Erasmus 38

Daniell, David, 48
Dante, 14, 27, 60, 114, 149, 154,
  182, 199n9
Devereux, E.J., 45, 213; Erasmus
  and English politics 45
Dilthey, Wilhelm, 171
dualisms, vii, viii, xi–xiii, 13, 14,
  15, 21, 32, 103, 143, 146, 147,
  148, 150, 152, 154, 156, 158, 160,
  161, 162, 164, 166, 168, 170, 172,
  174, 175, 177, 178, 180, 182, 183,
  189, 190, 191, 192, 193, 194,
  197n4, 200n13, 204n2, 208n3;
  Erasmus and Voltaire compared
  146 ff; Voltaire's attack against
  Rousseau 159–62; and war
  194

Erasmus (Desiderius Erasmus
  Rotterdam): and bastardy 25–6;
  and brother 26; and Christian
  scepticism 48, 155, 169; difference from Voltaire 36–7, 51; as
  educator 42; and England 36;
  historical gradualism and conciliation 155–7; influence under
  Catherine Parr 48–9; and literary influence 50; name change
  22, 24; optimistic period 92; and
  pessimism 93; and république
  littéraire 33–5; response to Dorp
  70–6; and rhetoric 27–9; sketch
  of Colet 40–1; and Tudor politics
  44; visits to England and John
  Colet 38–40
Erasmus's works: Adages 97;
  Christian folly 132–3; and Christian liberty 98; Colloquies 81–5,

85–104; The Complaint of Peace
  94–5; defence of Bierlaire 90–1,
  100; The Education of a Christian
  Prince 95–6; The Enchiridion 46–7;
  Erasmus in the 20th century 199;
  Julius Exclusus 5, 98; Letter to
  Latomus 166–8; letter to Marteen
  van Dorp 70; Letter to Martin
  Laurinus 129, 168–9; liabilities
  of learning 129–32; Mending the
  Peace of the Church 157, 207n1;
  opposed qualities 129–34; Praise
  of Folly 123–32; satire 126–9; selections of Bierlaire 89–91; selections of Rummel 89; selections
  of Thompson 89; and the Third
  Station 177–80; and translation
  of Bible 48; on war and peace
  91–2; women and marriage
  90–1

Ferguson, Wallace K., xiv, xv, 162,
  195n2, 205n7
Frederick II, xvi, 5, 9, 110, 120, 159,
  160, 161, 204

Gangoux, Jacques, 'les trois puissances', 206n3
Gibbon, Edward, 9, 11, 48, 170,
  195n1
Groos, René, 7

Haile G.H. 93
Haskins, Charles Homer, 43, 59,
  60, 199n10; on Luther 199n10
Hazard, Paul, 204n3, 206–7n4
Heidegger, Martin, xvi, 148, 149,
  178, 180–92, 208n3, 209n4; and
  Cassirer debate at Davos 178,
  180–91; description of debate
  181, 182; Heidegger's argu-

ments 185–8; later 'violence' in criticism 208n3; Letter on Humanism 189, 190

Howe, Neil. *See* Strauss, William

Huizinga, Johan, 8, 15, 16, 17, 23, 26, 32, 35, 68, 132, 133, 162, 171

Jaspers, Karl, 182, 188, 209n5

Judt, Tony, 178

Jusserand, J.J., 77, 202n6, 203n8

Kaiser, Walter, 134, 196n4, 206n2

Ladner, Gerhard, 201n1

Luther, Martin, 150, 151, 163–70

Mansfield, Bruce, vii, 11, 50, 76, 197n4, 199n6, 200n11

McConica, James K., 17, 40, 44–9, 196n4, 199n7

Mervaud, Christiane, 115

More, Thomas, 36, 38, 44, 69, 103, 124, 202n2

Naves, Raymond, 9, 63, 82, 141, 146, 153, 154, 196n2, 198n5, 200n12, 201n15

Nuttall, A.D., 201

O'Rourke Boyle, Marjorie, 22, 23, 216; Erasmus's change of name 22–4

Paulin, Roger, 28, 203

Pelikan, Jaroslav, 207

Rousseau, Jean-Jacques 152, 173–5; *Lettre à M. d'Alembert* 161: *Lettres écrites de la montagne* 161

Rummel, Erika, xvi, 26, 28, 32, 48, 68, 83, 86, 89, 101, 102, 155, 167, 200n13, 203n1

Safranski, Rudiger, 181, 182, 188

Sartre, Jean Paul, xi, xii, 6, 148, 149, 162, 149, 183, 189, 197, 198

Schalk, F., 4, 32

'second Reformation,' 11–12, 76–7, 116. *See also* Mansfield, Bruce

Seebohm, Frederic, 35, 37–41, 44, 45; Erasmus and the Oxford Reform 37, 40, 41, 44, 45

Strauss, William (and Neil Howe) 17, 18, 84

Tenhaeff, E.N., 195

Thompson, Craig, 37, 42, 43, 45–52, 85, 89, 134, 196

Trevor-Roper, H.R., xiv, xv, 37, 196, 204, 206, 209

Trousson, Raymond, 10, 151, 197, 200, 201

Tyndale, William, 47, 48

Voltaire (Francois-Marie Arouet): and bastardy 26; with Besterman 52, 53; le 'cas' Voltaire 159–62; contradiction and contrast 154–5; family tensions in *Oedipe* and parricide 29; and Frederick II 159; and his historical afterlife 198–9; with J.J. Jusserand 53; and Maupertius 159–62; mini-aesthetic conversion 81–5, 104–21; name change 24–5; recognition and recurrence192–3; relentless attacks on J.-J. Rousseau explained by dualisms 161–2; respect for tolerance and political liberties 52; with A.M. Rousseau 53 passim; and Shakespeare 52–63; and the Third Station 177–80; Voltaire's England 51f

Voltaire's works: *Appel a toutes les nations* 55; *Babouc* 106–7; *Candide* 137–42; *Cosi-Sancta* 106; *Le Crocheteur* 105; Les deux consoles 152–7; *Docteur Pansophe* 172; *Essai sur les moeurs* 76, 117, 145, 154,182; first shot in new campaign 142; formulator of North and South axis 120–1; *L'Ingenu* 112–15, 136–7; *Lettre de M. de Voltaire* and controversy with LeTourneur 58–60; *Lettres philosophiques* 55; Martin and Candide as two sides of Voltaire 141; *Memnon* 107–8; *Micromegas* 88–9; *La Princesse de Babylone* 118–21; Rousseau's singularity and 'inner voice' 173; the three clasps and Zadig and L'Ingenu 136–7; *Zadig* 109–12, 136

Welsford, Enid: on Erasmus and Shakespeare, 133–6
Woodward, William Harrison, 40